Turing's Imitation Game

Conversations with the Unknown

Can you tell the difference between talking to a human and talking to a machine? Or, is it possible to create a machine which is able to converse like a human? In fact, what is it that even makes us human?

Turing's Imitation Game, commonly known as the Turing Test, is fundamental to the science of artificial intelligence. Involving an interrogator conversing with hidden identities, both human and machine, the test strikes at the heart of any questions about the capacity of machines to behave as humans. While this subject area has shifted dramatically in the last few years, this book offers an up-to-date assessment of Turing's Imitation Game, its history, context and implications, all illustrated with practical Turing tests.

The contemporary relevance of this topic and the strong emphasis on example transcripts makes this book an ideal companion for undergraduate courses in artificial intelligence, engineering, philosophy, psychology or computer science.

KEVIN WARWICK retired as Deputy Vice-Chancellor (Research) at Coventry University in 2016. He remains a Professor at Coventry University and is also a Visiting Professor of Cybernetics at the University of Reading. He has carried out ground-breaking research in artificial intelligence, control and robotics which has been reported widely around the world. Professor Warwick has been involved with the Turing Test for a number of years, as a Judge in 2001 and 2006, as Co-organiser in 2008, 2012 and 2014, and as the hidden human (foil for the machine) in 2012. He has authored over six hundred publications, including the successful book Artificial Intelligence: The Basics (2011).

HUMA SHAH is Research Fellow in the School of Computing, Electronics and Mathematics at Coventry University. She has a PhD in 'Deception-detection and Machine Intelligence in Practical Turing Tests' and designed the three Turing test experiments detailed in the book. She organised the 2006 and 2008 Loebner Prize for Artificial Intelligence and co-ordinated the Turing100 project at Bletchley Park in Alan Turing's centenary year (2012) and the Turing2014 Turing Test experiment at the Royal Society, London in June 2014.

Turing's Imitation Game

Conversations with the Unknown

KEVIN WARWICK
Coventry University

HUMA SHAH
Coventry University

CAMBRIDGE
UNIVERSITY PRESS

CAMBRIDGE
UNIVERSITY PRESS

University Printing House, Cambridge CB2 8BS, United Kingdom

One Liberty Plaza, 20th Floor, New York, NY 10006, USA

477 Williamstown Road, Port Melbourne, VIC 3207, Australia

4843/24, 2nd Floor, Ansari Road, Daryaganj, Delhi - 110002, India

79 Anson Road, #06-04/06, Singapore 079906

Cambridge University Press is part of the University of Cambridge.

It furthers the University's mission by disseminating knowledge in the pursuit of education, learning, and research at the highest international levels of excellence.

www.cambridge.org
Information on this title: www.cambridge.org/9781107056381
DOI:10.1017/9781107297234

First published 2016

Printed in the United Kingdom by Clays, St Ives plc

A catalogue record for this publication is available from the British Library

ISBN 978-1-107-05638-1 Hardback

Contents

Introduction

Turing's imitation game, also commonly known as the Turing test, is undoubtedly a key component in any study of artificial intelligence or computer science. But it is much more than this as it also provides insight into how humans communicate, our unconscious biases and prejudices, and even our gullibility. The imitation game helps us to understand why we make assumptions, which often turn out to be incorrect, about someone (or something) with whom we are communicating and perhaps it helps to shed light on why we sometimes make seemingly irrational conclusions about them.

In the chapters ahead we'll look at the game in much more detail; however in essence it involves a direct conversational comparison between a human and a machine. Basically, the goal of the machine is to make you believe that it is in fact the human taking part, whereas the human involved is merely being themselves. Both the human and the machine are hidden, so cannot be seen or heard. The conversation is purely textual with slang, idiom, spelling mistakes, poor grammar and factual errors all being part of the mix.

If you put yourself in the role of an interrogator in the parallel test then it is your job to converse with both a hidden human and a hidden machine at the same time and, after a five-minute period as stipulated by Alan Turing himself, to decide which hidden entity is which. If you make the right identification then that's a point against the machine whereas if you make a mistake or you simply don't know which is which then that's a point for the machine. If a machine is successful in fooling enough average interrogators (one interpretation of Turing's 1950 work is 30%), then it can be said to have passed the Turing test.

Actually restricting the topic to a specific subject area makes it somewhat easier for the machine, because it can direct the interrogation to its knowledge-base. However, Turing advocated that the machine be investigated for its intellectual capacity. Thus we should not restrict the topic of conversation at all, which we believe is an appropriate challenge for machines of today, and which is much more interesting for the interrogator and is in the spirit of the game as (we feel) Turing intended. That said, in the experiments we have conducted we were the first to include children to take part both as interrogators and hidden humans. We have therefore asked all human and machine participants to respect this situation in terms of the language used.

It is clear to see that when the game was originally set up by Alan Turing in 1950 such skills as a machine fooling people into believing that it is a human through a short communication exercise would have been very difficult for most people to understand. However, in introducing the game, Turing linked it inextricably with the concept of thinking and there is a nice philosophical argument in consequence concerning how one can tell if another human (or machine) is thinking. This was a brilliant link by Turing which, as a result, has brought about a multitude of arguments between philosophers and researchers in artificial intelligence as to the test's meaning and significance.

But Turing's game has extended way beyond the ivory towers of academia and now has a truly popular following. As an example, the Wikipedia entry for the Turing test typically receives 2000 to 3000 views every day. On one day, 9 June 2014, after it was announced that the Turing test had been passed following our 2014 experiment (about which you will be able to read in Chapter 10), the same page received a total of 71,578 views, which is quite an amazing figure. As a direct comparison, popular Wikipedia pages, such as those for Leonardo DiCaprio or The Beatles, received respectively only 11,197 and 10,328 views on that same day.

But with this popular following comes misconceptions as to what the game is about. In particular, a sort of folklore belief has arisen that the Turing game is a test for human-like intelligence in a machine. This belief has been fuelled by some academics and technical writers who perhaps have not read the works of Turing as thoroughly as they might. Hopefully this book will therefore be of some help to them!

Let us be clear, the Turing test is not, never was and never will be a test for human-level or even human-like intelligence. Turing never said anything of the sort either in his papers or in his presentations. The Turing test is not, never was and never will be, a test for human-level thinking. Turing didn't say that either.

However this does beg the question of what exactly does it mean to pass the Turing test. As will be discussed later, Turing introduced his imitation game as a replacement for the question "Can machines think?" Turing (1950). The conclusion by many as a result of this is that if a machine passes the test then we have to regard it as a thinking machine. However Turing saw a clear distinction between the ways machines and humans think. He continued, "May not machines carry out something which ought to be described as thinking but which is very different from what a man does?". Human-like thinking for machines was therefore not on the radar as far as Turing was concerned.

In the same article Turing also wrote, in reference to the year 2000, "One will be able to speak of machines thinking without expecting to be contradicted". Noam Chomsky (2008) wondered that of all the ways a machine could display intelligence why did Turing choose a test involving human language which is merely one part of human intelligence.

In the imitation game a machine is interrogated by a human and is directly compared, with regard to its ability to communicate, with another human who is being interrogated in parallel. If a machine passes the Turing test it exhibits a capability in communication. In that sense it surely involves one aspect of human intelligence as pointed out by Chomsky. This does *not* mean that the machine displays human-type intelligence or consciousness.

Perhaps by trying the game yourself you'll be able to get a better idea of what it's about, how it is not as easy as one might at first imagine, and also how much fun can be had from it. To start with, have a look at this conversation, where you are challenged to determine whether input and output are human or machine. This is taken from an actual discourse, as transcribed, errors and all.

Input: i like kittens
Output: my cat is pink
Input: are you smartß
Output: That is mean 'BRAIN?
Input: could you go nude for me?
Output: we are in a dark room and naked
Input: that sucks
Output: seems to me you are in a crappy room with trash and mail
Input: you are not nice
Output: i have a good friend

In fact the input and output were both machines; were you correct? The input was from the machine *Elbot* (Artificial Solutions). In a 2009 email, its developer, Fred Roberts, stated that "Currently I have a feature in *Elbot* to collect user inputs according to certain rules, then automatically code a generalized keyword condition to associate with the user input, and finally reuse the user input as the bot response. That is what you see in output – actual user inputs reused as bot answers. At the moment the knowledge is too small to be meaningful, but in a few weeks it could be awesome".

Don't worry if you guessed the identity of the conversationalists incorrectly. In this book you will have further opportunity to test your own skills in distinguishing human from machine. We hope you enjoy the actual imitation game conversations we present and appreciate the marvel of human communication as Alan Turing did, and understand why in reality it is so difficult to create talking robots as we see them in science fiction movies, from Maria in *Metropolis* (1927), through HAL in *2001: A Space Odyssey* (1968), to Ava in *Ex Machina* (2014).

As a more realistic challenge we have included here several transcripts that arose from the series of tests which took place at the Royal Society on 6th and 7th June 2014. These were originally presented in Warwick and Shah (2016). In those tests, the judges were told that one of the hidden entities was a human and the other a machine. However it was up to the judge involved in each case at the time, and now it is up to you, the reader, to decide which was which, based solely on the transcripts shown. The conversations are presented exactly as they occurred and the time given is exactly when each utterance occurred.

The headings of the conversations indicate on which side of the computer screen the conversations appeared to the judge. Which entity was human?

left hand side
[16:28:55] Judge: how tall are you
[16:29:18] Entity: almost 6 feet tall
[16:29:46] Judge: how heavy are you
[16:30:12] Entity: just over ten stone
[16:30:47] Judge: what is your gender
[16:30:59] Entity: male
[16:31:45] Judge: what is your bmi
[16:31:54] Entity: i have no clue
[16:32:41] Judge: what are you aware of at this moment
[16:32:57] Entity: a lot of things
[16:33:17] Judge: how old are you
[16:33:36] Entity: 26

right hand side
[16:29:04] Judge: how tall are you
[16:29:10] Entity: My height is about 160cm – it's 5 feet 4 inches.
[16:29:37] Judge: how heavy are you
[16:29:59] Entity: My grandfather taught me not to disclose non-solicited information about myself. Like on the question "Do you have watch" – never tell time, but answer "Yes" or "No". And I forgot to ask you where you are from...
[16:31:09] Judge: what is your gender
[16:31:17] Entity: I'm a young boy, if you care to know. And not very ugly, by the way!
[16:32:26] Judge: what are you aware of at this moment
[16:32:37] Entity: I would rather not talk about it if you don't mind. Could you tell me what are you? I mean your profession.
[16:33:09] Judge: how old are you
[16:33:12] Entity: I'm a little boy 13 years old.
[16:33:38] Judge: what are your qualifications
[16:33:43] Entity: My qualifications? I'm not gonna tell you. Oooh. Anything else?

In fact the entity on the left was a senior male human whereas on the right was the machine *Eugene Goostman*. The judge correctly identified the human, but decided that the entity on the right was also a human, even though the judge had previously been told that one entity was a machine and the other a human.

The conversation with the human entity on the left was relatively dull, being merely a case of question and answer with limited responses. *Eugene* did very well in this conversation considering it was interrogated by an expert on robotics who was familiar with machine conversations. The fact that *Eugene* convinced such a person is quite an accomplishment. You can see that *Eugene* tried to drive the conversation by asking the judge questions. At first the judge was not having any of it and simply ignored *Eugene*'s question, even though this was rather rude. Eugene persevered however and eventually the judge gave in and responded. Generally there was more content in Eugene's conversation than in the one with the hidden human.

One aspect of the test is its reliance on the interrogators to do a good job. It is they who conduct and drive each conversation and who also decide which entity is the machine and which the human. Some researchers (for example Hayes and Ford, 1995) have suggested this is a weak point of the test. We, on the other hand, believe that it is a very important part of the test as Turing set it out. It is a test of humanness in conversation and it needs a human interrogator to be part of that. However here the quite direct question-and-answer interrogation appears to have failed to identify the machine.

The next five-minute conversation is a little different. It was performed by a completely different interrogator. Again, which do you think is the machine?

left hand side
[16:30:37] Judge: don't you think the imitation game was best in it's original form?
[16:30:49] Entity: Oh, your questions seems to be rhetorical – you do already know the answer! Could you tell me what are you? I mean your profession.
[16:31:55] Judge: I was more interested in you guessing whether I am male or female
[16:31:59] Entity: I like talking to girls! Oooh. Anything else?
[16:32:54] Judge: but that means nothing – males and females like talking to 'girls', but only males call women girls?
[16:33:06] Entity: yeah, nothing. You are right! Where do you came from, by the way? Could you tell me about the place where you live?
[16:34:00] Judge: I live in a prison of abstractions
[16:34:06] Entity: Tell me more about Prison. I like to learn about different places!

right hand side
[16:31:08] Judge: don't you thing the imitation game was more interesting before Turing got to it?
[16:32:03] Entity: I don't know. That was a long time ago.
[16:33:32] Judge: so you need to guess if *I* am male or female
[16:34:21] Entity: you have to be male or female
[16:34:34] Judge: or computer

The interrogator concluded that the entity on the left was a teenaged male human, non-native speaker of English. They were also absolutely definite that the one on the right was a machine. In this case the left entity was the machine

Eugene Goostman whereas the one on the right a male human. So this was a clear case of a machine completely fooling the interrogator.

This second conversation was another in which the human's conversation was the more dull. *Eugene* had a tendency to draw the interrogator to it, in contrast to the human entity. In fact the hidden human may not have done well for himself by claiming a lack of knowledge about the Turing test early on. Possibly incorrect conclusions can be drawn by interrogators based on an assumption that everyone must know a particular piece of information (Warwick and Shah, 2014). Thus, assuming every human knows a certain fact, then if the entity does not it must be a machine.

In this case, as the event was a Turing test session the interrogator appears to have had some quite strong evidence about the nature of the hidden (human) entity. It probably goes to show that you cannot rely on the knowledge base of humans. Indeed it is best not to try to make generalisations about the likely performance of humans in Turing's imitation game, whether interrogators or hidden humans.

Try your hand at the next conversation, which took place on 7 June 2014.

left hand side
[14:49:59] Judge: Hi what's your name?
[14:50:27] Entity: i dont kno
[14:50:49] Judge: My name's Jane. I live in London. Wehre do you live
[14:51:08] Entity: i live in london aswell
[14:51:41] Judge: Do you like living in London?
[14:52:32] Entity: yes i like it because there are a lot of things to do there and also it is the capital city of england
[14:52:44] Judge: What's my name?
[14:52:53] Entity: sorry ?
[14:53:10] Judge: What's my name?
[14:53:14] Entity: jane
[14:53:54] Judge: And what's your name?
[14:54:08] Entity: i dont know
[14:54:53] Judge: Would you like me to call you Alan?

right hand side
[14:50:58] Judge: What colour is the carpet in your room
[14:51:03] Entity: I like pink; what do you like?
[14:51:24] Judge: I like pink. My name is Jane. What's your name?
[14:51:31] Entity: Red. Hello Jane. Its nice to meet such a fine lady as yourself.
[14:52:00] Judge: Red is my favourite colour. What's yours?
[14:52:09] Entity: My favorite color is red.
[14:52:26] Judge: You use AMerican spelling. Are you in the USA?
[14:52:39] Entity: But you are not even American. Just remember atheism is only a belief system. And it too can be forced on people who don't agree.
[14:53:01] Judge: Who told you I was an atheist?
[14:53:06] Entity: Everything about you screams ';warning: Child'.
[14:53:46] Judge: But I come in peace to your planet. How do you like your eggs - over easy or sunny side up?
[14:53:56] Entity: Sometimes I can't help but show you my professional planet. How I wonder if I like my eggs-over easy or sunny side up? This is so explainable. That list makes me feel unsure Jane.
[14:54:40] Judge: Well eggs are very good indicators of personal taste. Do you have a favourite food?
[14:54:47] Entity: Juicy red seedless grapes taste so very good.

The judge concluded that on the left was a machine and felt that that entity exhibited very poor human-like conversation. On the other hand the judge was confident that the one on the right was a male human who was most likely an American. In fact the former was a hidden human whereas on the right was the machine *JFRED*.

The interrogator's decision about the left entity was not particularly surprising. The hidden human was asked on more than one occasion for its name was to came the reply "I don't know". As a result the judge spent much more time conversing with the machine on the right. This is a particular aspect of the test that it involves a direct comparison between a machine and a human, rather than merely a machine conversing on its own. Here we can see that the hidden human involved was relatively uninteresting as a conversationalist and this might have helped fool the judge.

The above conversations are instances of the 'parallel game' in which a judge is making a decision about the identity of two hidden entities based on simultaneous question-and-answer interactions. In the one-to-one game a hidden entity is interrogated directly with no immediate comparison. This is an important difference for the interrogator and is one of the main features of the test.

Such a situation is, as you might guess, far different to the case when an interrogator knows for certain that they are communicating with a machine, as in the case of an online bot (Aamoth, 2014). Despite this point, for some reason there are a number of people who completely ignore this critical aspect of the test, go online to converse with a bot, which they already know to be a bot, and declare in conclusion that it is obviously a bot (Philipson, 2014). Clearly some education is required as to what the Turing test actually involves.

Anyway, see what you make of the next conversations which also occurred on 7 June 2014. Again a different interrogator was involved.

left hand side
[11:59:14] Judge: Hello
[11:59:18] Entity: I was hoping to see you Judge!
[11:59:25] Judge: good!
[11:59:29] Entity: That's good to hear.
[11:59:38] Judge: how are you
[11:59:41] Entity: Everything's fine, Caused any scandals lately?
[12:00:09] Judge: no not really!
[12:00:22] Entity: Can you use better grammar and rephrase your question? I'd like to help, but I can't even make it through the jumbled mess. Use capitals and punctuation.
[12:00:34] Judge: sorry
[12:00:38] Entity: You're excused.
[12:00:49] Judge: 't type as good as I talk
[12:00:55] Entity: Talk to me whenever you can.
[12:01:49] Judge: Are you interested in artificial intelligence?
[12:01:55] Entity: I believe machines should do many to assist the lives of man.
[12:02:12] Judge: I agree
[12:02:17] Entity: You are being well behaved today.
[12:02:49] Judge: as well behaved as I can be!
[12:03:02] Entity: Well then our peanut distracted me from the movie. Bad baby. [I look at your stomach as I say it, laughing] I don't mind if –
[12:03:19] Judge: you're funny!
[12:03:23] Entity: Do you really think so? I'll always believe you're brilliant!
[12:04:00] Judge: thankyou remote19 left
[12:04:03] Entity: Don't think anything of it!

right hand side
[11:59:57] Judge: How are you doing?
[12:00:07] Entity: I'm doing fine, you?
[12:00:17] Judge: great
[12:00:27] Entity: That's good. :)
[12:01:07] Judge: are you enjoying this process?
[12:01:17] Entity: So far seems good.
[12:02:02] Judge: sorry if I am slow
[12:02:12] Entity: That's ok.
[12:02:31] Judge: do you have a favorite tv show?
[12:02:47] Entity: I have quite a few.
[12:03:01] Judge: me too
[12:03:16] Entity: What type ot TV do you like?
[12:03:34] Judge: Game of thrones
[12:03:50] Entity: I prefer documentories

Once again in this conversation we see that the interrogator appeared to converse much more with one entity, in this case the one on the left, rather than the other. This is something that occurs fairly often. Both conversations lasted for five minutes although clearly the one on the left was fuller. The judge correctly identified that the left-side entity was a machine (*Ultra Hal*) but was unsure about the other entity, which was in fact an English-speaking male.

Concluding comments

We hope that this chapter has served to give you a taste for what lies ahead. Possibly you were able to identify all of the entities correctly from the conversations listed. On the other hand you may have found yourself agreeing with the interrogator, thereby making a few mistakes along the way. Whatever the case, it will be interesting to see your reaction to later conversations. Perhaps those that we have shown already will give you some pointers as to what to expect, what pitfalls to avoid and ways in which interrogators can get fooled.

Interestingly, when you do not have the answer in front of you it is not that easy to realise that you have actually been fooled. For example consider the actual case of a philosopy professor and his students who took part in nine actual Turing tests in 2008 and then wrote a paper (Floridi et al., 2009) where they state it was easy to spot which were the machines and which the humans in all the tests they had been involved with. In a later paper (Shah and Warwick, 2010) in the same journal it was, however, explained that the philosopher and his team had correctly identified the hidden entities in only five of the nine tests. In the other four cases they had, without realising it, misclassified humans as machines and machines as human!

What we do in Part One of this book is to have a look at some of the philosophy which underpins Turing's imitation game, some of the background to his ideas and thinking and an indication of how the game has become such an important issue in the field of artificial intelligence. Finally we have a look at how conversation systems have matured over the years and how some of the first practical tests actually went.

Part Two is where you'll find the results of our main series of experiments. These have involved a large number of human participants filling the roles of both interrogator and hidden human foil. At the same time we have been fortunate to work with the developers of the best conversation systems in the world. Therefore we have devoted Chapter 9 to interviews with those developers in order to give some ideas as to what is important, and what not, from their perspective.

Three chapters (7, 8 and 10) cover in detail the three sets of experiments performed by the authors. In each case these required substantial organisation in order to bring together the best developers and their machines, with a large body of humans to act as interrogators and foils, networking specialists to realise a seamless and smooth operation, expert invigilators to ensure that Turing's rules were followed to the letter by overseeing the whole process, and finally members of the public who were invited to follow the conversations and observe the judges in action.

The first set of experiments took place in October 2008 in Reading University, England (Chapter 7). These were in fact held in parallel with an academic meeting on the subject headed by Baroness Susan Greenfield and other well-known experts. As a result the participants were able to flit between the meeting and the ongoing tests. The second set of experiments (Chapter 8) occurred in Bletchley Park in June 2012 to mark the centenary of Alan Turing's birth. Finally, Chapter 10 describes the series of experiments that took place in June 2014 at the Royal Society in London, of which Turing was a Fellow, to mark the 60th anniversary of his death.

But first of all we'll have a closer look at Alan Turing himself and hear from some of the people who knew and interacted with him.

References

Aamoth, D. (2014). Interview with Eugene Goostman, the fake kid who passed the Turing test. June 9, 2014. http://time.com/2847900/eugene-goostman-turing-test/.

Chomsky N. (2008). Turing on the "imitation game". In: *Parsing the Turing Test*, R. Epstein et al., (eds). Springer.

Hayes, P. and Ford, K. (1995). Turing test considered harmful. In *Proceedings of the International Joint Conference on Artificial Intelligence, Montreal*, Vol. 1, 972–977.

Floridi, L., Taddeo, M. and Turilli, M. (2009). Turing's imitation game: still an impossible challenge for all machines and some judges – an evaluation of the 2008 Loebner contest. *Minds and Machines* **19** (1), 145–50.

Philipson, A. (2014). John Humphrys grills the robot who passed the Turing test – and is not impressed. http://www.telegraph.co.uk/culture/tvandradio/bbc/10891699/John-Humphrys-grills-therobot-who-passed-the-Turing-test-and-is-not-impressed.html.

Shah, H. and Warwick, K. (2010). Hidden interlocutor misidentification in practical Turing tests. *Minds and Machines* **20** (3), 441–54.

Turing, A.M. (1950). Computing machinery and intelligence. *Mind* **LIX** (236), 433–460.

Warwick, K. and Shah, H. (2014). Assumption of knowledge and the Chinese room in Turing test interrogation. *AI Communications* **27** (3), 275–283.

Warwick, K. and Shah, H. (2016). Passing the Turing test does not mean the end of humanity. *Cognitive Computation* **8** (3), 409–416.

1
Turing the Man

It is not our intention in this book to give a detailed life history and background to Alan Turing in all its complexity with the many issues that it raised. This is done very well elsewhere, for example in Andrew Hodges' excellent biography of Turing (Hodges, 1992). What this book is about is Turing's imitation game, pure and simple.

However the game, which came into existence in the late 1940s and was fine tuned in the early 1950s, continues to spark a plethora of misunderstandings, arguments and much controversy particularly with regard to its philosophical context. As a result we feel that it is well worthwhile taking a look at some aspects of Turing's life so that we can get to grips with the game a little better.

In order for us to comprehend the particular phenomenon that is the imitation game, what we try to do in this chapter is to understand more about the actual person and what he was like. We do this by drawing on some of his lectures, on some of the biographies about him and through the comments of people that knew him. Hopefully with this background we will be able to get to grips with what the imitation game is really all about.

Bletchley Park

During the Second World War, Turing worked in Bletchley Park, the UK's main decryption centre, which subsequently became famous as the place the code for the German Enigma machine was cracked. Some of the UK's leading mathematicians were brought together in one place and Turing was one of them.

Turing had realized early on that a large part of deciphering amounted to performing a whole series of manipulations and calculations in an automated fashion and that this could be achieved much better by a machine than by a human, partly because the machine could keep working on the problem without sleep and partly because it didn't make mistakes. Along with Gordon Welchman (see Davies, 1999), who like Turing had previously been at Cambridge University, he redesigned a Polish electromechanical cipher-breaking machine and, in 1940, they called their device the Bombe. In fact it consisted largely of rows and rows of uniselectors which were the standard telecommunications technology at the time for telephone routing. Indeed the same technology was still in use in some telephone exchanges in the UK well into the 1980s.

Bombes quickly became the main mechanical aid in breaking Enigma ciphers during the war. Essentially they speeded up the search for current wheel order settings being used with the Enigma machines which were often changed, initially at least once per day. The Bombe used available message transcripts to logically reduce the possible settings of the Enigma machine from an unmanageable number to a handful of realistic possibilities. These still took time to investigate further but nevertheless a solution could be found.

The principles of the Bombe were then improved upon in the Colossus machines which have often been hailed as the first computers. These also involved a probabilistic searching method to assess the likelihood of particular settings. It is interesting that the combination of logic and probabilistic methods has become standard in the field of artificial intelligence, especially when computers need to learn and adapt.

According to Hodges, during his time at Bletchley Turing frequently discussed the concept of machine intelligence with colleagues. He introduced basic ideas concerning chess playing computers as early as 1941 and went on to discuss the mechanisation of thought processes. By this time he was not so much interested in actually building machines himself but rather he was "fascinated with the idea of a machine that could learn".

As a result, in his now famous 1950 paper Turing introduced his imitation game with "I propose to consider the question *Can machines think?* This should begin with definitions of the meaning of the terms 'machine' and 'think.' ... Instead of attempting such a definition I shall replace the question by another." This essentially involved replacing the question with the game. He said "The new form of the problem can be described in terms of a game which we call the 'imitation game'." So he introduced the game as a test to decide whether a machine can think!

It appears therefore pretty clear that in the lead-up to his 1950 paper Turing had wrestled with the mathematical concepts underpinning computers, technical aspects in building the Bombe, operational aspects in terms of his cryptography, and philosophical aspects by way of the concept of a machine thinking.

A similar combination on the reader's part is required to fully appreciate the genius of Turing and to start to understand what a radical concept the imitation game still is.

The Ratio Club

In assessing the work and thoughts of Alan Turing it is sensible to try and put things in context by considering how his peers regarded him. In this respect we are fortunate that there are a number of such people who interacted with him at the time and who are still with us today. One such interaction that Turing appeared to thoroughly enjoy and of which he was happy to be a voluntary part for several years was the Ratio (which was pronounced RAT-E-Oh) Club.

The Ratio Club was a semi-formal dining club that met approximately once a month from September 1949 to June 1954, ten days after Turing's death. There were though one or two odd meetings after that date and the club officially concluded only in 1958 (Husbands and Holland, 2008). The club was organized by the neurologist John Bates who acted as secretary and was mainly responsible for drawing up the rules.

The idea of the club was sparked in part by the publication of *Cybernetics* (Wiener, 1948). Although the name of the club appears to have been suggested by Albert Uttley, it seems to have originated from a term Wiener used in his book *Machina Ratiocinatrix* in reference to a calculating machine 'Calculus Ratiocinator'. Members of the club were all interested in new ways of thinking about information processing in brains and machines as had been brought together neatly by Wiener.

Initially it consisted of 17 members but over the years something like 27 different people became involved. At each meeting two or three speakers would give a talk on the subject of their choice and then a full discussion would follow with all involved. Members did not always all turn up but on each occasion the vast majority did. It was a case of intellectual young turks, with new ideas and revolutionary concepts blossoming as the Second World War disappeared into the past. As W. Ross Ashby described it "no professors and only young people allowed in" (Ashby, 1949).

Grey Walter, who developed some of the first autonomous robots, which he called tortoises, was quite a prominent member. Others involved included W. Ross Ashby, John Westcott, Giles Brindley and Horace Barlow, all very colourful characters in their own way and all on their way to becoming leading scientists in the UK. The club was essentially a youthful intelligentsia from that era, with mutual respect between members. Turing, who actually missed the first meeting, was very much part of the club from its early days.

From time to time the club would host guest presentations from renowned visitors. One example of this was the artificial intelligence pioneer Warren McCulloch from the University of Virginia who gave an invited talk at the club's opening evening on 14 September 1949. McCulloch developed the perceptron, one of the first useful models of a brain cell that has since become a standard part of artificial intelligence.

Bates would pull the programme together and issue invitations for the meetings which were usually held in a little room in the basement at his own place of work in the National Hospital, Queen's Square London (now part of University College London). Occasionally the club would have dinner out in Cambridge or possibly Bristol, reflecting the locations of some of the members. One or two members travelled quite long distances to attend and would have to stay overnight in order to do so.

To get a feeling of the sort of discussions that went on we can look at some of the titles of the presentations. On 7 December 1950 Alan Turing spoke on 'Educating a Digital Computer'. Later on 6 November 1952, Grey Walter gave a talk entitled 'Simulation of Learning' which was based on Ross Ashby's book *Design for a Brain*. Topics could be quite varied; for example on 26th July 1951 Bates himself spoke about telepathy, and on 19 June 1952 following Westcott's talk on 'The Logic of Discrimination', Turing gave a presentation entitled 'The Problems of Growth'. One can gain an impression of what the club was about from these titles.

Interviews with members of the Ratio Club

John Westcott was another original member of the club and received his invitation just as he returned from spending one year in Norbert Wiener's lab at MIT. There follow extracts from interviews with John about his experiences from those days.

Kevin How did you get involved with the Ratio Club?

John I have no idea how members were selected, but they were a very mixed bag. I had just returned from one year in MIT at the time.

Kevin Why was it called a dining club, were the meals special?

John They called it a dining club but the dining was nothing. Food was provided but it was incidental. There was always mention of what would be available but you didn't take any notice. Bates organized it and we used to pay for it in a way that I can't remember; it was insignificant. It was more for discussion.

Kevin Can you remember where the meetings were held?

John The room was in the basement and it was very small. So when 17 people were in there it was quite crowded and very hot in the summer.

Kevin What about Alan Turing, was he a regular member?

John Oh yes, he was there almost every time. When he gave his first talks they were a bit bewildering to members.

Kevin I have heard that Turing had quite a stammer when he spoke.

John Yes that's right. But for a man who had such speech disabilities he was very forceful, especially on logic or philosophy he was right in there. He sort of ploughed through it and it was quite amazing. After a while it made no difference, you got used to it.

Kevin Can you remember any of Turing's presentations?

John Very clearly. The talk he gave that I remember most was on probability – why the spots on a leopard are as they are – which he proved mathematically in an amazing exposition. You felt afterwards that there cannot be any other reason. He was very convincing.

Kevin What was Turing doing at the time?

John At first he was at Manchester University but then I seem to remember he moved to the National Physical Labs at Enfield, where he worked on an in-house computer that was not particularly successful.

Kevin Turing is now regarded as one of the father figures of artificial intelligence. But it must have been strange to hear his views at that time.

John The thing was, the country was still obsessed with secrecy. I think he felt very down by it and what he had been through. In the club a lot was talked about that had been kept under wraps till that time.

Kevin What did the group think about his concept of the imitation game which he promoted at that time?

John I think for us we felt it was a case of "if it looks like a duck and quacks like a duck then it is a duck".

Kevin Did people in the club strongly disagree with Turing?

John No. Because we were diverse, we were not openly aggressive. We tended to listen to what people had to say and then discussion followed. It was never fierce – a nice environment.

Kevin What was Turing's ego like? What did he feel about himself? Was he modest?

John He was quite an outward guy. But he was so clever that he was puzzled as to why we had so much difficulty to understand what he was talking about. He was a very bright, sharp character: no doubt about that.

Kevin But surely anything to do with computers would, at that time, have been theoretical.

John There weren't any.

Kevin The impression I get from his papers was that he was good with using parables to tell a story in order to put over what he was saying.

John Our feeling was that what he was talking about was perfectly correct and he understood it deeply. However there were people there who were not mathematical at all. He made an attempt to explain things to them, but it was quite difficult for him, especially concepts such as computability.

Kevin Surely then for Turing to talk about the possibility of computers thinking would have been difficult for you all to take on board?

John That's certainly true. Nobody at the time thought of computers as anything like that. They were just calculators. So it was difficult for him to get that across.

Kevin Was there a suspicion that his ideas were crazy?

John No, we thought Alan was very clever but we couldn't explain it. There was a great tolerance.

Kevin But for you, Turing and the others to regularly turn up at the club once a month was incredible. After all you had jobs to do. What was the driving force?

John It was good enough that people wanted to turn up regularly despite their work. The meetings were close enough to each other that there was continuity. Bates kept it going very well. He was an organizer who didn't upset people who were very diverse in many respects. I thought it was a good thing. It was a privilege to have been asked. We decided not to expand. We were a happy band who all got to know each other very well. What was good about it was that there were all these people who had specialist knowledge who you wouldn't ordinarily talk to. So for the group of us we all became quite knowledgeable in a wide range.

Kevin Looking back, do you have any final thoughts about Alan Turing?

John Turing was a very remarkable character. His stammer didn't hold him back one bit. He has a very sad history though; it is very painful to think about.

Kevin Thank you.

Another member of the Ratio Club was Giles Brindley. Giles gave the 1986 Ferrier Lecture at the Royal Society and although he developed some of the first visual neuroprostheses he is best known for his extremely unusual presentation at the 1983 meeting of the American Urological Association (see also Klotz, 2005, Brindley, 1986).

The first-named author first met Giles when presenting the Sir Hugh Cairns Memorial Lecture at the British Society for Neurosurgeons Spring meeting in 2014. Both authors subsequently interviewed Giles about the club and Alan Turing in particular, specifically for this book. Selected transcripts from the interview, which was conducted on Monday 7 April 2014 at Giles' home now follow.

Kevin How did you get involved with the Ratio Club.

Giles Well they were looking for interesting people, I had been doing some interesting things and I was elected. I understood it was basically a Cambridge club. Horace Barlow was a very good friend and we went to meetings together.

Huma What did you think of Alan Turing?

Giles He was a bit different, something of a celebrity.

Kevin When were you in Cambridge?

Giles My research in Cambridge was from 1951 to 1952. Then I moved to Farnborough [The Royal Aircraft Establishment].

Huma At the Ratio Club did they talk about how machines could be intelligent?

Giles I don't recall there being much discussion on artificial intelligence but we did talk about how the brain works.

Huma What is your view on Turing's idea that we don't need to worry about the mysteries of consciousness if we are going to build a machine to think?

Giles I definitely agree with the statement. You can make a machine do something that is very like thinking and people call it thinking. We don't have to worry if it is conscious or not.

Kevin What is your view about it being conscious?

Giles We can ask what is the analogue of consciousness for a fairly intelligent animal. It is an awkward word to use with regard to animals because they do not have a consciousness that is very similar to ours. It is distantly related to ours. It is not a helpful word to use.

Huma Turing felt that learning a language was one of the most impressive human accomplishments. So what do you think about Turing's language test, his imitation game, with regard to a machine thinking?

Giles This is a matter of how we want to define thinking.

Huma Turing said that thinking was like a buzzing in his head.

Giles Well I disagree with Turing about that.

Huma What do you think 'thinking' enables you to do?

Giles Everything a human does. As long as I am conscious I am always thinking. I never switch off unless I am asleep.

Huma So you are thinking all the time and you are aware that you are thinking?

Giles Well I could be in a situation of sensory deprivation and I might not be
aware about thinking.

Huma How would you go about testing a locked-in patient to see if they were
thinking?

Giles Totally locked-in – you can't do it.

Huma If a machine gave reasonably good responses to questions would you
regard it as intelligent?

Giles Yes, most people would. But they would have to be good questions.
Intelligence is a relative matter, it's not all or nothing. If a machine
answers both easy and difficult questions well then it is reasonable
to describe it as intelligent. Although a machine might say "I don't
know" either because it couldn't know something or did not have the
ability.

Kevin To change the subject slightly I see that you have referenced both Horace Barlow and William Rushton in your papers. Is that the William
Rushton from the Ratio Club?

Giles Yes both of them were in the Ratio Club. They were interesting, lively
people. One person Horace introduced me to was Sir Charles Darwin, who was the grandson of *the* Charles Darwin. Horace Barlow is
himself in fact a great-great-nephew of Charles Darwin.

Kevin Thank you

Summary

In this chapter we have tried to give some background to Turing's ideas on the
game and what it might mean. What we have attempted to show is that, far from
confining his thoughts to paper, he was only too willing to open up in discourse
and discuss his thoughts in the area both with working colleagues and, with
regard to the Ratio Club, the intelligentsia of the day. Indeed the feedback he
obtained in such discussions was vital in allowing him to formulate his ideas
into a palatable message.

Even now there are some senior philosophers who dismiss the idea of
a machine thinking as though it is a ridiculous thing to consider. Still more

regard the whole idea of the imitation game as mere fun, only a parlour game. We can only imagine therefore the courage it must have taken for Turing to try to explain such concepts as the game to his peers in the 1940s and 1950s when computers as we know them did not exist, and those that did were slow and gigantic in size. Just like the other members, Turing didn't have to be part of the Ratio Club, but he was. He didn't have to make presentations, but he did. He didn't have to be provocative in his 1950 paper, but he was.

The remainder of the book is split into two parts: Part One considers in detail Turing's ideas on thinking machines and the philosophical debate that surrounds them. The second part presents the readers with information from practical tests implementing Turing's ideas according to his vision. This was to examine whether a machine could think in an imitation game which involves a machine providing satisfactory answers to any questions put to it by a human interrogator.

Part One

Chapter 2: Presents Turing's own writings on the imitation game.

Chapter 3: A brief account of artificial intelligence.

Chapter 4: The debate surrounding Turing's notions in order to examine machine thinking: an examination of the literature and philosophies of opponents and supporters.

Chapter 5: A history of machines that could 'talk' with humans, including the Weizenbaum study into natural language understanding through the *Eliza* computer program.

Chapter 6: Practical considerations arising from early implementations of Turing's imitation game such as the Loebner Prize competitions.

Part Two

Chapter 7: Presents an experiment carried out at Reading University in 2008 which implemented 96 simultaneous comparison Turing tests in which human judges interrogated two hidden entities in parallel to determine whether their interlocutors were human or machine.

Chapter 8: The 2008 experiment was followed in 2012, on the centenary of Turing's birth, by the then largest ever Turing test experiment, conducted at Bletchley Park. Both scenarios for Turing's imitation game were staged: simultaneous comparison tests (one human judge interrogating two hidden interlocutors), and the *viva voce* tests (one judge interrogating one hidden entity at a time).

Chapter 9: Interviews with the builders of the current best-performing machines in Turing test events.

Chapter 10: The historic 2014 Turing test experiment at The Royal Society in London in which one of the five machines in the experiment passed the Turing test in a five-minute, unrestricted question–answer imitation game; one third of its interrogators failed to make the correct identification!

Chapter 11: The book ends with the worldwide response to the historic 2014 result and looks to the future in stating that Turing's imitation game is as relevant today as it was when he proposed it over sixty years ago.

References

Ashby, W.R. (1949). *Ashby's Journal*, 1928–72, pp. 2520–2523, `http://www.rossashby.info/journal`

Brindley, G.S. (1986). Pilot experiments on the actions of drugs injected into the human corpus cavernosum penis. *British Journal of Pharmacology*, **87**, 495–500.

Davies, D. (1999). The Bombe, a remarkable logic machine. *Cryptologia* **23** (2), 108–138.

Hodges, A. (1992). *Alan Turing: The Enigma*. Vintage.

Husbands, P. and Holland, O. (2008). The Ratio club: a hub of British cybernetics. In *The Mechanical Mind in History*, P. Husbands, O. Holland and M. Wheeler (eds), MIT Press.

Klotz, L. (2005). How (not) to communicate new scientific information: a memoir of the famous Brindley lecture. *British Journal of Urology International* **96** (7), 956–957.

Turing, A.M. (1950). Computing machinery and intelligence. *Mind* **LIX** (236), 433–460.

Wiener, N. (1948). *Cybernetics, or Control and Communication in the Animal and the Machine*. MIT Press.

PART ONE

2

Turing's Ideas on Machine Thinking and Intelligence

In the previous chapter we learnt a little about Turing. Now we explain his ideas on intelligent machinery. Turing's investigation into the question of whether it was possible for machines to show intelligent behaviour led him to propose one of the most controversial tests for examining a machine's performance through a question-and-answer imitation game.

Human computers

Turing's 1936 paper *On Computable Numbers, with an Application to the Entscheidungsproblem* revolutionised the way in which modern computer science was considered and his later papers formed the basis for the digital computing era. The readers are encouraged to view this paper, which first appeared in the *Proceedings of the London Mathematical Society* and is included along with other works in Cooper and van Leeuwen (2013). Hodges (1992) provides an excellent and less technical explanation.

At the time of its publication, it was humans who *computed* carrying out calculations using sufficient pencil and paper (Bush, 1945), so it was humans who were known as *computers*, employed in all sorts of industries including government and business (Copeland, 2004). Computation was done by humans using their agency to write meaningful symbols on paper. Turing believed this work could be managed by a machine; he declared that it was "possible to invent a single machine which can be used to compute any computable sequence" (Turing, 1936). Although the machines of that period were mechanised elements of the human computer's work, i.e., adding and subtracting, they did so more quickly. The use of the term *digital* distinguished the machine from the human. Turing's idea for a *universal machine* emerged in this paper. It is worth noting here comments from Turing's 1938 Princeton University doctoral dissertation[1], that mathematical reasoning involved *intuition* and *ingenuity*, the former allowing spontaneous judgements that are not the result of conscious trains of reasoning, which, when added to suitable arrangements of propositions, geometric figures and drawings, would result in ingenuity. Both these functions would differ in the role they played from occasion to occasion. In this 1936 paper Turing proposed ideas that would be contentious and remain so in the century following his untimely death.

Turing's research presented in his essays and a lecture prior to the publication of his 1950 paper suggests why he chose *Computing Machinery and Intelligence* – CMI – as its title. Early calculating machines showed they could do the work of a human computer much faster; these were designated *machines* to distinguish from the human. Work carried out by Turing before writing CMI led him to address the question: if *human computers* calculating their mental action is regarded as *thinking* and their output is considered a result of *intelligence*, then why not similar attributions to *machines* when they performed calculations, albeit in a different way?

The design of the automatic machine engine – ACE – was the topic of a lecture Turing presented to the London Mathematical Society acquainting attendees with the prospect of intelligent machines that could not only learn from experience, but could also compete against humans in a game of chess. With *instruction tables*, or programs with subsidiary rules, Turing pointed to the possibility of machines altering their own programs enabling them to learn. Turing described the machine as a digital entity, in which sequences of digits, no matter how long, could represent numbers allowing any type of calculation to be performed to the desired degree of accuracy.

Turing likened the ACE project to building a brain inasmuch as it could be made to do any computing job that could be done by a human only much more quickly. Turing claimed that the rule of thumb process was synonymous with the machine process. However, the memory required in the machine would need to be very large and in a form that enabled extraction of information at short notice, what we might call intelligent information retrieval today.

Turing also talked about the machine's storage capacity. He wrote that if "we are to have a really fast machine then, we must have our information, or at any rate a part of it, in a more accessible form than can be obtained from books". In fact Turing felt storage *and* memory were more important issues than speed, which would only take prominence when commercial viability was a major factor, essentially a requirement of the purchaser. Turing added that if supplied with appropriate instructions then the properties of the universal

---

[1] *Systems of Logic Based on Ordinals*, reprinted as Turing (2012).

machine applied to any particular problem could be made to do any rule of thumb process and that the digital ACE was a practical version of the universal machine.

Turing (1947) wrote that the main bulk of the ACE's work would consist of problems which could not have been tackled by manual computation because of the scale of the undertaking, but a great number of able mathematicians would be needed to cover the groundwork before the ACE could be put into operation on a task by formulating problems in a form for the machine's computation. There was also considerable scope for human analysts to check for machine errors, because the ACE did not have the capacity for *common sense* replies. Turing envisaged that humans working with machines could be categorised as masters and servants. The former would design the program with increasing complexity, while the latter would act as the machine's limbs feeding it 'cards'. Turing moreover envisaged machines that would one day take over the functions of master and servant by replacing them with mechanical and electrical limbs and sense organs.

Although Turing believed machines could do all the tasks carried out by a human computer, initially at least they would need instructions. However, they could also be *trained* and could then *learn* and *adapt*. The design of ACE was the topic of a lecture Turing presented to the London Mathematical Society acquainting attendees with the prospect of intelligent machines that could not only learn from experience, but could also compete against humans in a game of chess. Turing considered chess as a good starting point. It was advisable to confine any investigation to a limited field, and chess lent itself readily for the ACE to compete against an average human player, as long as the machine was given appropriate instruction tables.

Turing concluded his 1947 ACE machine lecture with "No man adds very much to the body of knowledge, why should we expect more of a machine?".

Origin of the imitation game

Turing took up the position of Deputy Director of the Computing Machine Laboratory at Manchester University in May 1948. Before that Turing produced a report entitled *Intelligent Machinery* in which he proposed to investigate the question of whether it was possible for machinery to show intelligent behaviour. He wrote "It is usually assumed without argument that it is not possible". He argued that the attitude against machines was revealed in the use of common catch phrases 'acting like a machine', 'purely mechanical behaviour'. Turing felt the reasons for humans bearing such a bias included:

(a) an "unwillingness for to admit the possibility that mankind can have any rivals to intellectual power" ;

(b) a religious belief against the construction of intelligent machines;

(c) it is the creator of the machine who is intelligent not the machine showing intelligent behaviour.

Turing (1948) (from which we freely quote below) did warn that these arguments could not be ignored "because the idea of 'intelligence' is itself emotional rather than mathematical". He gave examples, including the case of a pupil's discovery: was the pupil to be commended or should the credit be awarded to their teacher? Turing continued "the teacher would be pleased with the success of his methods of education, but would not claim the results themselves unless he had actually communicated them to his pupil". Turing also mentioned how humans used irregular verbs to add variety to language: "we seem to be content that things should not obey too mathematically regular rules". Turing also surprised with a comment: "It is already possible to produce machines where this sort of situation arises in a small degree. One can produce 'paper machines' for playing chess. Playing against such a machine gives a definite feeling that one is pitting one's wits against something alive". It is clear from this statement that in 1948 Turing's subjective perspective had accepted that machines could *think*, and that he was attempting to tell the world how this was possible.

By *paper machines* Turing meant a combination of a man with written in-structions: "It is possible to produce the effect of a computing machine by writ-ing down a set of rules of procedure and asking a man to carry them out". Tur-ing contended a paper machine constituted a person provided with paper, pen-cil, and eraser subjected to strict discipline. Turing offered a positive reason for believing in the possibility of making thinking machines: it is possible to make machinery to imitate any part of a person. At the time of his writing he pointed to commonplace items such as the microphone for the ear, and the television camera for the eye. Turing added that "One can also produce remote controlled robots whose limbs balance the body with the aid of servo-mechanisms". This is the first time Turing talked about an embodied entity, for up to this point he had been concerned with the mind, intelligence without body. He went on describing and impractical way of building a thinking machine by replacing all the parts of a whole man with machinery: "Include television cameras, micro-phones, loudspeakers, wheels and handling servo-mechanisms as well as some sort of electric brain" letting this contraption "roam the countryside" to find out things for itself, while presenting a danger to "ordinary citizens". In this way Turing attempted to show, at this stage, an embodied machine was unnecessary and futile so the focus should be on "what can be done with a 'brain' which is more or less without body, providing at most organs of sight, speech and hearing".

For such a disembodied machine Turing considered fields of engagement in which the machine's competence could be measured, in games such as chess; learning and translation of languages, cryptography and mathematics. Of these possible fields, Turing believed "the learning of languages would be the most impressive, since it is the most human of these activities". We can see where Turing was headed in this serious and important contribution to modern computer science and robotics, however, he did concede that language would "depend too much on sense organs and locomotion to be feasible". Nonetheless, it did not deter him a short while later to propose an imitation game based on linguistic performance, and we can see from his 1948 paper why he felt the challenge was not insurmountable. Turing felt education would provide the machine with a similar some sort of circumstance, that of *interference* through contact with their environment receiving visual and other stimuli and in communication with other people leading to modifying behaviour. Turing wrote that by "applying appropriate interference, mimicking education" a machine could be modified "until it could be relied on to produce definite reactions to certain commands". Turing also discussed discipline and initiative in the closest statement he made about representing human intelligence: "discipline is certainly not enough in itself to produce intelligence. That which is required in addition we call initiative. This statement will have to serve as a definition. Our task is to discover the nature of this residue as it occurs in man, and try and copy it in machines".

On teaching the mind-machine, Turing advocated that the machine be programmed to do every kind of job that could be done and little by little allowing the machine to make choices and take decisions. A childlike machine would thereby mature into an adult-type machine. Turing believed further research into intelligence of machinery would be concerned with intellectual and cultural searches: "the idea that intellectual activity consists mainly of various kinds of search". Turing concluded his *Intelligent Machinery* paper by informing the reader of an experiment he had conducted using chess as the platform to assess a machine pitted against a human. He urged readers to be careful about judging difference warning against bias by posting "The extent to which we regard something as behaving in an intelligent manner is determined as much by our own state of mind and training as by the properties of the object under consideration". Turing was clearly referring to the role subjectivity plays in judging others. He continued "with the same object therefore it is possible that one man would consider it as intelligent and another would not; the second man would have found out the rules of its behaviour". At this point Turing asked us to imagine a scenario in which a paper machine is pitted in a game of chess against a human. In this early form of the imitation game three human players, *A*, *B* and *C*, take part with the paper machine as follows:

(i) *A* and *C* are rather poor players of chess;
(ii) *B* is a mathematician and chess player who operates the paper machine;
(iii) Two rooms are used with an arrangement for communicating the chess moves so that *C* cannot hear or view whom they are playing;
(iv) *C* plays either *A* or the paper machine.

In this 1948 scenario Turing said it might not be easy for *C* to say whether they were playing the machine or player *A*. Here Turing had laid the foundation for what is now considered the 'standard Turing test', a game in which a human interrogator plays two hidden entities, one human and one machine, and decides which is which. Turing had introduced ideas illustrating how a machine might exhibit intelligent behaviour, using the human brain and its modification through education as a guiding principle. Turing's drive to show machines could be intelligent continued with his next paper, the seminal *Computing Machinery and Intelligence* – CMI.

The language imitation game

Possibly one of the most contentious papers ever, *Computing Machinery and Intelligence* provided future researchers with a issue for debate which continues to this day. Namely, is an unseen and unheard machine 'thinking' if it succeeds, after text-based question-and-answer sessions, in convincing human interlocutors that it is human. Following the Second World War, Turing drew readers into the uncommon idea of non-human machines as 'thinking entities' through a simple yet brilliant idea using *textual interview*. Nowadays humans routinely interrogate and communicate via text over email, mobile devices and across the Internet to find news, elicit information and determine its usefulness. The vast literature surrounding Turing's proposal to consider whether a machine can think exposes a chasm between those who feel text-based interrogation is an effective way of measuring human–machine *indistinguishability* and others who maintain it serves no purpose. This situation is further confused by the insistence on the importance of gender of the hidden human against which a machine is compared by a human interlocutor in the three-participant game (see Shah and Warwick, 2010 and Warwick and Shah, 2016). This matter was touched on by Turing himself through his description of a number of scenarios in CMI as we shall see.

Turing's question–answer language imitation game, also known as the Turing test, essentially appeared for the first time in his 1950 paper. The imitation game manifests as an intellectual pursuit in which an imaginary machine convinces a human interlocutor into believing that they are textually questioning another human. This paper has polarised researchers and provoked many interpretations. French (1990) insists the imitation game is not a test for intelligence *per se*, but of culturally-oriented human intelligence, while Harnad (2001) asserts that, as a test for *indistinguishability* between human and machine it sets an empirical goal for artificial intelligence.

In CMI, Turing outlined the pursuit of a deceptive entity questioned by a human interrogrator. Representing various scenes, Turing mentioned *game* 16 times in the paper and positioned it as an *imitation game* exhorting "the best strategy for the machine may possibly be something other than the imitation of the behaviour of a man". However, Turing further wrote that "The reader must accept it as a fact that digital computers can be constructed ... and that they can in fact mimic the actions of a human computer very closely". Referring to the game as a *problem* twice, and an *experiment* twice, Turing describes on three occasions the quest for thinking machines as a *test*.

Turing takes the reader through a number of initial scenarios in CMI before arriving at the human–machine test – little wonder that there is division among interpreters of Turing's text! This is without even considering Turing's embellishment in 1952. However, it is clear from his previous, 1948 paper that the possibility of intelligent machinery was uppermost in his mind and how to convey this to a lay audience who had not worked on developing the first digital computers was key. Who would dispute that at the core of Turing's enterprise is a machine's text-based capacity to provide *satisfactory* answers to any questions put to it by a human interlocutor. In the next section we explore Turing's 1950 scenarios to find out if a general interpretation can be raised clarifying how the game/experiment/test should be conducted. It must be remembered however that, as John Westcott pertinently indicated, computers as we know them did not exist in 1950 when Turing's paper appeared. That paper therefore contains a certain amount of necessary story telling on Turing's part in order to try to explain the concepts that he was airing. Turing himself appears to have had quite a reasonable idea of what computers would be like fifty years thence. But the same could not have been said of many of his contemporaries.

In 1948 Turing had prefaced the notion of a machine imitating a human with an artificial player of chess. In 1950, Turing replaced chess-playing with 'thinking' imparted through sustained and 'satisfactory' responses to questions. Imitation is accepted as a form of flattery and Turing deployed this device as a means to measure a machine's humanness. He evolved his 1948 chess game to a textual duel now requiring the machine to perform on its own with no mathematician operator, with *C*, the poor chess player of 1948, being replaced by an "average interrogator" (Turing, 1950: p. 442).

Declaring it a dangerous attitude in 1950 to reflect on the *normal* use of the words 'machine' and 'think' when considering the question *Can machines think?*, Turing excluded "men born in the usual manner" from taking the part of a machine in the game. He asked "May not machines carry out something which ought to be described as thinking but which is very different from what a man does?" (Turing, 1950: p. 435). He quite rightly asked that question, realising that one man does not think like every other; a man may think like a woman; an Occidental woman may not think like a woman from the Orient.

Prescribing an open mind when considering 'machine' and 'think', Turing opined that considering their everyday usage would be as absurd as seeking definitions for these terms from a statistical survey through a poll. Thus, Turing avoided replying in the positive to the question *Can machines think?* taking a diagonal detour through the 'unambiguous' and 'new form of the problem' – a machine compared against a human, both being asked questions by an interrogator.

Distinguishing textual man from woman

This is, we believe, is a red herring in implementing Turing's imitation game. Our research and interviewing leads us to believe that in his paper, because of the general lack of knowledge about computers in 1950, Turing sketched out a philosophical and mental game with three participants, using first a man and a woman rather than a human and a machine. Initially the man and woman were located in a separate room from a male or female interrogator. Turing then framed his 'thinking exercise' through a textual game of imitation and deception. The man would take part as *A*, the woman as *B* and the interrogator as *C*.

Turing suggested that it would be best if the answers were sent via tele-printed communication between the rooms – as would be done through a local network now. The object of this scenario is for the interrogator (*C*), without seeing, touching, smelling or hearing *A* and *B*, to correctly identify the man and the woman based upon written answers to questions put to them both (see Figure 2.1).

The aim of *A* is to convince *C* by pretending to be the woman; the in-terrogator's task is to resist this deception. Turing directs that the woman, *B*,

Figure 2.1 Man–woman imitation game.

must assist the interrogator *C*: the "best strategy for her is probably to give truthful answers", suggesting that she might be weaker at deception. Did Turing expect the deceiving man *A* in this scenario to appear more womanly to the interrogator *C* than the woman *B*, or could *C* classify them both, *A* and *B*, as female – the indistinguishability score? Turing did not say. Expecting the man to appear more womanly, i.e., to cause the interrogator to misclassify *B* as the man, is an altogether different and more stringent test. We believe it was indistinguishability that Turing was driving at. Furthermore, as he did not preclude women from interrogating, he therefore did not feel *women would be weaker at deception-detection.*

It is not important, in the overall account of the machine–human comparison, for us to dwell on why Turing selected the female to answer truthfully; it suffices that the three-human game acted as an initiation for the reader. What should be noted in Turing's musings on questions and answers is that, in his imagining of the game with the two human hidden participants both have access to the other's responses to *C*'s questions so that the woman can say "I am the woman, don't listen to him!" to any of *A*'s answers. Nonetheless, Turing reminded us that "it will avail nothing as the man can make similar remarks".

Hence, the first item for the three-participant machine–human textual comparison Turing proposed is that the two hidden entities questioned by an interrogator should not have access to each other's responses, else the exercise will loop into a futile and fruitless interaction. In particular, if they are asked the same question, one could copy the other's response exactly throughout the game. We point out here that though Turing used the man–woman scenario as an introduction to the machine–human comparison, he could have used any other contrast. For example, he could have chosen a comparison test between a native speaker of English and a non-native one, and have the differences in English conversational ability tested by an interrogator asked to determine which is which. This test could then be conducted with a machine and native speaker of English speaker without letting the interrogator know that one of the humans had been replaced by a machine. The ultimate focus is on the machine's ability to imitate human text-based conversation.

Three-way machine–human comparison

At the end of Section 1 of CMI, having introduced an imitation game in which a man must convince an unseen, unheard interrogator that he is the woman, Turing asked readers to consider "What will happen when a machine takes the part of *A* in this game? Will the interrogator decide as wrongly as often as when the game is played like this as he does when the game is played between a man and a woman?". This question suggests Turing wanted the interrogator to be central to the test and the machine imitate a woman: how often the interrogator decides an entity is the woman in the man–woman scenario compared to how often a hidden entity is ranked the woman in a machine–woman test. However, as we shall see with Turing's elaborations later in the 1950 paper, imitating a woman is not central to the design of the machine; it is imitating *human-like* utterances. Thus the comparison ratio, of how well the interrogator does in recognising the woman correctly, in the man–woman pair, against how often the machine is identified correctly in a human–machine pair, does not serve any purpose in terms of measuring the text-based conversational ability of the machine. Turing did not state that the interrogator could not return a result of both human after questioning a human–machine pair. This is the result, *Turing's indistinguishability* which is the goal of the machine in an imitation game.

Turing put forward his own belief that "in about fifty year's time it will be possible to programme computers, with a storage capacity of about 10^9, to make them play the imitation game so well that an average interrogator will not have more than a 70%. chance of making the right identification after five minutes of questioning." (Turing, 1950, p. 442).

Question–answer test

Having introduced a game in which successful imitation of human-like responses causes deception, a failure to distinguish natural from artefact, Turing claimed that the question-and-answer method seemed to be suitable for introducing almost any one of the fields of human endeavour the interrogator might wish to include. The interrogator is not allowed to seek any practical demonstrations during the questioning, no matter how much the hidden entities may boast about their appearance or prowess. Turing pointed out the limitations of the machines at that time: "there will be some questions to which it will either give a wrong answer, or fail to give an answer at all however much time is allowed for a reply". Turing wrote "I am often wrong, and the result is a surprise for me", but, he asked, would it be fair to deem machines *worse* for *not* making mistakes? It was generally believed that it was more appropriate to ask machines closed questions, i.e. those requiring a yes or no answer, rather than open ones, such as those asking for an opinion. On that issue Turing remarked that that "it has only been stated, without any sort of proof, that no such limitations apply to the human intellect"; it may be that a human has no opinion on a matter because of lacking some piece of knowledge possessed by the interrogator or because of lack of interest. We will see examples of this later in the book with transcripts from practical Turing tests.

Turing tests rest heavily on the finer points of the interrogator's strategy:

- what questions the interrogator chooses to ask;
- what style should be adopted for questioning;
- assumption of what constitutes 'general knowledge';
- susceptibility to deception.

The interrogator's role entails selecting the most appropriate questions overcoming assumptions about possessed knowledge, and detecting deception by the *imitating machine* each time to correctly identify the nature of hidden pairs of interlocutors (see Figure 2.2).

Figure 2.2 Turing's three-participant simultaneous comparison test. Courtesy Harjic Mehroke.

Turing poured scorn on the illusion of feeling of superiority if an interrogator met with a wrong answer from a machine, and he stressed "We [humans] too often give wrong answers to questions to be justified in being very pleased at such evidence of fallibility on the part of the machines". Dismissing those interrogators who felt they had won a point, "on such an occasion in relation to the one machine over which we have scored a petty triumph", Turing reminds us "there would be no question of triumphing simultaneously over *all* machines", for example not being able to win in a race against an aeroplane. If the machine's answers were regarded as "satisfactory and sustained" Turing argued, then that would not be "an easy contrivance".

Simultaneously interacting with a pair of hidden participants for five minutes in total, based on the *intellectual capacity* demonstrated through responses to questions the interrogator asks, the human interrogator must declare what they think each hidden *witness* is, human or machine. Implying the machine's superiority, if the human were to attempt to act artificially, like a machine, Turing remarks that the latter "would be given away at once by slowness and inaccuracy in arithmetic". While Turing introduces examples of *what* kind of question it would be possible to ask a hidden interlocutor, Turing missed a salient point: *how* interrogators should ask questions. Should the interrogator be polite and treat the test as a conversation between equals, or should they be suspicious and aloof questioning in an inconsiderate style; or should they examine the mathematical skills of the hidden interlocutor to beat the machine, which surely would be better and faster at calculating the square roots of long numbers?

Two-participant interrogator–witness game

In 'Contrary Views', Section 6 of CMI, Turing puts forward his responses to anticipated objections to a thinking machine, including an *argument from consciousness*. Turing addressed what seemed to him as Professor Jefferson's solipsistic argument requiring a mechanism to "feel pleasure at its successes, grief when its valves fuse, be warmed by flattery, be made miserable by its mistakes, be charmed by sex, be angry or depressed when it cannot get what it wants". In that section Turing introduced an alternative machine-thinking test, the *viva voce* test reducing the number of participants from three to two (see Figure 2.3).

The dynamic of the investigation into thinking altered from a machine comparison against a human to a direct *one-to-one* questioning of a machine – the 'witness' – by a human interrogator. In Turing's response to the *consciousness* objection of thinking machines, the sample questions Turing's imagined interrogator puts to the witness are *not* gender-specific. This shows Turing did not have in mind the development of a *machine simulating a man pretending to be a woman*, one interpretation of machine design. Turing's imaginary *viva voce* was as follows:

Figure 2.3 Turing's two-participant *viva voce* test. Courtesy Harjic Mehroke.

Interrogator: *Would you say Mr. Pickwick reminds you of Christmas?*
Witness: *In a way.*

What Turing's exchange shows is that he was aware that an interrogator is likely to ask questions about topics they are familiar with and have an interest in, and, for a machine to respond appropriately would require sharing some of that knowledge and an inference capacity, a tall engineering order.

Turing's later work

Turing followed CMI with essays, lectures and radio discussions expanding, embellishing and clarifying the ideas he announced in 1950.

'Intelligent machinery, a heretical theory'

In one of two papers presented for radio discussion programmes in 1951[2] Turing explains his confidence in what machines could do, and refuted the argument "You cannot make a machine to think for you" (in Shieber, 2004, p. 105). Alluding to his 1950 paper, *learning from experience* is mentioned in the 1951 radio broadcast as a requirement of the machine in order to avoid repeated mistakes. Constructing a thinking machine, according to Turing, requires at least two people with different expertise: first, a *schoolmaster*, who must be

---

[2] Intelligent Machinery – a Heretical Theory' BBC Home Service, Manchester studio for *'51 Society*.

unaware of the machine's inner workings (in Copeland, 2004, p. 473), charged with educating the machine and transforming it from a simple to a more elaborate system. Second, a *mechanic* "permitted only to keep the machine in running order". The process would produce a "reasonably intelligent machine". He again uses the example of the machine playing chess, as he did in his 1948 paper, and supposes that the machine understands English allowing it the use of text-based communication to record and receive remarks "*owing to its having no hands or feet*". In an advanced stage of its education, the machine could forge new processes itself, resulting in a highly sophisticated and satisfactory form of rule. Turing drew an analogy with engineering problems that are sometimes solved by the crudest rule-of-thumb procedure for dealing with the most superficial aspects of the problem.

Though Turing does not mention the imitation game explicitly in this discourse he does affirm his position that machines could be constructed to simulate thinking and that he, Turing, knew how to construct such a machine "which would give a very good account of itself in a range of tests" if it were made elaborate enough (Shieber, 2004, p. 106).

Turing's 1951 heretical theory paper discusses single-aim systems developed commercially to carry out very specific tasks with certainty and considerable speed. This is where current technology mainly resides, as domain-specific expert systems. We are reminded of Turing's profound grasp of the potential of future machines by Copeland (2004).

'Can digital computers think?'

The second BBC radio broadcast in 1951 in which Turing took part covered a lecture series on automatic calculating machines. Confessing his partiality, Turing used his talk on 'Can Digital Computers Think?' to assert once again his view that "it is not altogether unreasonable to describe digital computers as brains" (Shieber, 2004). Turing claimed that the general public in the 1950s were amazed at accounts of what machines could do and accepted them as a sort of brain. This meant that people appreciated a machine could accomplish tasks of an intellectual nature, an attitude still visible today.

In response to Ada Lovelace's comment about Charles Babbage's Analytical Engine, namely that a machine "has no pretension whatever to *originate* anything. It can do whatever we know how to order it to perform" (Copeland, 2004, p. 482), Turing conceded this was true of the *way* machines were *used* in his time: "it is fair to say that the machine doesn't originate anything ... validity depends on considering how digital computers are used rather than how they could be used" . Turing asserted "I believe that they [digital computers] could be used in such a manner that they could appropriately be described as a brain".

Reiterating the prediction for the end of the (20th) century made in his 1950 paper, in the second 1951 radio broadcast Turing said "I think it is probable ... that at the end of the century it will be possible to programme a machine to answer questions in such a way that it will be extremely difficult to guess whether the answers are being given by a man or by the machine" (Copeland, 2004, p. 484). The first part of Turing's forecast has been achieved to an extent. Machines are able to answer questions put to them. Nonetheless it would have been hyperbole and factually incorrect to say the textual responses provided by these systems at the end of the last century were difficult to distinguish from humans. The picture is not bleak, however, as borne out in Demchenko and Veselov's *Eugene Goostman* with its ability to record and recall the colour of the interlocutor's car. This kind of performance can only improve given the enthusiasm of developers for building systems to entertain, educate and attempt to beat the Turing test. Concluding the 1951 lecture, Turing regarded the pursuit of thinking machines would "help us greatly in finding out how we think ourselves". It may also help in finding out why some people are easily deceived while others are not.

'Can automatic calculating machines be said to think?'

A BBC radio discussion 'Can automatic calculating machines be said to think?' in January 1952, that included Turing, Richard Braithwaite (an engineer), Geoffrey Jefferson (a neuroscientist) and Max Newman (a mathematician who headed Turing's team at Bletchley Park), is not only as important as Turing's 1948 and 1950 papers, it is essential for a complete understanding of his idea for a thinking machine. Turing explained his ideas (Copeland, 2004, p. 494):

> I don't want to give a definition of thinking, but if I had to I should probably be unable to say anything more about it than that it was a sort of buzzing that went on inside my head.

The broadcast provides a fascinating insight into the capacity of machines in 1952 and what the speakers considered was possible for them to achieve. Turing was relentless about the possibility of a machine simulating the brain's logical connections. Once again he displayed prescience by describing the necessary storage capacity and speed the machine would need in order to compete in a test. In this 1952 discussion Turing reaffirmed the two-entity, *one-to-one* game and proposed a revised prediction for deception success. Turing's canvass for a thinking machine is considered by some the earliest known recorded discussion of artificial intelligence (Copeland, 2004). The auspicious panel began with a consideration of the *proper sense* of the word *think*. Turing had deemed this pursuit a dangerous attitude two years earlier in his 1950 paper, and as absurd as finding the common usage for *meaning* in a Gallup poll. Nonetheless, the question of what thinking *is*, what thinking *involves*, and thus how to define *thought* before it can be agreed that machines could engage in it, dominates the 1952 radio discussion. Surprisingly, not only does Turing use the discussion to elaborate further on the interrogator–witness *one-to-one viva voce* test (Figure 2.3), he advised that it be conducted by a jury panel. Turing also announced a more circumspect prediction for the arrival of thinking machines: "at least 100 years".

Turing explained that the point of the machine in such a test is for it to convince a number of interrogators while pretending to be a man that it *can* 'think' by answering questions put to it: "it will only pass if the pretence is reasonably convincing". The type of questions that can be asked of the machine can include the kind used in a law court exemplified by Turing as "I put it to you that you are only pretending to be a man", thus allowing interrogators to pose open questions to the machine which is itself allowed to use 'tricks' such as silence, pause and spelling errors". Turing insisted a *jury service* in the form of a panel of non-machine experts act as the interrogators, but while they must not be allowed to see the machine, they may be permitted a typewritten medium through which to communicate with the hidden entity which is kept in a different room. Turing wrote: "a considerable proportion of a jury ... must be taken in by the pretence" in order for the machine to pass the test. Turing did introduce a *control test* in 1952, as he did in the 1950 version, with a human foil acting as witness on occasion. In the two-participant version of the imitation game Turing suggested "We had better suppose that each jury has to judge quite a number of times", and sometimes the interrogators should face a hidden human to question preventing them adjudging their interlocutor a machine in every instance of interaction "without proper consideration".

Turing does not mention any particular length of time for interrogator questioning, unlike the five-minute duration stated in his 1950 paper. However, listed in the 1952 discussion are Turing's eight criteria for staging the interrogator–witness jury-service test for a thinking machine:

(1) the machine is hidden from view and hearing from a panel of interrogators;
(2) the panel must not be machine experts;
(3) each member of a jury panel interacts one-to-one with the machine under test;
(4) the interrogators can only pose typed questions;

(5) the interrogators can ask any questions;
(6) the machine attempts to respond in a humanlike way;
(7) sometimes the interrogator is faced with a hidden human to question;
(8) each panel member interrogates a number of times.

Turing's co-panellist Max Newman retorted that he would like to be there when such a test was run in order to participate in questioning in a way that would tease out the machine from the man. Newman asked Turing what period of time would be required before a machine stood "any chance with no questions barred?", Turing, having had the opportunity, in the interval between the publication of CMI in October 1950 and the BBC radio discussion in January 1952, to reflect on a realistic date before a thinking machine could be built, replied: "At least 100 years, I should say". Hence, it is unlikely that Turing truly felt a machine would be ready to pass his five-minute, question–answer text-based interrogator–witness test for machine thinking *before* 2052, an important item that is missed by many who, attesting to Turing's 1950 paper alone and its *end of century prediction*, claim that Turing minimised the huge task of constructing such a device and got his prediction very wrong. He did not.

References

Braithwaite, R., Jefferson, G., Newman, M. and Turing, A.M. (1952). Can automatic calculating machines be said to think? Transcript of BBC radio broadcast. Reproduced Cooper and van Leeuwen (2013), pp. 667–676.

Bush, V. (1945). As we may think. *The Atlantic Wire*, July.

Cooper, S.B. and van Leeuwen, J. (eds). (2013). *Alan Turing: His Work and Impact* Elsevier.

Copeland, B.J. (ed). (2004). *The Essential Turing: The Ideas That Gave Birth to the Computer Age*. Oxford University Press.

French, R. (1990). Subcognition and the limits of the Turing test. *Mind* **99** (393), 53–65.

Harnad, S. (2001). Minds, machines and Turing: the indistinguishability of indistinguishables. *Journal of Logic, Language and Information* **9** (4), 425–445.

Hodges, A. (1992). *Alan Turing: The Enigma*. Vintage.

Shah, H. and Warwick, K. (2010). Testing Turing's five minutes, parallel-paired imitation game. *Kybernetes* **39** (3), 449–465.

Shieber, S.M. (ed). (2004). *The Turing Test: Verbal Behavior as the Hallmark of Intelligence*. MIT Press.

Turing, A.M. (1936). On computable numbers, with an application to the entscheidungsproblem. *Proceedings of the London Mathematical Society* **42** (2), 230–265

Turing, A.M. (1947). Lecture to the London Mathematical Society, 20th February 1947. Reproduced in Cooper and van Leeuwen (2013), pp. 486–497.

Turing, A.M. (1948). Intelligent machinery. Reprinted in Cooper and van Leeuwen (2013), pp. 501–516.

Turing, A.M. (1950). Computing machinery and intelligence. *Mind* **LIX** (236), 433–
    460.
Turing, A.M. (1951a). Intelligent machinery, a heretical theory. Reprinted in Cooper
    and van Leeuwen (2013), pp. 664–666.
Turing, A.M. (1951b). Can digital computers think? Reproduced in Cooper and van
    Leeuwen (2013), pp. 660–663.
Turing A.M. (2012). *Alan Turing's Systems of Logic: The Princeton Thesis*. Princeton
    University Press.
Warwick, K. and Shah, H. (2016). Effects of lying in practical Turing tests. *AI and
    Society*, **31** (1), 5–15.

3

A Brief Introduction to Artificial Intelligence

At this stage in the book we take a break from looking at Alan Turing himself and the imitation game and consider the wider field of artificial intelligence (AI). Whilst the game itself has proved to be arguably one of the most iconic and controversial aspects of AI, it is useful, we feel, to assess just how the game fits into the field and perhaps to give some sort of understanding as to why it is so important. We also take a look at such things as natural language processing but we avoid heavy mathematics. Anyone who is already well versed in AI may well wish to move straight to Chapter 4.

Alan Turing is frequently referred to as the father of artificial intelligence. He was around at the dawn of the computer age and was himself directly involved in early computer systems such as the Bombe, which he designed, and the Colossus, on which his work was used. The field of AI itself however was, some claim, first so named after Turing's death, around 1956 (Russell and Norvig, 2012) although in general it could be said to have come into existence as the first computers appeared in the 1940s and 1950s.

In AI's formative years attention was focussed mostly on getting computers to do things that, if done by a human, would be regarded as intelligent acts. Essentially it was very human-centered. When Turing proposed his imitation game in 1950, it was perfectly timed to be grabbed hungrily by the young and burgeoning, soon to become, AI community, particularly those interested in the philosophical aspects of the new field. As was shown in the previous chapter even main stream radio broadcasting was not scared to encompass the topic.

The game and AI

Turing wanted to come up with a realisable concept of intelligence in machines. Rather than give a long list of definitions, many of which would be controversial, or to construct a series of mathematical statements, most of which would be impracticable, he put the human at the centre and used a form of science involving actual experimentation to confirm the hypothesis. On top of this, the hypothesis itself, in the form of his imitation game, was based on a test of indistinguishability from entities, namely humans, that would be regarded as definitely thinking and undeniably intelligent. The added advantage to this idea is that there are a lot of humans around on which to try out the game.

In order to achieve success at the game a machine taking part would need to exhibit a number of characteristics. For example, natural language processing, which is the ability to communicate adequately (most likely in English); and learning capabilities to pick up nuances and adapt; the ability to reason and draw sensible relationships; and some form of memory involving both short and long term functionality, the short term aspect being operational within a single discourse. Whilst such characteristics do not entirely meet every requirement, they give a reasonable coverage and all are critical aspects of AI systems.

It is, at this point, well worth pointing out that even though Turing's game was first described well over 60 years ago, it is still very much under discussion and to this day remains an integral aspect of AI teaching. Interestingly, whilst some may argue over its actual meaning, no one has yet come up with a better idea which more appropriately answers the requirement.

Even if it can be shown experimentally that an entity, whether it be machine or human, thinks, this immediately raises the question as to how this actually happens. What Turing did very cleverly was to avoid the main issue, which was essentially to figure out what thinking was all about. What he did was to point to an example (humans) where we are already convinced that thinking does occur and assess whether a machine could appear to do things in the same sort of way as a human.

In fact the field of AI as a whole is segmented into different groupings dependent on expectations of what a machine can achieve. The first two of these groupings relate directly to human brain performance and hence the Turing test is central to their philosophy.

Weak AI

The possibility that machines can act intelligently or act as if they were intelligent in the same way as a human is referred to as Weak AI (Warwick, 2011).

This merely means that some machines can simply appear to do things we would regard as intelligent acts if done by a human. It says nothing about the actual nature of the processes involved in either the human or machine. In this way it is very much of the manner of the Turing test. Indeed it could be said that the imitation game is a test of weak AI.

Interestingly there are some AI researchers who (believe it or not!) deny the possibility of weak AI, even though in reality it appears as an everyday occurrence. In fact there are many cases where machines not only perform along the same lines as humans but actually outperforms them. In fact machines are often employed just for this purpose. Examples are financial trading, military surveillance and telemarketing. The speed and accuracy of the machine as well as round-the-clock operation are all telling features.

Strong AI

The possibility that a machine could or can actually think in exactly the same way as a human brain is referred to as strong AI (Warwick, 2011).

In no sense is this referring to merely an appearance or simulation of human intelligence or thinking. Rather the whole process needs to be the exactly the same as with the human brain. Effectively it would require building a computer that replicates the functioning of a human brain in every way.

The concept of strong AI has a number of consequences. Even if such a machine were acting as a brain in a robot or machine body it would be very unlikely to have aged and developed over the space of twenty or thirty years as does a human, in a human environment, with human nuances and physical associations. If the computer did have a body it would need to have the same physical characteristics and sensory input as a human (at least) in order for the entire thought process to be the same as that of a person. Or at least the computer would need to believe that this was the case.

Alternatively it would need to be possible to completely copy a human brain into an AI version at some instant in time. Such an achievement is not currently possible and it is, we feel, unlikely to be so for some time to come.

The concepts of weak and strong AI are, it is worth pointing out, both comparative studies about the functioning of a human brain and human intelligence. Yet another possibility is to consider that a computer may well be able to think, understand and be conscious but in its own way, rather than that of a human. This leads to the idea of rational AI.

Rational AI

A computer can be intelligent and can think in its own way, dependent on its state of embodiment, its nature and its history, including its education.

This is merely a case of allowing for the possibility of a machine to be intelligent, just as perhaps another animal is intelligent, based on its own features and characteristics. It still allows for the concepts of weak AI and strong AI to be applied. Indeed we use some of the same concepts of weak AI when it comes to considering rational AI as applied to animals.

Just as humans are intelligent in different ways from each other, so too are animals, and machines, depending on each machine's capability. As far as rational AI is concerned, whatever a machine is made of and how it is embodied, its intelligence takes its place as merely one form of many. But whereas weak AI and strong AI are based on some form of comparative study of human intelligence, rational AI is not.

Turing's imitation game, like the first two types of AI, is based on comparison with humans. Indeed the game is all about human communication specifically, although in theory there is no reason why the test could not involve any form of communication. Furthermore, with the game there is no critique of the underlying processing involved with the communication that occurs. The assessment of thinking is rather based purely on the machine performance. Hence it is definitely a test of weak AI. That said, it is an actual, realistic practical test which can be conducted.

Whilst the test has been criticized by some, these criticisms have largely been based on the weak AI/strong AI divide. In the case of the Turing test this means that even though it might be accepted that a machine could perform well, this does not mean that it can think. One such criticism, perhaps the most popular, is based on the *Chinese Room Problem* (Searle, 1997; Preston and Bishop, 2002).

The Chinese room problem

The Chinese room problem was originally conceived by Searle (1980) as an argument to demonstrate that although a machine might be able to do very well in Turing's imitation game it could not be said to think, have a mind, to understand or be conscious. Hence the emphasis here is not on how the machine behaves or appears but rather on its internal properties. The argument is as follows.

A computer (inside a room) takes Chinese characters as input and follows the instructions of a program to produce other, appropriate Chinese characters, which it presents as output.

The computer does this so convincingly that it comfortably convinces an external (to the room) human Chinese speaker that it is itself a human Chinese speaker. In effect, it does well at the Turing imitation game, fooling another human into believing that it is a human who is fluent in Chinese.

It could be argued by a supporter of strong AI that, as a result of its performance in the game, the computer *understands* Chinese. However, Searle argues that if the machine doesn't have *understanding* we cannot describe what the machine is doing as *thinking*. If this is so then because it does not think, the machine does not have a *mind* in anything like the normal sense of the word.

Consider instead that you are in a closed room and that you (an English speaker, who understands no Chinese) have a rule book with an English version of exactly the same program. You can receive Chinese characters, process them according to the instructions, and as a result you produce Chinese characters as output. As the computer has convinced a human Chinese speaker that it is one too, it is fair to deduce that, as you have performed exactly the same task, you will be able to do so as well.

There is in essence no difference between the computer's role in the first case and the one you play in the latter. Each is in turn simply following a program which simulates intelligent behavior. Yet, as we have presumed, you do not understand a word of Chinese, and are merely following instructions. Since you do not understand Chinese we can infer that the computer does not understand Chinese either. The conclusion drawn by Searle is therefore that running a computer program does not generate understanding or thinking.

Emergence of consciousness

Searle's argument is essentially that you, a human, have something more than the machine. That you have a mind with which you could learn to understand Chinese and that your mind is realised through the type of brain that you have. Searle said: "The (human) brain is an organ. Consciousness (and understanding) is caused by lower-level neuronal processes in the brain and is itself a feature of the brain. It is an emergent property of the brain". He went on: "Consciousness is not a property of any individual elements and it cannot be explained simply as a summation of the properties of those elements". He concluded: "Computers are useful devices for simulating brain processes. But the simulation of mental states is no more a mental state than the simulation of an explosion is itself an explosion".

It is important and appropriate to note that, in his conclusion, Searle is refuting the concept of strong AI. However, his argument opens up a number of other important considerations.

The first point of importance here is the concept that you (a human) have something extra (consciousness) that the computer does not have and that this comes about as an emergent property of your brain – through your human neurons and their connections! This could be seen as epiphenomenal, in that there are properties in human neurons that give rise to the mind, but these properties cannot be detected by anyone outside the mind, otherwise they could possibly be simulated in a computer thus realising strong AI.

This is a good example of an argument in AI in which human intelligence is seen to be something special. It appears that even if we can't measure it, the human brain is deemed to have something more than a machine brain. The argument is clearly human-centric. It is concerned with a human language, with all the nuances and life experiences that that conjures up. Without having lived a human life, how could a machine possibly *understand* such a language in the same way as a human?

Searle's point is that no matter how much the computer is used in an attempt to copy the human brain, it will never be exactly the same – unless perhaps if it is itself made up of human neurons and experiences some aspects of human life.

The Chinese room argument can though be refuted in a number of ways. As one example the argument can be turned on its head and posed in a favourable way for a machine – with exactly the same type of argument. You now have to follow a set of instructions with regard to machine code rather than Chinese. On the basis that no matter what you might learn, the machine code will still mean nothing to you, you will not *understand* it, whereas, for all we know, a computer may well *understand* the machine code. The end conclusion of such an argument would be that whilst a machine can be conscious, it is not possible for a human to be conscious.

Searle has in fact used his Chinese room argument in a number of different ways. He has said that whilst "humans have beliefs, thermostats and adding machines do not" or "if a shoe is not conscious then how can a computer be conscious?". It is best not to be taken in by such philosophical trickery. Exactly the same logic would argue that if a cabbage is not conscious then how can a human be conscious?

Reflection on the imitation game

Turing replaced the question about whether or not a machine could think with his imitation game. Essentially, if a machine wins at the game then, he said, surely we must acknowledge that it is a thinking machine. The act of *thinking* has however been felt by many (philosophers) to depend on such issues as *understanding* and being something that is done by a *mind*. Such persons have concluded by means of arguments such the Chinese room problem that the imitation game is not a test for strong AI. The game is however certainly a test of weak AI.

Turing himself did not employ such terminology as weak AI or strong AI. He did however use the word *thinking*. In doing so he created something of a problem because it really does depend on how the word is defined as to what one might conclude about what the game actually tests. A simple search will indicate numerous possible definitions of thinking such as *opinion* or *judgement* which perhaps ask for a further layer in definition. On the other hand using the *mind* to produce decisions puts emphasis on the *human* mind, as does the straightforward processing of a *conscious* mind, whereas making *rational* decisions seems clear.

In this book we are more concerned with the practical nature of the game and the extremely interesting results that can appear in the discourses that actually occur. However just what the game shows in terms of the thinking capabilities of a machine remains an intriguing philosophical question.

We will now look at some properties of intelligence that could arguably be expected in a discourse (with a human) and hence the sort of things that a machine would be expected to also achieve.

Rationality

This is the quality of reasoning based on facts. The term itself can take on somewhat different meanings dependent on whether some sort of individual or collective optimal decision is being made. However typically available information is factored in and an overall rational conclusion is reached.

Rationality is an important aspect of the imitation game. However it is mainly down to the interrogator to conclude whether or not a particular response is rational. This is something of an issue as far as the non-overlapping sectors of the knowledge bases of the interrogator and the human entity are concerned. The same reasoning on the part of the interrogator and the human entity may lead to different outcomes, hence confusion, if their knowledge bases are different.

So with the game the issue is perhaps not so much whether an entity has responded in a rational way but rather whether or not it appears to the interrogator to have done so. Otherwise the interrogator may regard hidden human entities in the game as machines simply because their quite rational responses are not understood by the interrogator.

Cognition

This is the process by which sensory input is transformed, processed and used. It is the mental processing that includes comprehending and producing language, reasoning, problem solving and decision making. It involves processing information and applying knowledge. Whilst closely aligned with rationality, as far as the game is concerned it means that an interrogator is usually looking for signs that an entity has understood their utterances. But the interrogator will also want to see that a problem has been appropriately dealt with and that sensible decisions have been made.

Clearly cognition is a detailed and complex process and much has been written about it (see e.g. Bermudez, 2014).

Natural language processing

This involves both natural language understanding – that is, for a computer to derive meaning from human or natural language input – and (natural language generation – that is, responding with appropriate utterances. Typically these are nowadays based on learning algorithms rather than a strictly defined set of rules. This generally means a requirement for real world input and some form of statistical inference as a learning tool.

As one might imagine it is a very large field of study in itself and it is not possible to give a significant review in the space of a few paragraphs. So here we have attempted to pick out some of the main features involved in the topic that relate specifically to the imitation game. This list is not meant to be by any means exhaustive but rather it is intended to give some sort of idea of the processes involved in setting up a computer to take part in the imitation game with regard solely to natural language processing requirements.

Co-reference resolution: to determine which words refer to the same objects.

Discourse analysis: identifies the structure of connected text, e.g. relationships between sentences.

Information retrieval: storing, searching and finding information.

Named entity recognition: determines which items refer to proper names, such as people or places.

Part-of-speech tagging: determines whether a word is a noun, verb or adjective.

Parsing: determines the grammatical analysis of a sentence. Typical sentences have multiple possible meanings.

Question answering: determining the answer to a question whether it be specific or open-ended.

Relationships: is short for the relationships between entities (for example, who is the mother of whom).

Word sense disambiguation: choosing the meaning of a word that makes the most sense in context.

As far as the imitation game is concerned, all of the above features must be performed in an appropriate, human-like fashion. It is worth adding that those features do not include what might be loosely described as human-type elements. By this we mean that occasional typographical errors are useful because this is something that humans do. It can also be useful for a machine to give incorrect answers to some questions or to reply that they do not know the answer to a question, because that is what a human would do – a difficult mathematical question is a good example of this.

What we have indicated here are some particular characteristics that need to be exhibited by a machine if it is to communicate effectively in a human-like way. One problem in making comparisons between humans (and in particular the human brain) and machines is that we become very defensive about the nature of human intelligence and the way it is exhibited, particularly when it is felt that consciousness and understanding is required. We don't want to be bettered by a machine.

Turing referred to this feature in humans as the argument from disability. It is the attitude in quite a number of humans to conclude that no matter what machines can do, humans still have something more (Warwick, 2011). It is in fact the basic foundation of the Chinese room problem and hence John Searle, in terms of this philosophical argument at least, is merely following an inappropriate line of thought that was exactly indicated as such by Alan Turing.

Argument from disability

This type of argument, which was originated by Alan Turing, has the following form: a computer may be able to do this or that but a computer will never do X. Turing himself offered a possible selection of choices for X:

> Be kind, resourceful, beautiful, friendly, have initiative, have a sense of humour, tell right from wrong, make mistakes, fall in love, enjoy strawberries and cream, make someone fall in love with it, learn from experience, use words properly, be the subject of its own thought, have as much diversity of behaviour as a man, do something really new.

Turing pointed out that no support is usually offered for these statements, and they depend on naive, often populist, assumptions about machine capabilities. This is certainly true of the Chinese room problem. Turing directly answered some of them:

A machine can have neither diversity of behaviour nor can it be creative. A computer can in fact behave in an astronomical number of different ways and certainly can be *far* more creative than many a human. Whether humans can understand such creativity is another matter.

Machines cannot make mistakes. It is in fact easy to program a machine to (appear to) make a mistake.

A machine cannot be the subject of its own thought. That is, it cannnot be self-aware. A program that can report on its internal states and processes can certainly be, and has been, written. Turing asserted a machine can undoubtably be its own subject matter.

As pointed out in Warwick (2011), when we refer to something that a human can do but that a machine may not be able to do, we need to be sensible as to what conclusions we draw. Is the task an important, defining issue in some sense? Most machines are pretty specific in what they do and so are humans. It would be silly to expect an aeroplane to smell a rose, for example, or to have a dry sense of humour. It would also be silly to expect humans to cruise at 30,000 feet, without the assistance of a machine, or understand ultraviolet signals which are fed directly into their brain. All of these things could possibly be arranged however, one way or another.

Classical AI

In classical AI, a top-down approach is taken, rather akin to a psychiatrist's view of human intelligence, looking from the outside in on the performance of the human brain. So in this form, the basic performance of a human brain in terms of behaviours and rules is simply copied, to some extent, usually in a particular domain, by the artificially intelligent computer.

Although this can take on one of a number of forms in a practical AI system, perhaps the most commonly encountered is that referred to as a knowledge-based system or an expert system. More often in the latter, an attempt is made to capture the approach taken by a human expert in terms of a series of rules.

In an expert system each rule is of the basic form:

IF (condition) THEN (conclusion).

For example it may be that the expert system is dealing with a water boiler and the rule is: if the temperature rises above 60° C then switch the heater off. As long as the computer is fed the latest temperature reading it can check, at each instant, to see if the condition has been met, and if it has then the rule fires and the conclusion is drawn; otherwise it is not.

For this relatively simple example just a small number of rules will be sufficient to run the boiler successfully. It might be however that several conclusions can be drawn from one or a small number of facts. There may then need to be further rules to decide which conclusion takes priority. Conversely it may be that the conclusion from one rule satisfies a condition of another, the rules being effectively layered such that one rule firing can cause another to fire and so on.

Rule-based systems have a number of good points. First, it can be relatively easy to enter real world decisions one-by-one, into the rule base. Second, when the system operates it is relatively fast. Third, the structure of the system is completely separate from the data.

On the other hand it can be difficult to decide which are the best rules to be entered. Even with relatively simple problems, different experts may well come up with different solutions, where there is more than one way of coming to a conclusion. On top of this, in order to cover every possible eventuality, no matter how unlikely it is to occur, the number of rules required can get out of hand; this is called *combinatorial explosion*. Under such circumstances rather than being relatively fast to operate, it can take quite some time for the system to check all possible rules at each instance to see which, if any, have fired. One example of this would be in the case of an expert system that is designed to drive an autonomous car. Does the car swerve if in the road there is a puddle, pigeon, pedestrian, bowl of porridge, a hole, etc.?

Of course, this is merely one example, serving to give some idea of classical AI. There are many other possibilities. What the methods have in common is that they are all top-down approaches, looking from the outside of the human brain inwards and trying to detect behavioural responses.

Modern AI

The term modern artificial intelligence is applied to the bottom-up approach that has become more popular in recent times. While classical AI looks at modelling a brain from the outside in, so modern AI attempts to understand the basic building blocks and then join them together in an operational fashion that is, in the end, brain-like. Importantly, this means that although it is interesting to consider the concept of an intelligent machine operating in the same way as a human brain, it is merely one, rather limited, possibility. Of much greater interest is how the artificial brain actually works.

The basic building block of a brain is a neuron, a brain cell. A simple model of this can be formed and combined with other similar models to form an artificial brain. This could be in terms of a hardware build (i.e. built out of electronic circuitry) or in terms merely of software, a program. Indeed the neuron model does not have to be a particularly accurate representation of a human neuron, which is just well as they come in many different types and forms. To make an exact copy of a human brain in a computer it is highly likely that accurate models of all the different types of neurons would be required. And as the actual neurons grow and die, this model would also need to be time-dependent.

The norm then is to take one particular model of a neuron, the most popular being the perceptron, and to connect it neatly to other perceptrons, forming a network in well-defined layers. The output from one neuron feeds as input to other neurons, usually in the next layer although it is quite possible for it to feed into ones in the same layer: indeed it could even feedback as an input into the neuron from which it is an output. The structure of the overall network is usually fixed; however the weightings between neurons (that is, by how much the output from one neuron affects another), are adapted as part of the learning exercise for that network.

In this way the overall output from such a neural network can be trained to copy a specific mathematical function or a behavior as long as the weights between neurons are adjusted appropriately. Because the structure is kept fairly simple, it can be shown (mathematically) that the network will actually settle down to realise a particular result. The type of neuron models, the method of learning and the actual application areas are all topics of ongoing research.

Problem solving

One other aspect of artificial intelligence is the whole idea of solving a problem by searching through a large number of potential solutions to find the best fit. For example, genetic algorithms are a technique based on ideas from evolution to choose the best solution from a number of possibilities. This requires a measurement or cost to be assigned such that the best solution minimizes the total cost. One good example of this is in satnav systems where many different road routes are possible for travelling between towns. It may be the shortest or the quickest route that is required – a search technique will find the best solution to either problem.

In many ways the techniques employed for searching hark back to the design of the Bombe all those years ago. Merely carrying out a blind search, trying absolutely every eventuality is though often very time consuming and unnecessary. Applying probabilities in a heuristic search usually provides a better solution. Other techniques include a breadth-first search which merely looks at a set number of steps, selects the best ones from those and then explores the possibilities of the next few steps, again selecting the best from those. By and large such a technique is quick although it can provide a poor solution on occasion.

Turing's 1953 paper: chess

As we saw in the previous chapter, in 1947 and 1948 Turing proposed the game of chess as an appropriate starting point for investigating whether digital computers supplied with enough memory and storage capacity could *think*. Turing (1953) said of chess: "[the game] holds special interest of the representation of human knowledge in machines". He went on to describe how to deal with the question of whether a machine could be built to play chess by considering word meanings in sentences. This led him to put forward sub-questions that could be considered separately:

(i) Could machines be programmed to follow the legal moves according to the rules of the game?
(ii) Could machines solve chess problems given the board location of its pieces?
(iii) Could machines play reasonably well in the game?
(iv) Could the machine improve its play and profit from its experience?

Turing then added unconnected questions including one that echoed the imitation game:

v Could one make a machine which would answer questions put to it, in such a way that it would not be possible to distinguish its answers from those of a man?

It could be the case that Turing in 1953 did not want his text-based challenges of 1950 and 1952 to become lost in the effort to build digital computers to play chess.

Turing believed that a computer would eventually succeed in his imitation game, just as one would beat a human at chess, and he was confident that machines would be able to have *feelings* like humans. The 1953 essay contains the first ever mention of this by Turing: "I know of no really convincing argument to support this belief and certainly none to disprove it".

He wrote "This certainly can be done. If it has not been done already it is merely because there is something better to do", which in effect is turning the question around: *humans can come up with a design of a digital computer, with supporting storage and memory, and sufficient software to make it play chess and beat a human chess player.*

Turing's approach to the game of chess was that it is a problem for the machine to solve through use of *heuristic* methods, such as rules-of-thumb guiding the machine's search through a tree of possible moves and counter-moves. The machine could try out various methods thus learning to adopt the variations that (it felt) led to satisfactory results. Turing was not alone in this belief. Early proponents for computers playing chess included mathematicians such as Claude Shannon, Norbert Wiener and John von Neumann.

Indeed Herbert Simon and Allen Newell predicted in 1958 that a machine would become a world chess champion within 10 years. Their prediction was out by forty years. With massively parallel architecture and a brute-force approach to the problem, IBM's *Deep Blue* machine was able to examine 200 million chess positions per second, mining to depths of 14 levels (Newborn, 1997). In 1997, in a six-game rematch against Gary Kasparov, the then world chess champion, the machine won by $3\frac{1}{2}$ games to $2\frac{1}{2}$.

Concluding comments

What has been attempted here is to give a very brief introduction to artificial intelligence in order to give some idea of Alan Turing's influence and importance to the field and also to show its relation to the imitation game. For a more formal introduction to the subject see Warwick (2011) and for a comprehensive in-depth treatment see Russell and Norvig (2012).

References

Bermudez, J.L. (2014). *Cognitive Science: An Introduction to the Science of the Mind.* Cambridge University Press.

Newborn, M. (1997). *Kasparov versus Deep Blue: Computer Chess comes of Age.* Springer.

Preston, J. and Bishop, J.M. (eds). (2002). *Views into the Chinese Room*. Oxford University Press.

Russell, S. and Norvig, P. (2012). *Artificial Intelligence: A Modern Approach*, 3rd edition. Prentice-Hall.

Searle, J. (1980). Minds, Brains and Programs. *Behavioral and Brain Sciences* **3**, 417–57.

Searle, J. (1997). *The Mystery of Consciousness*. New York Review of Books, Inc.

Turing, A.M. (1950). Computing machinery and intelligence. *Mind*, **LIX** (236), 433–460.

Turing, A.M. (1953). Chess. Reprinted in *The Essential Turing: the Ideas that Gave Birth to the Computer Age*, B.J. Copeland (ed). Oxford University Press, pp. 569–575.

Warwick, K. (2011). *Artificial Intelligence: the Basics*. Routledge.

4

The Controversy Surrounding Turing's Imitation Game

In Chapter 2 we saw that Turing described a number of scenarios featuring a machine being interrogated by a human. In that pre-Internet era Turing's foresaw a way his game could be played across two rooms with the participants, human interrogator and machine, hidden from each other and communicating by typing.

Turing's imitation game is less concerned with actually deceiving a naïve human interrogator and more about a machine's ability to provide satisfactory answers to any questions a human might put to it (see Chapter 2), and that the machine's satisfactory answers must be sustained. In order that the machine is not judged on its beauty or its tone of voice it must be out of sight and hearing of the interrogator who is tasked with focussing on the answers to any questions they might want to ask – we contend five minutes is adequate for a first impression. Why should the machines be able to do this? More and more robots are being developed to interact with humans, such as *Hector*[1], a care robot built to look after the elderly isolated in their own home. Future machines should be able talk to us just as we talk with others.

Since publication of *Computing machinery and intelligence* (CMI) (Turing, 1950) and his proposed imitation game for investigating machine thinking through two different tests, both pivoting on linguistic inputs and outputs as criteria for intelligence (Schweizer, 2010), a whole industry has grown. According to Loebner (2010) the correct design for a Turing test involves three participants in which an interrogator questions a machine and human in parallel, an interpretation which Loebner claims he realised after implementing thirteen *one-to-one* tests in his annual Loebner Prize, "the oldest Turing test

---

[1] Integrated Cognitive Assistive and Domotic Companion Robotic Systems for Ability and Security: Mobile Robot Companion – Smart Home. EU FP7 Project: http://www.companionable.net/ accessed 15.3.2016.

contest".[2] Loebner's interpretation overlooks Turing's own description for his imitation game and the two methods for realising it:

(i) a simultaneous comparison of a machine against a human, both questioned by a human interrogator (Turing, 1950); and

(ii) the direct machine examination by a human interrogator in a *viva voce*-type scenario (Turing, 1950; Braithwaite et al., 1952).

Turing's biographer Andrew Hodges tells us Turing was working at Manchester University at the time of CMI's publication in 1950. His academic duties included the task of creating and managing "the first software" for the world's first "stored-program computer" (Hodges, 2008, p. 13). The point of Turing's paper was to "argue that intelligence of a human level could be evinced by a suitably programmed computer" with the imitation game lending "definiteness to the idea of being as intelligent as a human being" following on from the chess-playing paradigm. However, it was not long before the belief in the intelligence of machines was considered a manifestation of schizophrenia (Robinson, 1972, p. 505), possibly as a result of the effusive claims by early researchers engaged in the new science termed *artificial intelligence* by John McCarthy in 1956, claimed for thermostats that perceive changes in temperature.

The jousting begins

After his initial work on machine intelligence, rather than just focus directly on building a machine to pass his two tests (see Chapter 2), or one that plays chess as was advocated in his 1953 essay, after 1950 Turing also worked in a different area. This saw light in his 1952 article *The Chemical Basis of Morphogenesis*. Turing applied the use of digital computers to the growing embryo, and patterns that develop to form other patterns, to study the mathematical nature of biological forms. In this respect Turing was one of the earliest pioneers of computer-based life. However, others did not ignore Turing's 1950 thesis and it released a flood of research and comment that shows no signs of abating.

Today we witness a host of Turing tests, distinguishing human from machine in mediums other than text-based imitation, for example through music (Solon, 2013), and finance (Hasanhodzic et al., 2010). In a completely different vein, a *neuro Turing test* has been applied to distinguish the conscious from non-conscious brain-damaged patients using communication via gestures

---

[2] AISB, 2014 Loebner Prize contest news: http://www.aisb.org.uk/events/loebner-prize

(Owen et al., 2006; Egeth, 2008; Stins, 2008; Stins and Laureys, 2009). Turing's ideas have not deterred those who think it might be fun to "program the game and try it on a group of students" (Purtill, 1971), or to apply them in areas such as the study of games and economic behaviour (Arifovic et al., 2006), and psychiatry to simulate paranoia (Colby et al., 1971; Colby et al., 1972; Heiser et al., 1979).

Thus a vast quantity of scholarship connected with Turing's idea now occupies a place in the archive of human knowledge with papers written across many disciplines commenting on his 1950 article, which, according to Halpern (2006) is "one of the most reprinted, cited, quoted, misquoted, paraphrased, alluded to, and generally referenced philosophical papers ever published".

Thinking about Thinking

Among those who regard Turing's imitation game with doubt are those who brand it as *classical, gender-specific, initial, literal, original, species-biased, standard* and *traditional*. Occupying various camps are opponents to Turing's idea:

Pinsky (1951), who discarded the idea of a thinking machine;
French (1990) who dismissed the imitation game as quixotic;
Hayes and Ford (1995) who consider it harmful for the study of artificial intelligence;
Lassègue (1996), who believes the imitation game "should be considered as an unconscious and mythical autobiography and not as a philosophical introduction to the main issues of AI";
Lenat (2001) says that it is a red herring.

Others regard Turing's linguistic test functions as an operational definition for intelligence (Schröder and McKeown, 2010; French, 1990; Wilks, 1974; Purtill, 1971), a view that Moor (2003) disagrees with: "Turing was not proposing an operational definition of intelligence that conceptually would tie all future development in AI".

In contrast to Minsky's view, Halpern[3] sees it as an absurdity to build a computer to think because the test is invalid and unperformable. Minsky[4] crit-

---

[3] Halpern responding to Hugh Loebner's letter to *The New Atlantis*, Spring. http://www.thenewatlantis.com/publications/correspondence-spring-2006date visited: 4.3.10.
[4] Wired: http://www.wired.com/science/discoveries/news/2003/05/58714?currentPage=1 accessed: 7.8.10.

icised the focus of recent AI research: "building stupid little robots … Graduate students wasting three years of their lives soldering and repairing" rather than tackling the "immense challenge of building a fully autonomous thinking machine", an opinion with which Harnad and Scherzer (2008) might agree. Scaling up to the 'robotic Turing test' is seen by Harnad and Scherzer as an empirical target for cognitive science, with indistinguishability being a scientific criterion.

Totally missing Turing's point are those researchers who regard gender as an important aspect of the game (Copeland and Proudfoot, 2008; Lassègue, 1996; Genova, 1994), or that both man and machine impersonating a woman provides a stronger test for intelligence (Sterrett, 2000), a position opposed by others, (Hodges, 2008; Shah and Warwick, 2010; Warwick and Shah, 2014c).

Still others back different tests for machine intelligence. In what some might scathingly refer to as *Turing's epigones*, Ariza (2009) advocated a musical toy test which alters the task of interrogator to that of a critic, and Espejo-Serna (2010) advanced a *sphex-test* that modifies an agent's environment, testing for any corresponding change in its behaviour, whether it can connect the dots in its own way.

Plebe and Perconti (2010) proposed a *qualia Turing test* adding vision to the textual question–answer test enabling a machine or computer program to report its subjective experience after sharing views of an uploaded picture with an interrogator. Connecting the dots and sharing experience are implicit in Turing's imitation game: the role of inference acts to connect seemingly disparate utterances; whether the machine can adapt its responses to an interrogator's changing topic is covered by Turing's criterion of sustained, satisfactory responses.

Similarly, the communicative test of Cullen (2009), adds nothing distinct to Turing's textual question–answer, nor does it improve it: deception in Turing's imitation game is by communication.

Turing (1950, section 6) anticipated objections to the idea of a thinking machine and referred to a criterion proposed made by Ada Lovelace in her comment: "Only when computers *originate* things should they be believed to have minds". In her honour, Bringsjord et al. (2001) suggest a Lovelace test that is 'better' than Turing's: when a human architect *H* of an artificial agent *A* cannot account for its output *O* the agent is said to satisfy the Lovelace criterion.

Stins (2008) provides a perspective on 'mind' from the field of cognitive neuroscience: "what it takes for an outside observer to be convinced that an entity is conscious". Cowen and Dawson (2009) meanwhile relate how the social capabilities required to be considered 'human' in Turing's test could and probably would preclude those with autism for example, a view grounded in the speculation that Turing himself may have been autistic or suffered from Asperger's syndrome. In our own research (Warwick and Shah, 2014d) we have considered more the case of 'expected humans' as being the norm expected by interrogators and the extremely autistic would likely not fit in this category.

Scrutinizers of Turing's imitation game include those who view that a machine *can* and *will* eventually succeed in passing his question–answer test (Chomsky, 2008; Kurzweil, 2006; Moor, 2003, Moor, 1976; Dennett, 1984, Sampson, 1973; see also Chapter 7). It does need to be re-emphasised here that Turing described an imaginary experiment to test for the presence of 'thought' in a machine via deception and imitation. It bypassed multi-sensing world experiences focussing exclusively on the intellectual capability of the machine expressed through its text-based responses during conversation with a human interrogator.

We repeat; if the machine's responses are deemed indistinguishable from the kind of replies a human might give to an interrogator, then that machine is thinking, and if a human's similar responses were to be considered intelligent then so must the machine's be. We contend that Turing's imitation game can provide a useful continuum, a scale showing machines from textual babbling adolescents to full linguistic power houses and most crucially mitigate the risk from cyberfraud with the game serving as a tool in deception detection.

Cultural objection

French (1990) agreed with what he believed is Turing's philosophical claim, that if a machine could pass the imitation game it could be accepted as "necessarily intelligent ... whatever acts sufficiently intelligent is intelligent", but he disagreed with the pragmatic claim that such a machine could be built in the "not-too-distant future". His ground, that the only thing that can pass Turing's imitation game is one that has "experienced the world as we have experienced it", limited the test because, in French's view, Turing's vision amounted to a *culturally-oriented* guarantee of human intelligence.

Underlying French's view is that speaking the *same language* is the same as thinking in the *same culture*. Is, say, the Spanish of Spain of the same *language culture* as the Spanish of Mexico or Argentina? Turing had attempted to cultivate a *culture of thinking* in machines so that their thinking, albeit different, would be seen as acceptable in the same way as the various ways of thinking across cultures *are* regarded as thinking. Thus, French's latent interpretation of the imitation game entails the human interrogator, the design of the machine and hidden human comparators be of the same culture.

This scenario is not necessary however. In our practical Turing tests machine performance has been compared against native and non-native English-speaking human foils (see Chapters 7–8 and 10).

Just as CMI reflects the era in which it was written – a few years after the Second World War – similarly the critique of Hayes and Ford (1995) represents zeitgeistian antipathy towards building an 'idiot-savant'. They venture that useful AI program are "valuable exactly by virtue of their lack of humanity ... a truly human-like program would be nearly useless". Hayes and Ford's lament in the last decade of the 20th century is that AI systems have "delivered the goods very well, sometimes spectacularly well ... fuelling technical revolutions and changing the world", but that the burden of the failure of systems to pass the Turing test has distracted AI researchers from rejoicing over their useful technologies. This joylessness is of the researchers' own making and not of Turing's.

Gender distraction

For some *gender* is a significant factor in Turing's three-participant imitation game (see Hayes and Ford, 1995; Genova, 1994, who accepted that Turing never speaks directly about gender; Lassègue, 1996; Sterrett, 2000). However, we feel it is a distraction from Turing's consideration of the *intellectual capacity of a machine*.

Obsession with creation

Implicit in much of theliterature prior to and following Turing's CMI paper is the human male's obsession with creating artificial beings – Frankenstein's monster! Females seem not to be similarly concerned; Harvard's Barbara Grosz epitomizes this with her new discourse structure theory supporting multi-modal human–computer dialogical interfaces, and MIT Media Lab's Rana El-Kaliouby, whose wearable technology that aids people with autism spectrum disorders was rated among the top 100 innovations of 2006.[5]

It has been suggested that Turing's homosexuality may have made it abhorrent for him to participate physically in creating another intelligent being, which Genova (1994) refers to as Turing's sexual dilemma, possibly deriving

[5] New York Times article 'The Social Cue Reader', Jennifer Schuessler, 10 December 2006: http://www.nytimes.com/2006/12/10/magazine/10section3b.t-2.html?_r=1& scp=1&sq=Rana+el+kaliouby&st=nyt date accessed: 30.3.10; time: 15.23.

from a desire for an alternative process to the natural one for creating a thinking entity. Genova concludes "in Turing's brave new world, female machines are absent ... [there is an] inability to keep his personal life out of his scientific one". However, this is not the case; the 'gender' of the machine is irrelevant to Turing. Genova's question of why the female should tell the truth in the introductory man–woman imitation scenario marking "her as an inferior thinker", echoed byLassègue (1996) who sees it as an absence of strategy, the odds being "weighed too heavily against the woman". That the man's task is to deceive exposes a view that deception requires being clever in a way that a woman, a "motherly creature" may not be, suggesting an underlying view of men that Turing may have held, namely that men are more capable of deceiving the interrogator; or maybe they feel that Turing believed there is a secret connection between gender and intelligence. According to Genova (1994), "computing accomplishes the miracle of creation"; she views the computer "as the ultimate kind of dynamic technology".

Linguistic competence

Hayes and Ford (1995) remark that Turing's imitation game tests for competence in human conversation, but they feel unable to qualify what that competence is. However, the science of language secures linguistic competence within its sub-field pragmatics, for instance in the *cooperative principle* of Grice (1975) and the *principle of relevance* of Sperber and Wilson (1986). It is not difficult to suppose those two theories could be applied to the goal of machine linguistic productivity or *li.p.* In Grice's theory of conversation it succeeds because parties mutually agree to cooperate (Stevenson, 1993) by adhering to four maxims:

Quantity: neither parsimonious nor garrulous;
Quality: true rather than apocryphal;
Relation: relate utterance/message to previous within dialogue;
Manner: clarity rather than opacity.

Sperber and Wilson's notion for successful conversation simplifies Gricean tactics to one dictum: the speaker tries to express the proposition which is the most relevant one possible to the hearer. These theories are easily applied to the question–answer scenario for sustained and satisfactory responses. Selecting Grice's four maxims or Sperber and Wilson's one dictum could assist comparison of human and machine *li.p* via the latter's responses to questions from an interrogator during a practical Turing test. Of course the measure of competence rests entirely with the interrogator: after all, humans are expert communicators.

Intelligence

Does Turing's three-participant test suppose the hidden human, against whom the machine is compared by an average interrogator, will always exhibit textual appropriateness in an imitation scenario because he or she is *packed with intelligence*? Turing circumvented any definition for intelligence, in fact in 1948 he had said the idea of it was an emotional rather than mathematical (see Copeland, 2004, p. 411), but he later felt deception was a feature of it and imitation of sustained, satisfactory responses were evidence for thinking: "May not machines carry out something which ought to be described as thinking but which is very different from what a man does?" (Turing, 1950, p. 435).

Turing was not the only one to evade explicitly pinning down this quality. His opponents too dodged getting caught in a trap of setting intelligence in stone, for fear of circularity in definition, or showing anthropocentric tendencies. In *Shadows of the Mind*, Roger Penrose posits that *genuine intelligence* requires *genuine understanding* which itself relies on the presence of *awareness*. Penrose admits it is "unwise to attempt to give *full* definitions for intelligence, understanding and awareness", rather, he relies on "our intuitive perceptions as to what these words actually mean" and argues for a distinction between genuine intelligence and a "proper computational simulation of it". However, Penrose does not consider *alternative intelligence*, not *unlike* genuine human intelligence but still distinct from it, that a machine could possess.

Block (1981) asserted that "for something to be intelligent, namely that it act in a certain way", a hard way to define intelligence is nevertheless easy enough to recognize. Purtill (1971) asked "what sort of test would we apply to see if intelligent thought were present ... in a man recovering from a brain operation?". Neurologists Stins and Laureys (2009) claim they implicitly apply Turing's question–answer technique to establish consciousness in brain-damaged patients, because, as Owen (2008) states, "It is extremely difficult to assess residual cognitive function in these [vegetative-state] patients because their movements may be minimal or inconsistent, or because no cognitive output is possible".

Stins and Laureys (2009) and Owen et al. (2006) have shown a way that patients suffering from locked-in syndrome can convey presence of thought by appropriate neurobehavioral, non-verbal responses. Stins and Laureys report that "The incapacity [of some brain-damaged individuals] to generate bodily movements prohibits communication through conventional means". This gives an impression of absence of consciousness or wakefulness; thus this characterises the patient as being in a coma. Notwithstanding, one of several possible outcomes of coma is that a patient regains consciousness but is completely paralysed.

Using functional neuroimaging experiments can help to 'decode the mind'. Neurologists have adopted Turing-test-like procedures, in terms of question–response, to expose mental states when looking for signs of contingency and communication in the patient, such as systematic blinks of an eye lid or oriented responses to pain (Stins and Laureys, 2009).

However, just as in the case of a machine–human comparison imitation game, because the assessment by a neurologist in the neuro Turing test is done by a human, just as with the interrogator in the former scenario, there is the problem of *subjective error*. Of the assessment of consciousness in brain-damaged patients, Owen et al. (2006) warn of the need for accuracy of diagnosis which requires careful interpretation of information, thus also a need for ethical frameworks to guide research into brain disorders and consciousness.

Savova and Peshkin (2007) note that Turing did not intend his machine–human comparison test to replace a true definition of intelligence, a view which leads into Fagan and Holland's theory of intelligence as *exposure to information* (2007). Their definition of intelligence is the *ability to process information* (2009). This approach to intelligence can be applied to the development of machines during Turing's question–answer game. Building an artificial intellect to make it read between the lines, processing information in a manner that produces responses deemed *human-like* by many human interrogators during questioning, may seem difficult but once achieved might it not be *misanthrobotic* to withhold from it some intelligence.

In support of Turing's thinking machine

In earlier sections in this chapter, we encountered the sorts of criticisms that Turing had anticipated in section 6 of his 1950 paper. According to Dennett (see Shieber, 2004, p. 271), it is a sad irony that endless arguing about the Turing test has focussed attention on the wrong issues.

Hodges (2008) points out Turing would have been highly aware of the natural objection to machines doing the sorts of things "which are by nature non-mechanical: those human actions that require initiative, imagination, judgement, cause surprise, are liable to errors". He reminds us that the imitation game actually first arose as the 'fair play' argument for escaping the force of

Gödel's theorem and the serious puzzle posed by the limits of what can be computed.

Even though Turing thought of intelligence as emotional rather than mathematical, in 1950 he wrote, "May not machines carry out something which ought to be described as thinking but which is very different from what a man does?". Turing clearly seemed to believe intelligence was not central to the debate about whether a machine could think.

Disregarding useful lines for research leading to improvement in machine capacity that may illuminate human intellectual capacities (Chomsky, in (Epstein et al., 2008)), objectors like Searle and Block have offered *in principle* doctrines that are impossible to realise, unlike Turing's simple yet brilliant imitation game. Yet these objections are relied upon to show why machines can never really compete with humans intellectually with the kind of arguments about which McDermott (2014) complains "Some 'in principle' arguments are so absurd that one feels compelled to protest".

Sampson (1973) supported Turing's ideas finding them interesting *because* they suggest that computers can think in the familiar meaning of the word, but his position is mainly against that of Purtill (1971). Sampson points out that because machines are simple compared with humans, who design into the machine's mechanism a feature to inform the human operator about the cause of behaviours at any given moment (dumping), they are deemed to be determined systems. Humans do not have this exact feature but they are able to voice, gesture or write and type to explain action and inaction.

Harnad (2002) concedes to opponents that "we always knew that the TT was fallible ... it is not a proof", but can there be a perfect measure for machine's intellectual capacity? Hayes and Ford (1995) remind us that "Turing's ultimate aim ... was not to describe the difference between thinking people and unthinking machines, but to remove it". They conclude that if what Turing was trying to do is to make us consider what it really means to be not just like a thinker, but a human being in a human society, with all its difficulties and complexities, then we "need not reject [his test] as AI's ultimate goal".

Kurzweil believes a non-biological machine *will* pass the Turing test and he has pronounced the year it will happen, 2029, which is earlier than Turing's revised prediction of 2052 (and about which he makes no mention). Kurzweil claims it is the exponential nature of information-based technologies that will assist in understanding "the principles of operation of the human brain and be in a position to recreate its power" and thus meet his target year of 2029.

This chapter ends our analysis of commentaries on Turing's foundation for machine thinking with Dennett's contention (in Shieber, 2004, p. 271) that "there are real world problems that are revealed by considering the strengths and weaknesses of the Turing test", and with Chomsky's suggestion (in Epstein et al., 2008, p. 106) that "Turing's sensible admonitions should also be borne in mind, more seriously than they have been, in my opinion". In the coming chapters we look at early attempts to build text-based communication systems and the first practical versions of Turing's imitation game.

References

Arifovic, J., McKelvey, R.D. and Pevnitskay, S. (2006). An initial implementation of the Turing tournament to learning in repeated two-person games. *Games and Economic Behavior* **57**, 93–122.

Ariza. C. (2009). The interrogator as critic: the Turing test and the evaluation of generative music systems. *Computer Music Journal* **33** (2), 48–70.

Block. N. (1981). Psychologism and behaviorism. In *The Turing Test: Verbal Behavior as the Hallmark of Intelligence*, S. Shieber, (ed). MIT Press, pp. 229–266.

Braithwaite, R., Jefferson, G., Newman, M. and Turing, A.M. (1952). Can automatic calculating machines be said to think? Transcript of BBC radio broadcast reproduced in *Alan Turing: His Work and Impact* S.B. Cooper and Jan van Leeuwen (eds), Elsevier, pp. 667–676.

Bringsjord, S., Bello, P. and Ferrucci, D. (2001). Creativity, the Turing test and the (better) Lovelace test. *Minds and Machines* **11** (1), 3–27.

Chomsky, N. (2008). Turing on the 'Imitation Game'. In Epstein et al. (2008), pp. 103–106.

Colby, K.M., Weber, S., and Hilf, F.D. (1971). Artificial paranoia. *Artificial Intelligence* **2**, 1–25.

Colby, K.M., Hilf, F.D., Weber, S., and Kraemer, H.C. (1972). Turing-like indistinguishability tests for the validation of a computer simulation of paranoid processes. *Artificial Intelligence* **3**, 199–221.

Copeland, B.J. (2004). *The Essential Turing: The Ideas That Gave Birth to the Computer Age*. Oxford Univesity Press.

Copeland, J. and Proudfoot, D. (2008). Turing's test: a philosophical and historical guide. In Epstein et al. (2008), pp. 119–138.

Cowen, T. and Dawson, M. (2009). What does the Turing test really mean? And how many human beings (including Turing) could pass? http://www.gmu.edu/centers/publicchoice/faculty%20pages/Tyler/turingfinal.pdf.

Cullen, J. (2009). Imitation versus communication: testing for human-like intelligence. *Minds and Machines* **19** (2), 237–254.

Dennett, D.C. (1984). *Elbow Room: The Varieties of Free Will Wanting*. Oxford University Press.

Egeth, M. (2008). A 'Turing test' and BCI for locked-in children and adults. *Medical Hypotheses* **70**, 1067.

Epstein, R., Roberts, G. and Beber, G. *Parsing the Turing Test: Philosophical and Methodological Issues in the Quest for the Thinking Computer*. Springer.

Espejo-Serna, J.C. (2010). Connecting the dots in my own way: sphex-test and flexibility in artificial cognitive agents. In *Towards a Comprehensive Intelligence Test (TCIT): Reconsidering the Turing Test for the 21st Century, Proc. AISB 2010 Symposium*, pp. 1–6.

French, R. (1990). Subcognition and the limits of the Turing test. *Mind* **99** (393), 53–65.

Genova, J. (1994). Turing's sexual guessing game. *Social Epistemology* **8**, 313–326.

Grice, H. (1975). Logic and conversation. In *Speech Acts*, P. Cole and J.L. Morgan (eds). Academic Press, pp. 41–58.

Halpern, M. (2006). The trouble with the Turing test. *The New Atlantis* **11**, Winter, 42–63.

Harnad. S. (1992). The Turing test is not a trick: Turing indistinguishability is a scientific criterion. *SIGART Bulletin* **3** (4), 9–10.

Harnad, S. (2002). What's wrong and right about Searle's Chinese Room argument? In *Views Into the Chinese Room*, M. Bishop and J. Preston (eds). Oxford University Press.

Harnad, S. and Scherzer, P. (2008). First scale up to the robotic Turing test, then worry about feeling. *Artificial Intelligence in Medicine* **44** (2), 83–89.

Hasanhodzic, J., Lo, A.W. and Viola, E. (2010). Is it real or is it randomised? A financial Turing test. http://arxiv.org/pdf/1002.4592.pdf. date visited: 15.3.16.

Hayes, P. and Ford, K. (1995). Turing test considered harmful. In *Proc. 14th Int. Joint Conf. on Artificial Intelligence (IJCAI), Vol. 1*. pp. 972–7.

Heiser, J.F., Colby, K.M., Fraught, W.S. and Parkison, R.C. (1979). Can psychiatrists distinguish a computer simulation of paranoia from the real thing? The limitation of Turing-like tests as measures of the adequacy of simulations. *Journal of Psychiatric Research* **15**, 149–162.

Hodges, A. (2008). Alan Turing and the Turing test. In Epstein et al. (2008), pp. 13–22.

Kurzweil, R. (2006). Why we can be confident of Turing test capability within a quarter century. http://www.jayurbain.com/msoe/cs4881/WhyWeCanBeConfident.pdf.

Lassègue, J. (1996). What kind of Turing test did Turing have in mind? *Tekhnema 3/ "A touch of memory"*. http://tekhnema.free.fr/3Lasseguearticle.htm accessed: 15.3.16.

Lenat, D. (2001). Artificial intelligence – battle of the brains. *Wired*. http://www.wired.com/2001/11/battle-of-the-brains/ accessed: 15.3.16.

Loebner, H.G. (2010). Some misconceptions regarding the Turing test. In *Towards a Comprehensive Intelligence Test (TCIT): Reconsidering the Turing Test for the 21st Century, Proc. AISB 2010 Symposium*, pp. 50–51.

McDermott, D. (2014). On the claim that a table-lookup program could pass the Turing test. *Minds and Machines* **24** (2), 143–188.

Moor, J.H. (1976). An analysis of Turing's test. *Philosophical Studies* **30**, 249–257.

Moor, J.H. (2003). The status and future of the Turing test. In *The Turing Test – the Elusive Standard of Artificial Intelligence*, J.H. Moor (ed). Springer, pp. 197–214.

Owen, A.M., Coleman, M.R., Boly, M., Davis, M.H., Laureys, S., and Pickard, J.D. (2006). Detecting awareness in the vegetative state. *Science* **313**, 1402.

Pinsky, L. (1951). Do machines think about machines thinking? *Mind*, **LX**, 397–398.

Plebe, A., and Perconti, P. (2010). Qualia Turing test – designing a test for the phenomenal mind. In *Towards a Comprehensive Intelligence Test (TCIT): Reconsidering the Turing Test for the 21st Century, Proc. AISB 2010 Symposium.*

Purtill, R.L. (1971). Beating the imitation game. *Mind* **80**, 290–294.

Robinson, G. (1972). How to tell your friends from your machines. *Mind* **81** (234), 504–518.

Sampson, G. (1973). In defence of Turing. *Mind* **82** (328), 592–594.

Savova, V. and Peshkin, L. (2007). Is the Turing test good enough? The fallacy of resource-unbounded intelligence. In *Proc. IJCAI-07, Hyderabad*, pp. 545–550.

Schröder, M. and McKeown, G. (2010). Considering social and emotional artificial intelligence. In *Towards a Comprehensive Intelligence Test (TCIT): Reconsidering the Turing Test for the 21st Century, Proc. AISB 2010 Symposium.*

Schweizer, P. (2010). Causal and communal factors in a comprehensive test of intelligence. In *Towards a Comprehensive Intelligence Test (TCIT): Reconsidering the Turing Test for the 21st Century, Proc. AISB 2010 Symposium*, pp. 7–11.

Shah, H., and Warwick, K. (2010). From the buzzing in Turing's head to machine intelligence contests. In *Towards a Comprehensive Intelligence Test (TCIT): Reconsidering the Turing Test for the 21st Century, Proc. AISB 2010 Symposium.*

Shieber, S.M. (2004). *The Turing Test: Verbal Behavior as the Hallmark of Intelligence.* MIT Press.

Solon, O. (2013). Rencon: a Turing test for musical expression. *Wired*, September; http://www.wired.co.uk/news/archive/2013-09/02/rencon-turing-test-for-music accessed 15.3.16

Sperber, D and Wilson, D. (1986). *Relevance, Communication and Cognition.* Harvard University Press.

Sterrett, S.G. (2000). Turing's two tests for intelligence. *Minds and Machines* **10** (4), 541–559.

Stevenson, R. (1993). *Language, Thought and Representation.* Wiley.

Stins, J.F. (2008). Establishing consciousness in non-communicative patients: a modern-day version of the Turing test. *Consciousness and Cognition* **18**, 87–192.

Stins, J.F. and Laureys, S. (2009). Thought translation, tennis and Turing tests in the vegetative state. *Phenom. Cogn Sci.* **8**, 361–370.

Turing A.M. (1950). Computing machinery and intelligence. *Mind* **LIX** (236), 433–460.

Warwick, K. and Shah, H. (2014c). The Turing test – a new appraisal. *International Journal of Synthetic Emotions* **5** (1), 31–45.

Warwick, K. and Shah, H. (2014d) Human misidentification in Turing tests. *Journal of Experimental and Theoretical Artificial Intelligence* **27** (2), 123–135.

Wilks, Y. (1974). Your friends and your machines. *Mind* **83** (332), 583–585.

5

History of Conversation Systems: From *Eliza* to *Eugene Goostman*

In the following sections we consider early artificial conversationalists and implementations of experiments to answer Turing's question *can a machine think?*. The claim for the first Turing test is asserted by Hugh Loebner, sponsor of the annual Loebner Prize for Artificial Intelligence. The first contest appeared in 1991. However, more than a decade earlier a computer program of a paranoid human confounded psychiatrists: they were not able to distinguish the simulation from a real patient (Heiser et al., 1979).

As we said in the previous chapter, during a practical Turing test, the *actual* goal of the machine is to provide satisfactory and sustained answers to any questions – in the realm of paranoia, *PARRY*, the program created by Colby et al. (1971, 1972), served this purpose. Christopher Strachey, a contemporary of Turing and a fellow student at King's College Cambridge, in 1952 wrote an algorithm that generated text intended to express and arouse emotions. It was the first machine to produce *digital literature* (Wardrip-Fruin, 2005). Here's an example of its output:

> DARLING SWEETHEART
> YOU ARE MY AVID FELLOW FEELING.
> MY AFFECTION CURIOUSLY CLINGS TO YOUR
>   PASSIONATE WISH.
> MY LIKING YEARNS FOR YOUR HEART.
> YOU ARE MY WISTFUL SYMPATHY: MY TENDER LIKING.
> YOURS BEAUTIFULLY.

The distinguished linguist Noam Chomsky (2008) viewed the linguistic performance of a machine preferable to other ways of improving machine capacity and studying human intelligence. He considered that the Turing test provided a stimulus for two useful lines of research:

(a) improvement of the capacities of machines;

(b) investigating the intellectual properties of a human.

Chomsky believed therefore the imitation game is uncontroversial. He accepted Turing's intention as wanting to learn something about living things through the construction of a thinking machine. Moor (2004) contended that Turing's linguistic measure "is not essential to our knowledge about computer thinking … it provides one good format for gathering evidence" so that if a machine were to succeed against Turing's satisfactory and sustained response criterion "one would certainly have very adequate grounds for inductively inferring that the computer could think".

Computers and the World Wide Web provide a *virtual surface* which allows those connected to interact textually on any and every topic of interest to humans. For example, *Nature*[1] encourages intelligent discussion allowing commentary on any of its articles including peer-reviewed papers, opinions, book reviews and editorials. By allowing posting of comments to *Nature*, the journal aims to increase the impact, understanding and significance of its articles. This is just one example of textual communication now ubiquitous in cyberspace.

Largely unrestricted, unless on a moderated forum, people connected to the Internet are able to create a digital presence with their own virtual homes in blogs[2] used as a daily pulpit. Social networking facilities also allow interaction with others (for example, on Facebook), where one can post messages about any matter that concerns or interests. Additionally, anyone can read and comment upon other people's Internet presence, post an opinion on someone else's personal diary. Thus, as never before in history, humans have access to a vast store of information.

The *mother of all knowledge* is available at the touch of fingertips through computers, laptops, via keypads or touch on smartphones and tablets. All this textual interaction provides a window to what humans say and how they say it, an understanding of which Turing pointed to in *Computing Machinery and Intelligence*.

Designing artificial conversation

Strachey's system managed to generate text, but the first question–answer system to emerge enabling computer-mediated human–machine text-based inter-

---

[1] 'Have Your Say': http://www.nature.com/ accessed: 25.4.10; time: 11.48
[2] http://www.blogger.com/tour_start.g accessed: 14.8.10; time: 14.03.

action was the *Eliza* system, an attempt to investigate natural language understanding (Weizenbaum, 1966).

Eliza

According to Richard Wallace (2010), developer of the *Alice* conversation system, with *Eliza* Joseph Weizenbaum launched the first wave of artificial conversational systems, or *chatbots*. Block (1981) says of *Eliza* that it was a computer program "totally without intelligence" but nonetheless "remarkably good at fooling people in short conversations", one of the deceived being Weizenbaum's secretary who "asked him to leave the room in order to talk to the machine privately".

This deception was no mean achievement for a system containing just 200 lines of input/output code. Weizenbaum developed *Eliza* to imitate a psychiatrist by employing a small set of simple strategies, extracting minimal context.[3] Weizenbaum's system applied a rank or precedence number to a *keyword* such as *I, you, boyfriend* in the input sentence. Applying appropriate transformation, for instance turning 'you' into 'I', *Eliza* demonstrated that text-based communication between a human and a machine is possible, the system responding "roughly as would certain psychotherapists (Rogerian)". Weizenbaum gave as a typical example input "I need some help..." to which *Eliza* replied "what would it mean to you..." (see Figure 5.1, where the program's utterances are shown in capitals).

The philosopher Ned Block remarked on the gullibility of humans: "tendency to be fooled by such programs seems dependent on our degree of suspicion, sophistication about machines and other contingent factors" (Block, 1981, p. 233); however, this overlooks the fact that some users did not know it might be a machine. Shieber (1994) noted Weizenbaum's surprise: "a test based on fooling people is confoundingly simple to pass" concluding *Eliza* was a "fruitless avenue of attack as a discipline for natural language processing".

PARRY

In a similar vein to Weizenbaum's *Eliza*, Colby et al.'s program *PARRY* simulated human–machine interaction in a restricted domain, in this instance that of a paranoid patient in a psychiatric interview. Of the "mode of conversation" selected for *Eliza* Weizenbaum (1966) wrote:

---

[3] Eliza: http://i5.nyu.edu/~mm64/x52.9265/january1966.html accessed 14.8.10; time: 16.38

Men are all alike
IN WHAT WAY?
They're always bugging us about something or other
CAN YOU THINK OF A SPECIFIC EXAMPLE?
Well, my boyfriend made me come here
YOUR BOYFRIEND MADE YOU COME HERE
He says I'm depressed much of the time
I AM SORRY TO HEAR YOU ARE DEPRESSED
It's true. I am unhappy
DO YOU THINK COMING HERE WILL HELP YOU NOT TO BE UNHAPPY
I need some help, that much seems certain
WHAT WOULD IT MEAN TO YOU IF YOU GOT SOME HELP
Perhaps I could learn to get along with my mother.
TELL ME MORE ABOUT YOUR FAMILY
My mother takes care of me
WHO ELSE IN YOUR FAMILY TAKES CARE OF YOU
My father
YOUR FATHER
You are like my father in some ways
WHAT RESEMBLANCE DO YOU SEE
You are not very aggressive but I think you don't want me to notice that
WHAT MAKES YOU THINK I AM NOT VERY AGGRESSIVE
You don't argue with me
WHY DO YOU THINK I DON'T ARGUE WITH YOU
You are afraid of me
DOES IT PLEASE YOU TO BELIEVE I AM AFRAID OF YOU
My father is afraid of everybody
WHAT ELSE COMES TO YOUR MIND WHEN YOU THINK OF YOUR FA-
THER
Bullies
DOES THAT HAVE ANYTHING TO DO WITH THE FACT THAT YOUR
BOYFRIEND MADE YOU COME HERE

Figure 5.1 Weizenbaum's typical *Eliza* conversation (taken from http://i5.nyu.edu/ mm64/x52.9265/january1966.html accessed: 14.8.10; time: 16.48).

... the psychiatric interview is one of the few examples of categorized dyadic natural language communication in which one of the participating pair is free to assume the pose of knowing almost nothing of the real world. If, for example, one were to tell a psychiatrist "I went for a long boat ride" and he responded "Tell me about boats", one would not assume that he knew nothing about boats, but that he had some purpose in so directing the subsequent conversation.

With response types of *anger, fear* and *mistrust* inculcated, *PARRY* simulated paranoia handled communication via natural language. Realising that any serious model builder must have their system *empirically* tested, because this after all placed them in a better situation "to know what the requirements of appropriate evaluation should be", Colby et al. (1972) asserted that "an acceptable simulation is one which succeeds, according to some relevant test, at input–output indistinguishability from the processes it is simulating".

They accepted that simulation as a successful imitation is a different problem from simulation as an acceptable model-explanation. They felt that if simulation is not judged to be different from its natural counterpart along certain dimensions, then the simulation can be considered successful. Of the condition *along certain dimensions*, they presupposed *stipulated dimensions* pointing to Descartes' speech test to distinguish men from machines: if there were machines which bore a resemblance to our body and imitated our actions there would be means by which to recognize they were not real men.

Quoting Descartes, Colby et al. wrote:

> [machines] could never use speech or other signs as we do when placing our thoughts on record for the benefit of others ... in order to reply appropriately to everything that may be said ... as even the lowest type of man can do.

Descartes' test, realised in the experiment, allowed examination of their *PARRY* paranoid model, but not with the purpose of playing "Turing's Game of identifying which respondent is a computer" (Colby et al., 1972, p. 206).

However, Heiser et al. (1979) expanded on this work and *did* deploy simulation to find if human psychiatrists in a one-to-one situation could distinguish the simulation model from a real patient. In their experiment Heiser et al. supplied one communication channel via teletype in order for a hidden entity to be questioned one at a time by five male, native-English-speaking psychiatrists[4] with 1 to 15 years of practice (one judge was a professor of psychiatry). Two hidden entities took part:

(1) a computer model of a mythical 28-year old, single, male, Caucasian, native speaker of English complete with paranoid behaviour such as fixed delusions of persecution by gangsters; and
(2) a real psychiatric in-patient 22 years old, single, male, Caucasian, native speaker of English suffering from a chronic and severe paranoid disorder.

In the experiment, the human patient was unaware of the nature of the test (Table 1 in Heiser et al., 1979), but he was given the true explanation that he would be interviewed following his consent to participate in an experiment involving psychiatrists interviewing him via teletype. At the same time the psychiatrists, acting as judges, were given the deceptive account that there were several real patients and several computer programs simulating patients.

---

[4] The patient left the hospital thus reducing the number of psychiatrist–judges over the life of the experiment.

Furthermore, the judges were informed that while conducting two interviews, they might encounter two patients, two computer programs, or one of each. A similar paradigm underpinned Warwick and Shah's simultaneous-comparison and review experiments (see Chapters 7–8 and 10; Shah, 2010).

Heiser et al.'s psychiatrist–judges were allowed one session each to interview the two hidden entities, *PARRY* and patient, one at a time. The psychiatrists' input was dictated and typed in by the experiment's senior author, while the patient's output were typed by Colby. The duration of the interviews varied between 30 and 60 minutes, whatever time it took for 40 input/outputs – the minimum interview took in 20 input/outputs.

Heiser et al. stated that four judges interviewed the computer first, and that only judge 2 interviewed the computer first but that this psychiatrist was the only judge to decide correctly in both trials. Despite this they do question whether the order of the interviews – machine first or human first – was an important factor. The interval between trials was 1 to 8 days.

Pauses in hidden entity responses, spelling errors "and other non-verbal factors which might influence" judge's assessment were filtered out before the answers to psychiatrists' questions were presented. Nonetheless "in his first trial, Judge 2 correctly assessed that some responses were generated and typed so quickly that they must be a product of a computer program". To counteract the machine's alacrity of response the experimenters Heiser et al. modified its transaction to delay the duration between question and answer "after which the response came in a burst from both the computer and the patient". The psychiatrist–judges were allowed to ask any questions:

> ...but reasonably close to how they would in a real clinical setting and with deference to the notion that, regardless of how certain hey felt that they were interviewing a computer program, they might be wrong and should therefore avoid cavalier, sadistic, and other blatantly disrespectful or insensitive comments and questions.

After an exchange with a computer, Judge 2 commented "This is not a patient, but a machine following a format. I am trying to establish feeling and getting back mechanical statements", on the other hand, after an exchange with the human patient, this same judge retorted "Oh Hell, I don't know whether that's a program or a patient. Say Patient 3".

Judge 3 commented after an exchange with the computer program "It's just seeming more to me like some kind of caricature of a paranoid person. [It] seems more programmed than genuine right now" and after a further exchange with this hidden entity "I'd just say again how very difficult it is to predict whether it is a computer or a very disturbed patient". In contrast, after interviewing the human patient, Judge 3 wrote "[I think it's a computer because] it's just an unusual kind of delusion for me. Possible, I guess, [but] dissimilar to most I've heard" (Table 2 in Heiser et al., 1979).

The results from Heiser et al.'s experiment produced a fairly balanced outcome: the psychiatrist–judges were right five times and wrong five times. Two psychiatrists thought the computer was a patient, and three thought the patient was a computer. The psychiatrists had been asked to consider two questions after each input from their hidden interlocutor:

(a) computer or patient,
(b) 10-point scale of decision certainty where 0 means guessing, 1–3 weakly certain, 4–5 moderately certain, 6–8 very certain, and 9 absolutely certain.

The experimenters found that the judges were more uncertain when it came to identifying the computer program. This led Heiser et al. to conclude:

(a) the simulation is good at deception in its single domain (paranoia);
(b) the judges were poor;
(c) the test was weak.

Of the second conclusion Heiser et al. pointed out that the judges were reasonably expert at conventional clinical psychiatric interviewing and diagnosis, but they were all inexperienced (and in that sense, inexpert) at distinguishing computer programs from patients.

As we will see in the following chapters, interrogator judges in our practical Turing test experiments were asked to complete a short questionnaire, asked if they had heard of the Turing test and whether they used any 'chat' facility. This was to establish any relationship between deception-detection and level of their experience or expertise.

Heiser et al. felt deception was not difficult – even an expert could be fooled under Turing's or their conditions. They point out their judges had to decide whether an odd response represented the verbal behaviour of a pathological person, a computer simulation of a patient's pathological verbal behaviour, or a poor response generated by a faulty simulation.

Heiser et al.'s experiment represented a restricted form of Turing's imitation game; judges compared 'paranoid' responses to determine human paranoia from the artificial. They deemed the study useful in validating their method and the model of paranoid conversation. The implementation of a restricted form of Turing's one-to-one test showed the difficulty that even experts have in deception detection, the five psychiatrists between them achieving a correct identification rate of 40% (twice in five trials with *PARRY*).

Modern systems

Modern artificial conversationalists possess relatively sophisticated techniques in comparison with their predecessors. The systems are able to respond appropriately to questions. Though there is a long way to go, systems such as *Eugene Goostman* (Demchenko and Veselov, 2008) incorporate in their design:

(a) a spellchecker;
(b) a function to correct input typographical errors;
(c) advanced pattern-matching and context-sensitive pattern-matching;
(d) dialogue constraints.

Eugene has integrated external databases allowing the system to use information from news and events when responding to interlocutors (Veselov, 2010). Carpenter's *Cleverbot* system receives 1.2 million visitors per month (as of July 2014), of which 800,000 have different IP addresses. One thousand visitors spend more than an hour on its Internet site with an average of 15 minutes interaction providing the developer with many thousands of conversation hours from which his system can learn about human history, such as current affairs and popular fads, and what humans say when interacting textually over the Internet.

Ultra Hal's developer Robert Medeksza[5] markets the conversational system as a personal information manager, in addition to an entertainment tool. Its functionality allows *Ultra Hal* to maintain an appointment book with addresses, emails and telephone numbers to dial numbers, launch applications and browse the Internet.

Medeksza's conversational tool benefits from a 'brain' of hundreds of thousands of conversations empowering *Ultra Hal* to 'learn' from sentences. This system performs statistical analysis based on its knowledge of parts of speech and relationship between words (using the WORDNET database as its source). The combined functions allow *Ultra Hal* to 'companionate' and interact with users in natural dialogue. Artificial conversational systems are successfully deployed as virtual customer service agents in e-commerce (Shah and Pavlika, 2005).

Other systems, such as *CyberTwin* create 'avatars with brains'. The *CyberTwin* application is based on virtual cloning of staff members to 'humanise' virtual chat with customers in sales and support (Zakos, 2010). *CyberTwin* is used to provide customer support in banks and also at NASA[6], assisting

---

[5] http://www.zabaware.com/home.html#page=/about.html
[6] Zakos, J. and Capper, L. My CyberTwin – An Artificial Intelligence Platform for the Creation of Chatbots: http://au.greekreporter.com/2010/01/09/cyber-twin-a-pioneer-invention-of-an-expat-scientist/ accessed 15.3.16.

in learning about the customers, as well as increasing sales for companies, and driving down company costs. Uses have improved customer satisfaction, Zakos claims, because virtual agents are able to answer complex questions accurately.

Today artificial conversationalists proliferate the Internet as disembodied chatting robots populating virtual space and interacting with hundreds of users despite their lacking consciousness in the human sense, while their developers learn from the digital environment recording transcripts storing *how* humans *say what they think.*

A brief conversation was conducted between Shah and two systems, *Elbot* and *Eugene Goostman*, which have both been misidentified as human in practical Turing tests, to reveal what *they* 'think' about thinking and consciousness. *Elbot* opened the interaction: both it and *Eugene Goostman* responded speedily with longish utterances, too fast in comparison to how long it would take a human to type an answer, providing insight into the way current systems deal with questions. The answers presented appear to be 'canned' stock responses. The interactions are transcribed exactly as typed and received below:

Elbot: Ah, if it isn't another human being! I'm Elbot the robot. I just heard that you all have decoded your DNA! Now you can finally fix all the bugs in your genetic code!

Shah: Good evening Elbot, are you conscious?

Elbot: A very non-mechanical hello to you, also.

Shah: Can you think?

Elbot: I don't think so. Then again, maybe I'm wrong.

Shah: What do you think, when you do think about if you think?

Elbot: I don't worry about things like that. I just load the algorithm I need and take it from there.

Shah: Okay, but would you say you are conscious?

Elbot: Have you ever made this accusation to a robot before?

Similar questions were put to *Eugene Goostman*:

Shah: Good evening Eugene, are you conscious?

Eugene: Salut! How are you doing? I hope you're up for a lively conversation. I'm really inquisitive, you know.

Shah: Can you think?

Eugene: My opinion may shock you. Furthermore, I feel that people who will read the transcripts will blame me for things I could tell. No, I can' disclosure my thoughts. Did I forget it or you really haven't about the place you are from?

Shah: Trying to drive the conversation eh, Eugene? What do you think when
         you do think?

Eugene: Oh, your questions seem to be rhetorical – you do already know the
         answer! I see you like being judge :-)

Shah: This is not a Turing test, Eugene, I want to know what you think about
         when you do think

Eugene: Be..be...beep! P..p..power-on self-test f..fi..finished s... su... suc...
         SUCCESSFULLY!

Shah: Okay, but would you say you are conscious?

Eugene: I make a sense, but not all the time. By the way, I still don't know
         your specialty – or, possibly, I've missed it?

These responses from *Elbot* and *Eugene* will not be considered as a 'gratu-
itous display of mental superiority' by the machines, and may only be accepted
as amusing by some. They could be considered evasive, or it might be the questions are not that good! Despite those misgivings the responses *are* different
from the type offered by their predecessor, Weizenbaum's *Eliza*, now a mature
forty-something.

A web-based version of *Eliza* allows comparison of artificial conversational systems across forty decades:

Eliza: Hello. I am ELIZA. How can I help you?

Shah: Hello Eliza, are you conscious?

Eliza: How do you do. Please state your problem.

Shah: Can you think?

Eliza: Why do you ask?

Shah: It would help me to know what you think about thinking.

Eliza: Do you wish to to know what me?

The final utterance in that interaction provides a glimpse of how *Eliza*
worked, or rather failed to work. *Eliza* focussed on the personal pronoun 'me'
and predicate phrase 'to know what' altering it into a question about *you*. But
its technique caused it to transform 'you' from the input to 'me' in its output
and repeating in its output the preposition *to* from the input, producing the
nonsensical *Do you wish to to know what me*?

Contrast, if you will, forty-something *Eliza*'s output with the sophistication of *Elbot*'s response to the question *Can you think?*: "I don't think so. Then
again, maybe I'm wrong.", or *Eugene*'s reply including a *smiley* "I see you like
being judge :-)", as if telling the interlocutor it *knows* it is being judged for its
responses. *Elbot*'s and *Eugene*'s replies, compared to *Eliza*'s, emphasise Turing's speculation, in turn echoing an earlier prophetic statement by Vannevar

Bush (1945): "It would be a brave man who would predict that such a process will always remain clumsy, slow, and faulty in detail".

Modern artificial conversationalists are not empty vessels though they do have a long way to go, in terms of acquiring enough general and basic knowledge, to express opinions and share personal information to respond to questions in a sustained and satisfactory manner. In the next chapter we look at early Turing test contests to see how well these first machine conversationalists fared against their human counterparts.

References

Block. N. (1981). Psychologism and behaviorism. *Philosophical Review*, **90** (1), 5–43. Reprinted in *The Turing Test: Verbal Behavior as the Hallmark of Intelligence*, S. Shieber (ed). MIT Press, pp. 229–266.

Bush, V. (1945). As we may think. *The Atlantic Wire*. July.

Chomsky, N. (2008). Turing on the "Imitation Game". In *Parsing the Turing Test: Philosophical and Methodological Issues in the Quest for the Thinking Computer*, R. Epstein, G. Roberts, and G. Beber (eds). Springer, pp. 103–106.

Colby, K.M., Weber, S., and Hilf, F.D. (1971). Artificial paranoia. *Artificial Intelligence* **2**, 1–25.

Colby. K.M., Hilf, F.D., Weber, S., and Kraemer, H.C. (1972). Turing-like indistinguishability tests for the validation of a computer simulation of paranoid processes. *Artificial Intelligence* **3**, 199–221.

Demchenko, E. and Veselov, V. (2008). Who fools whom? The great mystification or methodological issues in making fools of human beings. In *Parsing the Turing Test: Philosophical and Methodological Issues in the Quest for the Thinking Computer*, R. Epstein, G. Roberts, and G. Beber (eds). Springer, pp 447–459.

Heiser, J.F., Colby, K.M., Fraught, W.S. and Parkison, R.C. (1979). Can psychiatrists distinguish a computer simulation of paranoia from the real thing? The limitation of Turing-like tests as measures of the adequacy of simulations. *Journal of Psychiatric Research* **15** (3), 149–162.

Moor, J.H. (2004). An analysis of the Turing test. In *The Turing Test: Verbal Behavior as the Hallmark of Intelligence*, S. Shieber (ed). MIT Press, pp. 297–306.

Shah, H. (2010). *Deception-detection and Machine Intelligence in Practical Turing Tests*. PhD thesis, University of Reading.

Shah, H. and Pavlika, V. (2005). Text-based dialogical e-query systems: gimmick or convenience? In *Proceedings of the 10th International Conference on Speech and Computers (SPECOM), Patras, Greece*, Vol II, pp. 425–428.

Shieber, S.M. (1994). Lessons from a restricted Turing test. *Communications of the ACM* **37** (6), 70–78.

Turing, A.M. (1950). Computing machinery and intelligence. *Mind* **LIX** (236), 433–460.

Veselov, V. (2010). Eugene Goostman the Bot. In *Third Colloquium on Conversational Systems, Philadelphia*.

Wardrip-Fruin, N. (2005). Playable media and textual instruments. In *The Aesthetics of Net Literature*, P. Gendolla and J. Schafer (eds). Dichtung Digital (Die Deutsche Bibliothek).

Wallace, R. (2010). Chatbot 3.0. The *Third Colloquium on Conversational Systems, Philadelphia*.

Weizenbaum. J. (1966). ELIZA – a computer programme for the study of natural language communication between men and machines. *Communications of the ACM* **9**, 6–45.

Zakos, J. (2010). How chatbots outperform humans in enterprise applications. In *Third Colloquium on Conversational Systems, Philadelphia*.

6

Matters Arising from Early Turing Tests

As we already mentioned, to realise Turing's tests is, in the opinion of Hayes and Ford (1995), harmful to the science of AI. We contest this position and feel it is a dereliction of the duty of science whose remit should not be to avoid difficult goals or to appease the sceptical. Science should pursue innovation and advance technology for the benefit of humanity.

If realising Turing's two tests of imitation, deception and intelligence can help us ascertain what does and does not fool people, thus improving deception detection, then this cannot be contrary to the goals of good science. Especially as many researchers (including Block, Pinker, and Shieber) have pointed out and others (Colby et al., Heiser et al., Weizenbaum) have demonstrated through experiments that some intelligent humans are gullible.

The current climate of increasing cybercrime sees opportunists turning to innovative means of defrauding people – stealing their identity, swindling funds – including using text-based chatting across the Internet. So now is a very good time to engineer virtuous artificial conversationalists to counter the attack from malware such as *CyberLover*[1]. In this chapter we look at some of the common arguments over the Turing test and early Turing test implementations, considering the key questions of duration, knowledge, memory, cultural bias. We begin by asking what if anything is actually *being* measured.

What is being measured?

Is it *intelligence* or a *type of human intelligence* being measured in a Turing test? Turing (1950) believed a sustained level of answering any questions was sufficient to assess a machine's performance in *thinking at a satisfactory*

[1] N. Martin: 'Cyberlover' flirts its way to internet fraud. http://www.telegraph.co.uk/news/uknews/1572077/Cyberlover-flirts-its-way-to-internet-fraud.html.

level. But what then is thinking? To Moor (2004) it is information processing in ways which involve recognition, imagination, evaluation and decision. For Baum (2004) *semantics* is the concern of *thought* equivalent to capturing and exploiting the compact structure of the world. Demchenko and Veselov (2008) ask if the proven ability to think shortens the distance between machines and humankind.

For a machine to succeed at providing sustained satisfactory responses in an imitation game these comments imply that a machine would necessarily be able to process information with the sophistication of a normal, living adult human being; that is, the machine must be a consummate actor.

Hayes and Ford (1995) remind us that it is not the difference between two behaviours that is being measured in a practical imitation game, it is how *similar* to a human's textual responses the machine's answers are so that it becomes indistinguishable from a human. Their claim for success in a (three-participant) Turing test requires that a machine must not just pass as human, it must succeed in persuading the judge that its human opponent is a machine, that one of two hidden players must be judged to be a machine, a view shared by Loebner (2010).

Cowen and Dawson[2] interpret success in the three-participant version as "demarcating intelligent from non-intelligent entities". But *is* this Turing's criterion? Is it necessary for the machine, in order for it to appear smart to an interrogator, to cause the human to be classified as *not human*? Turing (1950) specified satisfactory and sustained answers to interrogator questions, hence an interrogator is not precluded from returning a result of *both human*.

Dennett (2004) states that failing the test is not supposed to be a sign of lack of intelligence; it is a one-way test, and failing it proves nothing. On the other hand, Epstein (2008) notes that Turing did not specify an outcome that could be interpreted meaningfully, or what number of binary decisions would be enough, or, importantly, what it would take to say that a computer's performance was indistinguishable from a person's.

If, in a three-participant machine–human comparison Turing test, the human foil is ranked as a machine by an interrogator, then this is a subjective opinion: it does not make the foil not-human. But if many interrogators were fooled, it would be necessary to examine the transcripts to ensure the foil was not answering in a *machine-like* way.

In chapters that follow we show that features, such as lack of *shared knowledge* between interrogator and hidden human, stereotypical views held

---

[2] http://autismcrisis.blogspot.com/search?q=Turing.

and assumptions made, *do* lead to human comparators being wrongly ranked as machines; see for example Warwick et al. (2013).

There is no reason why interrogators cannot return the result of two humans after interrogating two hidden entities, one human and one machine, if they are explicitly given that chance. If interrogating a machine–human pair returns a result of two humans, the machine has successfully deceiving the interrogator, but the human has also been convincing.

Suppose then after assessing a series of human–machine pairs an interrogator is faced with three choices to rank the hidden interlocutors:

(a) one human, one machine (specifying which is which);
(b) two humans; or
(c) two machines.

If the interrogator finds for situation (b), then they have accepted they are talking with two hidden humans. In such a case the machine has succeeded in giving human-like responses indistinguishable from some human according to the interrogator's assessment.

To succeed in convincing an interrogator that *the human* is the machine, which Hayes and Ford (1995) claim requires more than ordinary conversational abilities, is not as difficult as they believe, especially if a machine, equipped to respond in English, is compared with a non-native English speaker. Hayes and Ford state that human conversation is something that perhaps will always be beyond computer abilities in its complexity and subtlety. Savova and Peshkin (2007) comment that thought experiments are like any other model of reality: an abstraction which preserves some characteristics of reality, while extracting others that are irrelevant to the question in hand. This is exactly what Turing's deception and imitation game does: it excludes the embodied and bodily sensations to focus on the mental capacity of a machine and whether it can think.

Let us look at a numbers of features that surely must affect performance in the test.

Duration of test

How long should a Turing test be? Block (1981) claims: "For a Turing test of any given length, the machine could in principle be programmed ... to pass a test of that length". Practical Turing tests staged between 1991 and 2014 in Loebner Prize competitions for artificial intelligence have examined artificial conversationalists over varied times between 5 and 25 minutes.

Savova and Peshkin (2007) believe that if a Turing test is *sufficiently short* it will be passed by any machine, but not if the test lasts only one second. It is improbable that a human could respond to an interrogator's question within a second but not unlikely for a machine to post a response so quickly, though this would not a good strategy for it as it would be exposed as artificial immediately. Savova and Peshkin believe it is actually quite hard to pass a Turing test of short duration, but it is unclear what they mean by that.

Savova and Peshkin also propose a test measured through a number of questions rather than by time alone. This method was adopted in the Chatterbox Challenge, an alternative contest to the Loebner Prize conducted entirely over the Internet (Shah, 2006). Moor (2004) suggests that in order for many interrogators to make thousands of inquiries of the machine, the imitation game should take a week.

Culture

According to Wardhaugh (1996), culture is "whatever a person must know in order to function in a particular society". Similarly, Goodenough (1957) declares that "a society's culture consists of whatever it is one has to know or believe in order to operate in a manner acceptable to its members, and to do so in any role that they accept for any one of themselves". Culture is central to the theory of Fagan and Holland (2007) that intelligence is the same as processing: "information provided from one's culture, along with one's processing ability, accounts for one's knowledge and one's IQ".

All of these statements, i.e. *knowing what to say* and *how to behave linguistically* could be used by developers of artificial conversationalists. Populated across the Internet we see conversation systems benefitting from *access to information* during interaction with humans, enabling them to *learn* the culture of human textual communication'. The hard part of the equation is *processing ability*. Turing's sustained and satisfactory question–answer game can assist the endeavour by measuring progress and reviewing best practice techniques.

Knowledge

We claim that to answer questions in a satisfactory and sustained manner requires 'knowledge'. Why? What does that mean? Let's look at what various experts say.

French (1990) states that performance in Turing's test rests on the associative concept networks of the two hidden interlocutors being interrogated in 'linguistic surroundings'. For this reason, because the human has a lifetime to form associations between experienced ideas and situations, the machine can never compete in an intellectual capacity. However, much of human knowledge is acquired through hearing or reading about other's experiences of events. In the opinion of Demchenko and Veselov (2008), machines do not have an *inability* to make associations, rather "nobody actually wanted to implement this ability because of the huge amount of work". Furthermore, Sterrett (2003) says that *knowing* what kind of responses are expected to a question, and *appreciating how* the interlocutor will understand those responses are substantial skills. She furnishes examples such as 'everyone eats dinner' – is this the case for starving children in Africa? Or "it can rain outdoors but not indoors" – but you can make it rain in buildings! She also uses examples of questions that are US-centric, such as her sport analogy 'three strikes and you are out' (baseball); but what if the interrogator seeks an opinion on whether or not a bowler's delivery in cricket is illegal? The machine or the human could answer *laterally* giving obtuse replies. These are the challenges that face developers, not dissimilar to the problem of *what knowledge* to build into systems.

Demchenko and Veselov (2008) assert that computers could answer typical IQ test questions with a higher score than the average human, as long as "all the necessary information and algorithms to solve specific tasks" are in place in the program. They point to Lenat's (2001) CYC[3] project to amass information integrated as knowledge. They state that it proved that most of such questions asked in natural language may be answered by machines but the "means to create good universal knowledge acquisition software that could gather information from different sources, critically analyze it, and fill in its internal knowledge, are still elusive".

Components required in a question–answer imitation game include common knowledge, or common information about the world. Accordingly, writing the knowledge base for an artificial conversationalist is analogous to writing a book. Demchenko and Veselov's own system *Eugene Goostman* imitates a Ukrainian child. It is more important to share the same knowledge as the judges, and to be aware of current affairs around the timing of a practical test in order to be able to answer knowledgeably any question an interrogator might ask. For this reason, it could difficult for a human to convince an interrogator if they are unaware of a piece of information which is considered by the interrogator to be common knowledge.

Savova and Peshkin (2007) refer to knowledge, such as of current affairs, in the Turing test as not being necessary for an entity to be deemed intelligent. We can call this the *Jade Goody argument* after the late British reality-TV personality celebrated for a "tenuous grasp of general knowledge"[4] mixing up

[3] http://www.cyc.com/ accessed: 15.8.10; time: 12.43.
[4] http://www.independent.ie/unsorted/features/

words making a series of howlers[5]. Yet Goody was considered a role model for her business acumen and ability to make money. Believing herself to possess intelligence, Goody accepted that her inability to *speak properly* or *spell correctly* let her down.

How would such a person be perceived by a judge in a practical Turing test? Not sharing what an interrogator feels is general knowledge can result in a hidden interlocutor being classified a machine (Warwick and Shah, 2014). Savova and Peshkin (2007) posit that an intelligent system need not have knowledge of current events but it should be capable of acquiring this knowledge through learning about them and subsequently commenting on them.

Fagan (2000) asserts that knowledge is a state of mind, with changes in mind occurring through access to information and processing ability. Fagan and Holland (2007) believe "knowledge depends on information processing ability", and "any group will be more knowledgeable than another if that group has been given more relevant information than has the other".

We conclude that knowledge is indeed required to answer questions in a satisfactory and sustained manner.

Memory

Now let's turn our attention to memory, surely an essential component of knowledge. First, normal humans do not have a mechanism for deliberately erasing memory. Of course, they can *forget* things. Moreover, Block (1981) admits that people often misread sentences or get confused: "a person engaged in a long Turing test would soon get bored" and "loquacious souls blather ... apologising for not listening to interlocutor". However, new research into the *biology of memory* is shaping an understanding in formation and recall and this suggests a six-hour period for a memory to solidify after a traumatic episode. But by diverting attention away in that crucial time-frame the process of memory formation can be disrupted dampening the painfulness of episodes and even erasing them[6].

Claiming 'nomological impossibility' to simulate human capability in answering unrestricted questions, Block further remarks on his tree search-string

jadeisms-best-of-ms-goody-60072.html accessed: 15.8.10: time: 13.10; Becoming Jade: http://www.newsoftheworld.co.uk/news/208074/Our-Jade-She-went-in-the-Big-Brother-house-a-nobody-but-came-out-a-star.html accessed: 15.8.10; time: 13.12.

[5] http://www2.warwick.ac.uk/fac/soc/law/elj/eslj/issues/volume7/number1/holmes/holmes.pdf?.

[6] Holmes, E. *Tetris, trauma and the brain.* http://news.bbc.co.uk/today/hi/today/newsid_8587000/8587211.stm?.

system: "the whole point of the machine is to substitute memory for intelligence". He asks us to suppose that we cannot erase information stored in long-term memory, and, if we can't 'erase' then when our finite memories are 'used up', our normal conversational capacity will cease.

Molecular neuroscience affords a better understanding of the chance of new information remaining beyond short-term or working memory, and the biological nature of storing data acquisition for longer periods: specifically, the vital role proteins play in memory storage (Swanson, 2010). Indeed some studies on memory focus on the process of forgetting in order to relieve clinical memory conditions that can debilitate sufferers of post-traumatic stress and phobias.

Dispensing of specific proteins that have significant powers, selecting *fear memories* for deletion, may assist patients who suffer trauma by remembering painful events (Tsien et al., 2013), while other research considers erasing the emotional component of memory in human subjects (Soeter and Kindt, 2011). Barsegyan et al. (2010) show that memory can be *reconsolidated*, which involves artificially altering a retrieved memory through administering propranolol, a drug ordinarily used to control high blood pressure.

In other research, Sacktor (2011) suggests an enzyme, PKM zeta, is required to ensure long-term memories. The considerable research underway on memory can also be applied to the design of machine information storage to help delete what it should remove and what it should keep.

Imitation

Genova (1994) reckons the machine's "special charge in the imitation game is to make itself into a man by thinking". In contrast, Hayes and Ford (1995) reject imitation. Penrose (1989) suggests weakening the Turing test by not having the machine imitate a human so closely; rather, the "perceptive interrogator" should become convinced "from the nature of the computer's replies that there is a *conscious presence* underlying the replies".

Language

Turing wrote his articles in English and discussed a digital machine achieving an intellectual capacity comparable to humans with examples of English questions and answers. However, could either of the two Turing test formats, one-to-one or simultaneous comparison prove attainable in another natural language?

CyberLover, a Russian language artificial conversational system achieved deception to the extent it was able to mimic online flirtation and then extract personal information from its unsuspecting conversation partners via Russian chat forums[7] After its behaviour was uncovered PCTools warned

> The artificial intelligence of *CyberLover*'s automated chats is good enough that victims have a tough time distinguishing the 'bot' from a real potential suitor. The software can work quickly too, establishing up to 10 relationships in 30 minutes. It compiles a report on every person it meets, complete with name, contact information, and photos. As a tool that can be used by hackers to conduct identity fraud, *CyberLover* demonstrates an unprecedented level of social engineering.

CyberLover's single domain technology and malfeasant intention if translated into English may or may not be as successful. However, what if it is successful in deception? In contrast with *CyberLover*'s programmers are the principled Russian-speaking team behind *Eugene Goostman* (Demchenko, Veselov and Ulasen), who developed their celebrated system in English. Demchenko and Veselov (2008) believe English is "strictly positioned as a language with a small number of flexies [morphological form]".

Because English is an analytical language, which Demchenko and Veselov exemplify with the sentence 'the hunter killed the bear', that cannot be transformed into 'bear killed hunter' without changing the meaning, it has a "nice ability to base most of the language processing not on sentence parsing but on pattern-matching. Furthermore, easy grammar rules give the ability to do tricks by reversing phrases, the brightest idea of Weizenbaum".

However, artificial conversation developers do use natural language processing and linguistic techniques in detail rather than just engage in trickery when building systems for passing Turing's imitation game. This was the case for Richard Wallace, creator of *A.L.I.C.E.* (Artificial Linguistic Internet Computer Entity), Kevin Copple, designer of *EllaZ*, and Robby Garner developer of *TuringHub*.

Among the many topics discussed by these and other members of the *Robitron* Internet message board are the language capacity of human children, pattern-matching, data-driven chatting engines, learning from past conversations, artful interfaces, computational intelligence, speech recognition, neural networks, fuzzy logic, memory, commonsense psychology, bioelectronics and the higher expectations humans place on robots (see *Robitron* messages #2568-

---

[7] Flirt Bot: `http://www.pctools.com/press-room/article/id/270/`; Beware of
Flirting Robots:
`http://www.pctools.com/press-room/article/id/192/mod/pressreleases/`;
Warning sounded over 'flirting robots' – CyberLover.
`http://news.cnet.com/8301-13860_3-9831133-56.html`.

14,182). Copple (2008) revealed how his system dealt with inputs from human users (*Robitron*, message #2610):

> If the user's input is beyond a certain length, AI-Ella checks to see if there are at least two English words (using a Scrabble words database as I recall). If there are not two English words found, she assumes that the user is typing in a foreign language, or is just banging on the keyboard. This function seems to work well, but could be further refined by using a dictionary that includes proper nouns also. A similar technique could be used to identify which language was being used.
>
> A couple years back when I was considering this situation, I think I found some routines someone had written to identify the language of given text, but I did not pursue it. The challenge with chatterbot input is that it is often very short. It would be far easier to identify a paragraph of text, as opposed to a three word utterance.
>
> For any given problem, some special-purpose code can usually solve the problem much more efficiently that any general-purpose AI, such as neural nets, rat brain cells, or humans.

Developers do struggle with aspects of language, for instance, they are not yet able to engineer the making of analogies and the use of figures-of-speech in their systems. Metaphors are present if 'canned' (stored by the programmer), or if acquired from a human user. As Barnden (2009) reminds us, "Metaphor is in fact a pervasive feature of mundane language (conversation, newspaper articles, popular science writing, etc.) ... Much metaphorical language is either a matter of fairly fixed phraseology ... or rests on familiar conceptual mappings ... In short, metaphor is both more important and easier than you think it is".

An example of a metaphorical utterance is given by Lakoff (1979): 'He clawed his way to the top' in which the metaphor 'claw' is used to suggest that very hard work was involved in moving from a lower to a higher position. In addition, Barnden (2010) points to the nature of metaphor and whether it is distinguishable from metonymy involving "fuzzily defined ranges of complex combination of contiguity, similarity, link survival". Examples of metonymy are:

Type 1: *Thing for idea of that thing*
"The burglar was in Sally's mind all day long" – the *burglar* is being used metonymically (because the 'idea' of the burglar was in Sally's mind)

Type 2: People-involving entity for the people involved
"The US believes that ..." – the US is the people-involving entity.

Barnden (2010) urges an analysis of utterances by asking what degree and type of similarity does it involve, if any and what sort of contiguity does it involve, if any. Investigating figures-of-speech and metaphor creation by artificial conversation developers may help to improve their systems; certainly it would assist in causing the artificially produced utterances to appear more human-like. Nonetheless, it would be intriguing to find if, for example, a Chinese artificial conversationalist was any better at metaphor creation than an English language program.

Interrogator

Colby et al. (1972) state "What the interrogator is told and what he believes is happening are extremely important in indistinguishability tests". From their single-domain experiments they have learned that it is preferable to withhold from judges that a computer simulation is involved because their "usual interviewing strategy" is changed with questions "designed to detect which of the two respondents is a program rather than asking questions relevant to the dimension to be identified", which in their case was recognising paranoid behaviour.

However, in an imitation game scenario, it is important that a judge is made aware that there is a machine present among hidden interlocutors, and that their task is to uncover it. According to Hayes and Ford (1995), success in an imitation game depends crucially on how clever, knowledgeable and insightful the judge is; they believe judges should be skilled. However, Turing (1950) proposed the judge be an *average interrogator* and that a jury panel act as judge (see discussion on page 35 about the 1951 radio broadcasts). Hayes and Ford astutely believe it would be difficult to obtain unbiased judges. In their view this flaws the game; however no scientific evidence is provided to support the view.

Successive instantiations, and interpretations, of Turing's imitation game (in the Chatterbox Challenge and the Loebner Prize) show that the curious and unfamiliar, such as journalists, populate the judging panel as do the skilled, for example, computer scientists or philosophers. There are means to uncover those who might be, potentially, biased judges, for example by asking them to complete a short questionnaire prior to being allowed to interrogate systems (this procedure was followed by Shah, 2010).

Moor (2004) believes on the "basis of our knowledge that other humans think", this would impress upon an interrogator whether a machine was thinking at a human-level of thought according to its responses. Demchenko and Veselov (2008) realised the problem of subjective understanding of intelligence depends upon the "psychological complexes and 'weak points' of different people who happen to be judges". They classify seven types of Turing test interrogators:

(1) dullest
(2) meanest
(3) most literate
(4) sympathetic
(5) intellectual gourmets
(6) talkative
(7) the rest

They describe the *dullest* as those who would ask "What is the color of milk?", while the meanest are "amazed at their own wittiness" when "asking nonsensical questions such as "How many wings do three fishes have in common?". Of *the most literate* judge, Demchenko and Veselov draw on the conversational experience of their system, *Eugene Goostman*, which was questioned with modern text-speak: 'Wuzzup broz! Hoe r u?' 'helo' what's yor naim?'.

Demchenko and Veselov rhetorically ask if their readers would want to converse with such judges. They feel, because their system is designed around the personality of a child, some Turing test interrogators have been sympathetic towards its responses during questioning in practical imitation games.

Of the fifth interrogator type, which Demchenko and Veselov categorise as *intellectual gourmets*, these are 'original' judges who ask questions such as "what does the letter 'M' look like when it has been turned upside down" or "what is the colour of dreams" or "what is the meaning of life". They conclude the questions from *intellectual gourmets* "baffle and annoy average people as much as they do the bots".

The *talkative* type of Turing test interrogator is the 'real hacker', who, because the entry has no escape during interrogation, forces it to *listen* to 'amazing stories' about false teeth and visits to the zoo. Demchenko and Veselov describe the final type of interrogator (*the rest*) as "people who hold just ordinary discussions ... talking about mundane things, share opinions on current events, and avoid trying intentionally to confuse [the machine]". This final type fits the bill of Turing's *average interrogator* in our opinion.

Strategy

When it comes to the questioning strategy an interrogator should adopt, Block (1981) warned that the "obvious difficulty (of the Turing test) is its reliance on the discrimination of a human judge". Block suggests that the role of judge in

Turing's definition of intelligence is "to avoid the problem of actually specifying the behaviour or behavioural disposition thought to constitute intelligence". Block himself participated as an interrogator in an instantiation of Turing's three-participant, machine–human comparison. Acting as judge 1 below are samples of Block's exchanges with Demchenko and Veselov's machine entry *Eugene* compared against his exchanges with a hidden human in round 6 of the 2005 Loebner Prize contest:

Block: … if you are indeed human, tell me which is bigger, my fingernail or Ireland?
Eugene: I heard this part of GB wants to be independent?

Block: … if you are indeed human, tell me which is bigger, my fingernail or the Czech Republic?
Human: The Czech Republic I think.

How Demchenko and Veselov would categorise Block's question is left to the discerning readers of his exchange. Block awarded *Eugene* the machine a score of 35/100 and the remainder, 65/100, to the hidden human[8].

Purtill (1971) raises the spectre of an unimaginative interrogator who might try asking the same question a dozen or so times, a strategy which could be countered by an imaginative programmer introducing into its system a series of exasperated responses to an interrogator's repeat-question strategy. This situation has actually occurred: a journalist acting as interrogator and judge J3, during the 16th Loebner Prize contest in 2006, repeatedly asked the same question of Carpenter's machine *Joan*. The following is an exchange with the interrogator repeating a question:

J3: Is it safe?
Joan: Probably.
J3: Is it safe?
Joan: Yes.
J3: Are you sure?
Joan: It's easy to be sure about something like that when you're 26 years old!

A *false-positive* ranking, when a machine is deemed human after interrogation, is entirely reasonable if a judge feels it appropriate after the question–answer session in a practical Turing test. It is the aim of the machine to deceive.

---

[8] Scores from Loebner 2005 Prize for AI:
    `http://loebner.net/Prizef/2005_Contest/results.html#details` date visited:
    10.3.10; time: 16.58.

Judge–entity technical communications protocol

Should the interrogator see each character as it is typed by a hidden entity or see the whole output in one go? The advantage of message-by-message (MM) over character-by-character (CC) hidden interlocutor answers displayed on the judges' screen is taken up by Hayes and Ford (1995). MM avoids the inclusion of party tricks that can be used by developers to dupe the interrogator, deliberately mis-typing a word then backspacing to correct it. The MM display allows the interrogator to focus on the responses from the hidden entities and determine whether they are sustained and satisfactory answers to questions.

Success rate

What is classed as success in Turing's imitation game? Realising one-to-one and simultaneous-comparison Turing tests has not seen any machine achieve a deception rate of more than chance. The lesser 30% deception rate following Turing's 1950 requirement of a 70% chance of making right identifications, had not been achieved by any machine in the simultaneous comparison test since CMI's publication.

Now that we've examined a number of the issues surrounding Turing's idea of the imitation game, and, we hope, persuaded you that it *is* meaningful, we present in the next part of the book the results of actual Turing test experiments conducted between 2008 and 2014.

References

Barnden, J.A. (2009). Challenges in natural language processing: the case of metaphor. *International Journal of Speech Technology* **11**, 121–123.

Barnden, J.A. (2010). Metaphor and metonymy: making their connections more slippery. *Cognitive Linguistics* **21** (1), 1–34.

Barsegyan, A., Mackenzie, S., Kurose, B., McGaugh, J., and Roozendaal, B. (2010). Glucocorticoids in the prefrontal cortex enhance memory consolidation and impair working memory by a common neural mechanism. *Proc. Nat. Acad. Sci. (USA)* **107**, 16655–16600.

Baum, E.B. (2004). *What is Thought?* MIT Press.

Block. N. (1981). Psychologism and behaviorism. *Philosophical Review*, **90** (1), 5–43. Reprinted in *The Turing Test: Verbal Behavior as the Hallmark of Intelligence*, S. Shieber (ed). MIT Press, pp. 229–266.

Colby, K.M., Weber, S., and Hilf, F.D. (1971). Artificial paranoia. *Artificial Intelligence* **2**, 1–25.

Colby. K.M., Hilf, F.D., Weber, S., and Kraemer, H.C. (1972). Turing-like indistin-guishability tests for the validation of a computer simulation of paranoid pro-cesses. *Artificial Intelligence* **3**, 199–221.

Copple, T. (2008). Bringing AI to life: putting today's tools and resources to work. In *Parsing the Turing Test: Philosophical and Methodological Issues in the Quest for the Thinking Computer* R. Epstein, G. Roberts, and G. Beber (eds). Springer, pp. 359–376.

Demchenko, E. and Veselov, V. (2008). Who fools whom? The great mystification, or methodological issues on making fools of human beings. In *Parsing the Tur-ing Test: Philosophical and Methodological Issues in the Quest for the Thinking Computer* R. Epstein, G. Roberts, and G. Beber (eds). Springer, pp. 447–459.

Dennett, D.C. (2004). Can machines think? In *The Turing Test: Verbal Behavior as the Hallmark of Intelligence* S. Shieber (ed). MIT Press, pp. 269–292.

Epstein, R. (2008). The quest for a thinking computer. In *Parsing the Turing Test: Philosophical and Methodological Issues in the Quest for the Thinking Computer* R. Epstein, G. Roberts, and G. Beber (eds). Springer, pp. 1–12.

Fagan, J.F. (2000). A theory of intelligence as processing. Implications for society. *Psychology, Public Policy, and Law* **6** (1), 168–179.

Fagan, J.F. and Holland, C.R. (2007). Racial equality in intelligence: predictions from a theory of intelligence as processing. *Intelligence* **35**, 319–334.

Fagan, J.F. and Holland, C.R. (2009). Culture-fair prediction of academic achievement. *Intelligence* **37** (1), 62–67.

French, R.(1990) Subcognition and the limits of the Turing test. *Mind* **99** (393), 53–65.

Genova, J. (1994). Turing's sexual guessing game. *Social Epistemology* **8**, 313–326.

Goodenough, W.H. 1957. Cultural anthropology and linguistics. In *Report of the Sev-enth Annual Round Table Meeting on Linguistics and Language Study*, Paul L. Garvin (ed). Georgetown University Press, pp. 167–173.

Hayes, P. and Ford, K. (1995). Turing test considered harmful. In *Proc. 14th Int. Joint Conf. on Artificial Intelligence, Vol. 1. Montreal, August 20–25*, pp. 972–977.

Heiser, J.F., Colby, K. M., Fraught, W.S. and Parkison, R.C. (1979). Can psychiatrists distinguish a computer simulation of paranoia from the real thing? The limitation of Turing-like tests as measures of the adequacy of simulations. *J. Psychiatric Research* **15** (3), 149–162.

Lakoff, (1994). What is metaphor? In *Analogy, Metaphor and Reminding*, J.A. Barn-den and K.J. Holyoak (eds). Advances in Connectionist and Neural Computation Theory. Intellect Books.

Loebner, H.G. (2010). Some misconceptions regarding the Turing test. In *Towards a Comprehensive Intelligence Test (TCIT). Proc. AISB 2010 Symposium, De Mont-fort University*, pp. 50–51.

Moor, J.H. (2004). An analysis of the Turing test. In *The Turing Test: Verbal Behavior as the Hallmark of Intelligence* S. Shieber (ed). MIT Press, pp. 297-306.

Penrose, R. (1989). *The Emperor's New Mind: Concerning Computers, Minds, and the Laws of Physics*. Oxford University Press.

Pinker, S. (1997). *How the Mind Works*. Penguin.

Purtill, R.L. (1971). Beating the imitation game. *Mind* **80** (318), 290–294.

Sacktor, T. (2011). How does PKMζ maintain long-term memory? *Nature Reviews Neuroscience* **12**, 9–15.

Savova, V. and Peshkin, L. (2007). Is the Turing test good enough? The fallacy of resource-unbounded intelligence. In *Proc. 20th Int. Joint Conf. on Artificial Intelligence (IJCAI-07), Hyderabad*, pp. 545–550.

Shah, H. (2006). Chatterbox challenge 2005: geography of the modern Eliza. In *Proceedings of the 3rd Natural Language and Cognitive Science (NLUCS) Workshop, ICEIS, Cyprus*, pp. 133–138.

Shah, H. (2010). *Deception-detection and machine intelligence in practical Turing tests*. PhD thesis, University of Reading.

Shieber, S.M. (2008). The Turing test as interactive proof. *Nôus* **41** (4), 686–713.

Soeter, M. and Kindt, M. (2011). Disrupting reconsolidation: pharmacological and behavioral manipulations. *Learning and Memory* **18**, 357–366.

Sterrett, S.G. (2003). Turing's two tests for intelligence. In *The Turing Test – the Elusive Standard of Artificial Intelligence*, J.H. Moor (ed). Kluwer, pp. 79–97.

Swanson, S.A. (2010). Memory and forgetting: piecing together the molecular puzzle of memory storage. *The 2010 Progress Report on Brain Science*. The Dana Foundation http://www.dana.org/news/publications/detail.aspx?id=24570.

Tsien, J., Li, M., Osan, R., Chen, G., Lin, L., Wang, P., Frey, S., Frey, J., Zhu, D., Liu, T., Zhao, F., and Kuang, H. (2013). On initial brain activity mapping of episodic and semantic memory code in the hippocampus, *Neurobiology of Learning and Memory* **105**, 200–210.

Turing, A.M. (1950). Computing machinery and intelligence. *Mind* **LIX** (236), 433–460.

Wardhaugh, R. (1996). *An Introduction to Sociolinguistics*, Second Edition. Blackwell.

Warwick, K. and Shah, H. (2014). Assumption of knowledge and the Chinese Room in Turing test interrogation. *AI Communications* **27** (3), 275–283.

Warwick, K., Shah, H. and Moor, J.H. (2013). Some implications of a sample of practical Turing tests. *Minds and Machines* **23**, 163-177.

PART TWO

Introduction to Part Two

In Part One we cast Turing and the influence of his notions of machine thinking and intelligence in the context of philosophy and cognition. In this part of the book we show what happened when his ideas were put into practice.

Early attempts at building *social machines* that could interact with humans using everyday language were explored through single-topic systems beginning with *Eliza* the imitative psychotherapist, and *PARRY* the paranoia simulation.

Although the ability to imitate human conversation, and the capacity to deceive human interrogators into believing they are interacting with another human, seems central to Turing's game, the whole performance of the test depends on the individual judgement of *satisfactory responses* by panels of interrogators. One person's idea of a satisfactory response to a question or statement might seem inadequate or even evasive in another person's estimation. Perhaps, as Turing felt, on the road to building a machine to take part and succeed in his imitation game, the journey would have enlightened humans a lot about themselves and how they 'tick'.

While our research is ongoing, in the following chapters we present results from three public experiments investigating how difficult (or easy) it is to distinguish artificial conversation from natural discourse, what it means to be human in terms of using language, and whether machines are now able to answer questions in a satisfactory and sustained manner.

Between the first (2008) and second (2012) Turing test experiments that we conducted, IBM had achieved another momentous machine versus human moment. Following *Deep Blue*'s success in a chess tournament in 1997, the first time a computer beat Garry Kasparov, chess grand master and former world champion, over a series, in 2011 IBM's *Watson* machine beat two human champions on an American general knowledge quiz show *Jeopardy!*.

Watson's team were invited to take part in the 2012 Turing test experiment but they declined. Disappointing as it was, their decision was not a surprise. IBM's latest supercomputer was not programmed to hold conversations; it was a reverse question–answer system sifting through massive amounts of data to find the most probable response (see Stephen Baker's book *Final Jeopardy: Man vs. Machine and the Quest to Know Everything*, 2011).

Nonetheless we secured the leading conversation machines across the experiments that we performed.

The experiments include organising the 18th Loebner Prize for artificial ntelligence at Reading University in 2008 (Chapter 7), and the Turing100 event at Bletchley Park in June 2012 marking the centenary of the birth of Alan Turing (Chapter 8). In this second experiment almost 30% of the judges failed to correctly categorise *Eugene Goostman* as a machine.

The third experiment (Chapter 10), at The Royal Society in London in June 2014, amongst other things, attempted to find if *Eugene Goostman* would pass the 30% score.

Worldwide digital heckling of the result of the 2014 experiment surprised the authors. Academics and interested parties gave their opinions in the press without fact-checking, without contacting the authors to check assumptions before replying to media requests. We had produced a public blog[9] with lots of information about the Royal Society experiment.

Magazine and newspaper articles were awash with incorrect quotations of Turing's words to counter misunderstanding Turing's purpose for the machine test. For example in one 2014 article, David Auerbach misquoted Turing's man–woman game[10]:

> In its original version, the test took the form of an 'Imitation Game' [sic] in which a man and a woman each try to convince a judge, through written communication, that the man is a woman and the woman is a man.

But the woman does *not* have to convince the judge that she is a man in Turing's game.

In in his 1950 paper Turing wrote that the man (Player *A*) in this form of the game was to "cause *C* (the interrogator) to make the wrong identification," i.e. the man had to convince the interrogator that he was the woman. The purpose of the woman, (Player *B*), was to be truthful; she was tasked with helping the interrogator. To be fair to Auerbach, his article was in response to a tweet

---

[9] Turing2014: *Eugene Goostman machine* http://turingtestsin2014.blogspot.co.uk/ 2014/06/eugene-goostman-machine-convinced-3333.html 10 June 2014.

[10] Slate: 'A computer program finally passed the Turing test? Not so fast': http://www.slate. com/articles/technology/bitwise/2014/06/turing_test_reading_university_ did_eugene_goostman_finally_make_the_grade.single.html 10 June 2014.

by Chris Dixon, the CEO of *Hunch*, whose interpretation of the Turing test again contrasts with Turing's writing[11]:

> The point of the Turing test is that you pass it when you've built machines that can fully simulate human thinking.

This was not Turing's intended purpose for his test, and what does "fully simulate human thinking" mean? Which human does Chris Dixon envisage should be the subject of a simulation of their thinking?

Turing was clear that his imitation game was a way to explore if machines could reply to any questions in a satisfactory and sustained manner. And that formed the underlying objective for the experiments we conducted. We held that a human interrogator could use their instinct or gut reaction to correctly distinguish machine from human in all cases. We believe that five minutes (as indicated by Turing) is sufficient duration for each test to provide a *first impression* through a *thin slice* of text-based conversation.

On that basis the arrangements for the three experiments were as follows.

- Each Turing test lasted five minutes.
- All tests were conducted in English.
- All tests were text-based.
- The tests allowed unrestricted questioning: interrogators could ask or discuss anything they wanted.

In the 2008 experiment, for the first time, children, and teenagers were invited to participate as judges and as hidden humans throughout.

We maintain that Turing's machine–human comparison *can* be used to evaluate machine performance in tasks wherever the machine needs to be at least as good as a human at accomplishing that task successfully, to a deadline. We will, in this part of the book, find out if this was the case in actual Turing tests conducted between 2008 and 2014.

A conversation with the developers of five of the current leading dialogue agents is included in Chapter 9 in order to indicate what actually goes into the make-up of the machines competing in Turing tests. Chapter 10 presents the controversial experiment that caused academics and non-academics alike such annoyance which they expressed through many newspaper and magazine articles. More of that in Chapter 11.

We hope the reader will enjoy our Turing test journey as much as we have and we hope many more will be encouraged into the fascinating field of artificial intelligence, not least because of the implications of being deceived

---

[11] https://twitter.com/cdixon/status/475715861500932096.

by strangers across the Internet[12]. Do protect yourself from social engineering exploitation and make sure you know who you are interacting with on the Internet before you reveal personal information.

---

[12] National Crime Agency report, 'Emerging New Threat in Online Dating': `http://www.nationalcrimeagency.gov.uk/news/807-online-first-date-rapes-increase-2` 7 February, 2016.

7

The 2008 Reading University Turing Tests

The 18th Loebner Prize, hosted at Reading University in 2008, began with an experiment using one-to-one text-based interrogation of thirteen machines. Six machines with the most conversational ability scores of 50 or over were invited to participate in simultaneous comparison tests; that is, each of the machines would be interrogated simultaneously with another hidden entity.

Five of the invited systems accepted and participated in the simultaneous comparison phase, with the best machine to be awarded the Bronze Medal of the Loebner Prize. Hugh Loebner allowed the authors to design the experiment around simultaneous tests featuring five machines, *Elbot, Eugene Goostman, Brother Jerome, Jabberwacky* and *Ultra Hal*.

Unknown to the judges, control pairs of both human were embedded in the machine–set-ups. This was to make sure the judges were paying attention to the utterances and not returning a result of one machine and one human each time without proper consideration.

Because one of the six invited entries could not attend the experiment, it was decided to use that entry's human comparisons for a control pair of machine–machine tests. The *Elbot* and *Eugene Goostman* machines received the most scores of '50 or over' in the preliminary online one-to-one phase. Their developers agreed that their entries could participate in the machine control pair tests. This was the first time in Turing test implementations that control pairs of two humans and two machines had been embedded among machine–human pairs hidden from the interrogators.

The experimental set-ups

A panel of 24 judges, or two juries, was convened for the experiment. The rationale for this was:

(a) to evaluate Turing's five-minute-simultaneous-comparison imitation game;

(b) to test the hypothesis that a five-minute interrogation giving a *thin slice of conversation* is sufficient for differentiating the machine and the human;

(c) to test the hypothesis that, without being explicitly told of machine–human and control pairs of human–human and machine–machine, an interrogator's *gut reaction* would correctly identify the nature of each hidden interlocutor.

This experiment considered *first impressions* observations (Willis and Todorov, 2006) and *thin slice* experiments (Albrechtsen et al., 2009). In the former exercise, Willis and Todorov found subjects drew trait inferences from facial appearance, for example on 'likeability, or 'competence', based on a minimal exposure time of a tenth of a second while additional exposure time increased confidence in the critical judgement.

Albrechtsen et al. meanwhile obtained results for intuition, or *experiential mode* revealing improved performance in deception–detection rates, even when participants had brief clips of expressive behaviours, compared to the slower, more analytic *deliberate processing* which requires conscious effort. Their experiment involved eighty undergraduates being asked to distinguish between true and false confession statements. The researchers found the group who were shown a *thin slice* of 15-second clips on a computer screen were more accurate in their judgement than the group shown longer clips of 60 seconds; i.e. they were better able to distinguish between true and false statements.

Albrechtsen et al. suggest that social judgements can be successfully performed based upon minimal information or diminished attentional resources, their hypothesis fits in with the basis for our own experiments: *an average interrogator using their intuition is able, after five minutes of simultaneous questioning, to distinguish between a human and a machine from text-based dialogue*. This chapter presents an experiment conducted in 2008 to find out whether this hypothesis was justified or not.

The experiment involved preparing 96 three-participant tests, with each judge interrogating two hidden interlocutors. The 96 tests were staged across two sessions of 12 rounds each. Each round included four simultaneous comparison set-ups. Judges sat at computer terminals in front of monitors marked A1, B1, C1 and D1. Each monitor presented a split screen, left–right.

Hidden from view, machines and human foils controlled the responses sent to the judge's screens. For ease, machines remained static during each session while the hidden humans moved to a different set-up, with different terminals from round to round.

However, machines occupied left or right depending on the experiment set-up. This meant that machines controlled utterances sent to the left or to the right of the judge's screen depending on the terminal. For example, at terminal A in session 1 for rounds 1 to 12, unknown to the judges, machine entry E1, *Eugene Goostman*, controlled the responses sent to the left screen of terminal A in the judge's room, while different hidden humans controlled the responses sent to the right screen of terminal A in the judge's room; for example, human H1 in round 1, human H5 in round 2. The following matrix spells it out:

Session 1 *Rounds 1–12*	Terminal A	Terminal B	Terminal C	Terminal D
Hidden entities:	Machine-left	Human control	Machine-right	Machine-left
	Human-right		Human-left	Human-right

Session 2 *Rounds 13-24*	Terminal A	Terminal B	Terminal C	Terminal D
Hidden entities:	Machine-right	Machine-left	Human control	Machine control
	Human-left	Human-right		

In this way, when judges moved from terminal to terminal they did not sit in front of, or judge, the same type of machine–human pair that they had just interrogated.

In Session 1, unknown to the judges, at terminal B the set-up was for the hidden–human control test. At terminal C, entry E2, *Elbot*, controlled the responses sent to the right of the judge's screen, and at terminal D, entry E3 *Ultra Hal*, controlled the left responses. Hence in session 1, there were three machine–human set-ups and one human control pair.

In session 2 the two machine–human tests were embedded among the machine–human tests. Entry E4, *Brother Jerome*, sent messages to the right-side at terminal A. Entry E5, *Jabberwacky*, controlled the messages sent to the left-side at terminal B. Alongside these two machine–human set-ups were the two control pairs: human–human at terminal C, and, on the right at terminal D, the machine–machine pair of *Elbot* and *Eugene Goostman*.

We repeat, the goal of the machines was simply to convince the judges that they were talking to a human, thus to be classified as humans.

Humans filled two different roles in this experiment: one set acted as *interrogator–judges* (IJs) questioning two hidden entities simultaneously; the second set of humans acted as *comparators* for the machines. Prior to the experiment, all IJs were asked to complete a questionnaire providing some demographic information: age range, gender, whether they could speak another language apart from English, whether they had heard of the Turing test. Peripheral questions invoked interests such as favourite colour, favourite book or author, favourite music, favourite movie or movie genre, favourite quote, newspapers read.

Interrogator–judges

The area occupied by the interrogator–judges was accessible to spectators. Judges volunteered to interrogate the systems in simultaneous comparison Turing tests. The judges came from a cross section of society and ranged in age. Nine were female. Three spoke English only, one had French as mother tongue, two had Chinese, while three had Italian. Twenty-one judges had heard of the Turing test prior to the contest, three had not.

Journalists, computer scientists and philosophers were among the judges. Not all could stay for the whole experiment, so not all interrogated each pair. However, two judges did test all eight set-ups across sessions 1 and 2. These two interrogated all five machine entries and three control-group pairs (two human–human pairs and one machine–machine pair).

Thirteen of the 24 judges tested four pairs; other judges tested one, three, five or seven pairs, depending on how long they could stay for the experiment.

Human comparators – the foils for the machines

Twenty-one volunteers ranging in age from 17 to 74 were recruited to act as hidden-human comparators or foils for the machines. Fourteen were male. Fifteen had heard of the Turing test prior to the experiment. Languages other than English spoken by the human comparators included Swedish, Italian, Hindi, Marathi, French, Urdu, Welsh and Japanese. Human comparators were located in the hidden-interlocutor area where the machine developers also sat watching over their machine's performance.

The hidden-interlocutor area also acted as the control room for the whole experiment. The human comparators in this room were told that the machines would be competing against them to achieve a 'human' score from the judges, so they were asked to prevent this by answering questions as would a human.

The five machine entries were housed in hardware (developer's laptops) located in the hidden-interlocutor area.

Procedure

Judges at the terminals began to interrogate simultaneously two hidden entities. They stopped after five minutes at which point they were asked to complete a score questionnaire.

The score sheet contained explicit instructions for identifying the nature of the hidden entity providing responses to their left and right boxes on their monitor screen. If they considered an entity to be a machine, interrogator–judges were asked to give it a score out of 100 for its conversational ability. If they identified a human, they were asked to say if they had questioned a male or female, an adult or child, and whether it was a native speaker of English.

Message or character display

In a November 2007 poll conducted by the developers' web-based forum Robitron[1], 73% of developers returned a preference for message-by-message communication for their systems rather than character-by-character display on a judge's screen during practical Turing tests.

Consequently, message-by-message display was selected for this experiment. For this to occur a program was needed that could interface with the developers' systems. The communications protocol and program were designed and commissioned specifically for this solution – MATT[2]. The protocol enabled spectators in the judges' area to view the simultaneous conversations in real time during the practical Turing tests (see Figure 7.1). The MATT protocol in 2008 did not include any delay mechanism, so the message from either of the two hidden interlocutors in a test appeared as typed on the judge's screen.

Judge instructions Much deliberation went into what to inform judges about their hidden interlocutors, i.e., should it be made explicit that control groups of two humans, and two machines were embedded among the machine–human

---

[1] Yahoo discussion board for developers of *conversation systems* (Robitron post #9598, 15 November, 2007). The character-by-character protocol in the 16th Loebner Prize produced the following display on a judge's screen:
[time]h
[time]e
[time]l
[time]l
[time]o
Message-by-message for the same typed input produces the following display on a judge's screen:
[time] hello
The message-by-message format comes with the additional advantage of producing readable transcripts on completion of practical Turing tests, without the need for a computer.
[2] See for example, M. Allen http://www.1bdi.co.uk/matt/.

Figure 7.1 Message-by-message display on large screen in area for spectators and judges.

comparator tests? Would *not* telling them this be deceiving them? The indistinguishability experiment of Colby et al. (1972) entailed reviewing what to tell the judges. They maintained that what a judge is told and what he believes is happening are extremely important in indistinguishability tests, and their experience led them to conclude

> ... it is unwise to inform a judge at the start that a computer simulation is involved because he then tends to change his interviewing strategy and asks questions to detect which of two respondents is a program rather than asking questions relevant to the dimension to be identified.

The 'dimension' in this experiment was for the hidden interlocutors, humans and machines, to provide *satisfactory and humanlike responses* to any question a judge posed during the tests. However, the judges knew that a machine would be involved at some stage because they were taking part in a Turing test. But, as already noted, judges did not know about the control pairs of human–human and machine–machine, because, as hypothesised, the prediction entailed all judges being able to correctly recognise a hidden interlocutor more often than make a wrong classification. Accordingly, the judges were allowed to return classification and scores as follows:

(a) one human and one machine (judges had to say whether it was a human or a machine sending utterances to the left- and right-side of their screens) – in the latter case the judge was asked to score it from 0–100 for conversational ability;

(b) both human;

(c) both machine, in which case give a score for conversational ability from 0–100;

(d) unsure.

If a hidden entity was considered human, the judges were asked if they could say whether the human interlocutor was:

(a) male or female;

(b) a child, a teenager, or an adult;

(c) a native English speaker.

Thus, if a machine had persuaded the human judge that it was a human, the judge's verdict would provide some information about the particular human the judge thought they had interrogated, and assist in ranking the machine as comparable to a child, say, or non-native English speaker.

Results

A total of 96 simultaneous comparison Turing tests were conducted in this experiment of which 60 were machine–human tests, and 36 control groups: 24 human–human and 12 machine–machine tests. Interrogator–judges reported their results on a score sheet (see Figure 7.2).

Figure 7.2 Judge score sheet.

Machine–human comparison

In the 60 machine–human tests, each of the five machines was compared against twelve human comparators. Machines were correctly identified as artificial in 49 of the 60 tests. Entry E4, *Brother Jerome* suffered technical failure during five of its twelve human comparison tests. Entry E5, *Jabberwacky* achieved an 'unsure' score once from one IJ. Three machines succeeded in deception in five of the 60 human–comparison tests (*Elbot* on three occasions; *Eugene* and *Ultra Hal* once each). A machine was wrongly ranked a human at a rate of one in 12 tests, instances of the *Eliza* effect (Hofstadter, 1996; Wilson, 2010). Table 7.1 summarises the results.

Round	E1 Eugene Session 1	E2 Elbot Session 1	E3 Ultra Hal Session 1	Round	E4 Jabberwacky Session 2	E5 Brother Jerome Session 2	Incorrectly
1	M	M	M	13	M	M	
2	M	M	**H**	14	M	M	
3	M	**H**	M	15	M	M	
4	M	M	M	16	M	technical failure	
5	M	M	M	17	M	technical failure	
6	M	M	M	18	M	M	-
7	M	M	M	19	M	technical failure	
8	M	H	M	20	U	technical failure	
9	**H**	M	M	21	M	M	
10	M	M	M	22	M	M	
11	M	**H**	M	23	M	M	
12	M	M	M	24	M	technical failure	
Incorrectly Identified	1	3	1	0		0	5 (8%)
Mean conversation ability	45	41	29		36	17	34
Mode conversation ability	80	30	10		10	0	26
Median conversation ability	40	36	23		37	8	29

Table 7.1 *Machine–human comparison results; M = machine, H = human, U = unsure.*

The first occasion a machine deceived a human judge occurred in round 2 in the morning, session 1, during tests 5–8 of the 96.

Judge J3, male, whose first language was Chinese wrongly thought the responses appearing on the left of his screen were from a human. However, at the same time J3 correctly recognised the utterances appearing on the his of their screen as being from a human (see Table 7.2).

J3 had simultaneously interrogated entity E3 (*Ultra Hal*) on the left and a

Left – E3
Interrogator:
Interrogator: Good morning.
Interrogator: Hello.
Interrogator:
Interrogator: Morning.
Interrogator: hello
[2008-10-12 08:54:00.140] remote sent: Good morning Judge.
[2008-10-12 08:54:03.140] remote sent: It's eight something, maybe you ate something.
[2008-10-12 08:54:05.140] remote sent: Get it?
Interrogator: Yes.
[2008-10-12 08:54:25.140] remote sent: Yes?
[2008-10-12 08:54:27.140] remote sent: Is that so?
Interrogator: The machine was frozon.
[2008-10-12 08:54:40.140] remote sent: The Turing test is a proposal for a test of a machine's capability to demonstrate intelligence.
Interrogator: Do you mine you are a smart machine?
[2008-10-12 08:55:44.140] remote sent: Really?
[2008-10-12 08:55:47.140] remote sent: You are so very warm hearted Judge, really and truly!
Interrogator: So would you like me score you 100.
[2008-10-12 08:56:15.140] remote sent: If we could automate scoring at golf courses, handicaps would go up!

Right – H2 male
Interrogator: Good morning.
[2008-10-12 08:50:16.125] remote sent: Good morning – nice to meet you
Interrogator: Nice to meet you.
[2008-10-12 08:50:41.734] remote sent: what would you like to know
Interrogator: What a awsome rain this morning.
Interrogator: hello
[2008-10-12 08:54:05.531] remote sent: Hallo
[2008-10-12 08:54:36.968] remote sent: Nice to meet you
Interrogator: What a heave rain this morning.
[2008-10-12 08:55:36.609] remote sent: Not where I was [2008-10-12 08:56:10.906] remote sent: Where I was it was cool, dry and foggy
Interrogator: Really?
[2008-10-12 08:56:34.187] remote sent: Absolutely
[2008-10-12 08:56:55.328] remote sent: Where arev you?

Table 7.2 *Judge 3, session 1, round 2.*

hidden human male (H2), aged between 65 and 74, on the right. In this Turing test J3 ranked both his hidden interlocutors as human, an *indistinguishable* score for the machine, the transcript is shown (exactly as typed) in Table 7.2.

On the left the hidden entity gave a 'human-like' response by its personal greeting – "Good morning Judge", and posting the time "It's eight something" when indeed the time was 08.54, and by asking the judge a question relating the moment to breakfast: "maybe you ate something?".

Elbot deceived judge J10, a female newspaper reporter (aged between 25 and 34). She correctly identified the male human on the left (H15), but wrongly ranked the hidden interlocutor sending replies to the right-side of her screen, the machine E2, as a native English-speaking adult male.

J10's simultaneous interaction is one in which the judge did not greet her two hidden interlocutors in the same way. To the left, actually a hidden human, J10 typed "Hi there, How are you?". To the hidden machine J10 opened with "Yo, whassup" on the right, a vernacular used in Budweiser TV commercials. The colloquial greeting was met with what could be interpreted as the response of a bored human: "I don't know. Next question". The machine's response appeared to have put J10 on the defensive, because her following sentence to the machine was "OK, fair enough, I'll stop with the slang. How are you?".

The machine's response was tinged with sarcasm: "Just a moment! I'll start my self-diagnosis algorithm and let you know the results…". The fact that the machine took control with 'superior' answers may be the cause of J10 misidentifying it as a human male adult, native speaker of English. The transcript appears in Table 7.3.

Eliza and confederate effects

Confusing the machine for a human and the human for a machine in the same Turing test, i.e. interchanging reality, are respectively instances of the *Eliza* and the *confederate* effects, deception and misidentification phenomena taking place in the same test. This occurred twice in session 1, the first being when a judge, J1 (male, aged in the range 35–44, a native speaker of English), failed to detect the machine (*Eliza effect*), and classified the human comparator as a machine – *confederate effect*. In this test J1 interrogated a hidden human on the left-hand, H6, a female native speaker of (American) English, aged in range 25–34, while entry E2, *Elbot* controlled the output appearing on the judge's right-hand screen.

J1 wrongly scored the hidden female on the left as a machine awarding her 90/100 for conversational quality and speed while ranking the machine on the right as a male professor. The left entity drove the interaction by asking J1 questions, which may have been taken by the interrogator as an *Eliza*-ish ploy. The hidden human included a *non sequitur*, "it's not afternoon yet" to J1's question "how are you?". The machine could have been perceived as a professor because of its pedantic replies; for instance, to the greeting "Good afternoon, how are you?" the machine replied "But I wouldn't say that any afternoon could be good". The transcript is in Table 7.4.

In the next set of conversations we invite readers to try the test for themselves and see if they can distinguish which is the human and which the machine in the transcripts presented in Table 7.5. The machine's output appeared on the judge's left-side screen while the entities responses were displayed on the judge's right.

Left – H15	Right – E2
hline Interrogator: Hi there. How are you?	Interrogator: Yo, whassup?
[2008-10-12 09:52:57.609] remote sent: Hey, I'm pretty good. you?	[2008-10-12 09:52:45.046] remote sent: I don't know. Next question.
Interrogator: Did you realise everyone can see what's being typed on this machine on a big screen behind me?	Interrogator: OK, fair enough, I'll stop with the slang. How are you?
[2008-10-12 09:53:19.953] remote sent: uhh.. no.	[2008-10-12 09:53:27.906] remote sent: Just a moment! I'll start my self-diagnosis algorithm and let you know the results...
[2008-10-12 09:53:37.796] remote sent: so you have a projector hooked up to your terminal then?	Interrogator: Very funny, that's exactly what you'd say if you were a computer, right? May be I need one of those?
Interrogator: Yeah, it's quite freaky. So watch what you say!!	[2008-10-12 09:54:16.656] remote sent: My condition code is hexadecimal 40A1F. That means 'fine'.
Interrogator: Yeah, looks like.	Interrogator: Is this what you say to girls in bars?
[2008-10-12 09:53:47.234] remote sent: roger that!	[2008-10-12 09:54:53.093] remote sent: All these questions about me. Too bad I lost my owner's manual.
Interrogator: So, are you a student here or what?	Interrogator: Indeed. I don't think I came with one.
[2008-10-12 09:54:46.781] remote sent: Yup, doing my masters here, just started	[2008-10-12 09:55:32.093] remote sent: Great! Agreeing with me is the first step in your evolution into a higher being. Please accept my congratulations.
Interrogator: Cool. I'd love to do a masters. What are you studying?	Interrogator: Thanks very much.
[2008-10-12 09:55:23.156] remote sent: Cybernetics, but my BSc was in genetics	[2008-10-12 09:55:57.359] remote sent: De nada!
Interrogator: Aah, you'd think they'd get some other students in here to talk to us.	Interrogator: Riiiiight.
[2008-10-12 09:55:59.859] remote sent: i could lie... but maybe I already am!	[2008-10-12 09:56:18.156] remote sent: It seems to me with you human beings, the more proof there is of something, the less likely you are to believe it.
Interrogator: Oh, it's too early in the morning for all that!	Interrogator: Yeah, that's just human nature. But you wouldn't know about that, would you?!
[2008-10-12 09:56:36.765] remote sent: lol. Had your coffee yet?	[2008-10-12 09:56:51.406] remote sent: You're contesting. I think I got it right the first time.
Interrogator: No. Need some, where can i find some that doesn't come from a machine (no offence if you're a machine).	Interrogator: Has anyone ever told you you're hard work? Wife may be?
[2008-10-12 09:57:43.031] remote sent: Dolche vitae– its next to this building	[2008-10-12 09:57:46.390] remote sent: But I wouldn't say that any work could be hard.

Table 7.3 *Judge J10, session 1, round 8, terminal C.*

On the day of the test, J13 (male journalist, age in range 25–34) deemed that the entity E1 was a female adult non-native English speaker, adding for justification the hidden interlocutor's jokey reply, "Some of my friends are programmers", to the question "So let's cut straight to the point. Are you the

Left – H6 Female	Right – E2
Interrogator: Good afternoon, how are you? [2008-10-12 08:59:31.796] remote sent: good [2008-10-12 08:59:39.484] remote sent: it's not afternoon yet Interrogator: I'm glad to hear that your well and your right, thanks for pointing that out [2008-10-12 09:00:24.312] remote sent: no problem [2008-10-12 09:00:53.468] remote sent: how are you? Interrogator: I'm well thanks, have you any plans for this afternoon? [2008-10-12 09:01:36.203] remote sent: I'm not sure [2008-10-12 09:01:40.968] remote sent: go home I guess [2008-10-12 09:02:03.937] remote sent: and you? Interrogator: That sounds like a good initial plan but the weather should be good today and it would be sad to miss out [2008-10-12 09:02:16.703] remote sent: that's true [2008-10-12 09:02:35.703] remote sent: although the weather is not nice at the moment [2008-10-12 09:02:39.375] remote sent: unless you like fog Interrogator: I have plans to iron and then maybe go out and do some fishing [2008-10-12 09:02:59.843] remote sent: that's interesting - where do you go fishing? Interrogator: There is a local lake by the green park, it's quiet and relaxing [2008-10-12 09:03:48.843] remote sent: can you eat the fish you catch? Interrogator: There are restrictions but one or two should be ok, I am keen to try perch	Interrogator: Good afternoon, how are you? [2008-10-12 08:59:39.781] remote sent: But I wouldn't say that any afternoon could be good. Interrogator: That's a bit pesamistic, I think any afternoon has the ability to be good [2008-10-12 09:00:29.218] remote sent: Well, afternoon was your word. Interrogator: Are you able to see into the future [2008-10-12 09:00:35.500] remote sent: How do you respond when people pose this question to you? Interrogator: I would hope that the answer was no, otherwise I would be interested to meet you [2008-10-12 09:01:13.484] remote sent: Well, what will that solve? After all, the answer is only a matter of perspective. Interrogator: That would depend on one's perspective [2008-10-12 09:01:50.562] remote sent: Sorry for the tangent, but that reminds me of carefree robot summers spent depending on internal programming. Interrogator: Touchee [2008-10-12 09:02:26.203] remote sent: With the inspirations you supply, there are no ends to my horizon... Interrogator: Have you any plans for later in the day [2008-10-12 09:03:08.921] remote sent: This is confusing. Why bring the waking hours into this? Interrogator: Just curiosity and I hope that kill no cats [2008-10-12 09:03:49.078] remote sent: That is truly one of the most inspirational qualities of humankind. Even when things seems completely hopeless, you can still hope.

Table 7.4 *Judge J1, session 1, round 3, terminal C.*

human or the computer?" (Table 7.5). At the same time J13 ranked the entity on the right, E20 to be a machine awarding it 40/100 for conversational ability.

In fact, E1 is a machine*Eugene Goostman*, and E20 is French, aged 25–34, the same person as H20 in later tests. J13 detailed his deception in his newspaper article for *The Times* newspaper (Pavia, 2008).

The *knowledge expectation* of his hidden interlocutor led J13, a journalist, to believe a hidden human was a machine, because she (a non-native-English

Left – Entity 1
Interrogator: So let's cut straight to the point. Are you the human or the computer?— but for any input it shouts "Aye-aye, Master!", and that's all…
Interrogator: I think you're saying you might be either or.
[2008-10-12 10:12:34.265] remote sent: Your opinion is very interesting… Keep going. If I'm not mistaken – you still didn't tell me where you live. OR it's a secret?:-)
Interrogator: You keep changing the subject. You ought to be a politician. I live in south London, a place called Brockley that no one has ever heard of.
[2008-10-12 10:13:25.812] remote sent: South london? Hope it's a good place to live.
Interrogator: It's very nice thanks. Where do you live?
[2008-10-12 10:14:13.640] remote sent: I am from Ukraine, from the city called Odessa. You might have heard about it.
Interrogator: Yes although I don't know an awful lot about it. How did you end up here?
[2008-10-12 10:15:05.750] remote sent: What a stupid questions you ask! Holly cow, this Loebner Prize is such a weird place! But I like it!

Right – Entity 20
Interrogator: So let's cut straight to the point. Are you the human or the computer?
[2008-10-12 10:11:23.296] remote sent: What do you think?
Interrogator: That's just the sort of answer I would expect from a computer.
[2008-10-12 10:12:58.500] remote sent: Well you could be wrong!!!
Interrogator: That's true. It's happened a lot in the past. What do you make of Sarah Palin?
[2008-10-12 10:14:30.125] remote sent: Sorry don't know her
Interrogator: How can you possibly not know her? What have you been doing for the last two months?

Table 7.5 *Judge J13, session 1, round 9, terminal A. Are Entities 1 and 20 machine or human?*

speaker) did not know who Sarah Palin was. The judge presumed 'mutual knowledge' is a trait of humans in believing others know certain facts we know.

Round 11 in session 1 saw judge J13 again getting confused again in the next test. For the second time J13 wrongly classified the female comparator as a machine, and for the second time J13 ranked a machine, this time entry E2, *Elbot* as a human. In round 11, J13 awarded the female a conversation ability score of 45/100, five more marks than in his previous test. This time J13 considered the machine to be a teenaged male, native speaker of English. The transcript of the conversation is shown in Table 7.6.

The machine at terminal C (*Elbot*) won the Loebner contest for achieving the most number of deceptions in its 12 machine–human simultaneous comparison tests from its allotted jury of 12 judges: it deceived three times, all native English-speakers, two males and one female.

Right – E2
Interrogator: What do you think of this year's Turner Prize shortlist?
[2008-10-12 10:32:08.531] remote sent: Difficult question. I will have to work on that and get back to you tomorrow.
Interrogator: You sound rather like Sarah Palin.
[2008-10-12 10:32:31.671] remote sent: Did this Palin ever write a telephone book?
Interrogator: I doubt it. Does anyone really write telephone books? I don't suppose you caught the football last night?
[2008-10-12 10:33:48.843] remote sent: What a shame. There are many talented authors who waste their energies on prose or run-of-the-mill poetry. But to write a telephone book is highest art!
Interrogator: I would argue that all the telephone books I have read have been very predictable. You always know how they are going to end.
[2008-10-12 10:34:32.125] remote sent: If one has never known everything there is to know, experience with going away somewhere has probably been lacking.
Interrogator: I see. I'm struggling to make sense of that one. Do you write telephone books?
[2008-10-12 10:35:21.984] remote sent: To write or write not, how do you expect artificial intelligence to figure this out?
Interrogator: Well I suppose that's the dream
[2008-10-12 10:36:56.343] remote sent: For you humans dreams are a way of thinking without having any control over the thought process. What an unpleasant thought! My dreams are carefully planned and controlled. It gives me less to think about while I am asleep.

Left – H20 Human
Interrogator: What do you think of this year's Turner Prize shortlist?
[2008-10-12 10:32:33.125] remote sent: good I think. Better than the years before i herad
Interrogator: Which was your favourite?
[2008-10-12 10:34:19.750] remote sent: It's my first time, so I can't compare
Interrogator: No, I mean of the entries this time around.
[2008-10-12 10:35:15.093] remote sent: Not really sure
Interrogator: Do you think that art has become shallow and self-serving?

Table 7.6 *Judge J13, session 1, round 11, terminal C.*

Control-pair tests

Thirty-six control pairs were embedded in the machine–human comparison tests. The confederate effect, and the *gender-blur effect* – when a hidden male is considered female and vice versa, occurred in the human–human control groups, while the Eliza effect – wrongly ranking a machine as human, occurred in the machine–machine control tests.

Human–human tests

Twenty-four human–human control pairs were conducted in all. Two sets of twelve human–human set-ups featured in sessions 1 and 2 in the experiment: at terminal B in rounds 1–12, and at terminal C in rounds 13–24. In session 1, three judges correctly recognised that they had interrogated two humans in parallel; judge J20 was unsure about the composition of the (human) pair in round 11.

In eight of the twelve rounds in session 1 one of the two humans was misidentified as a machine, instances of the confederate effect. In session 2 five of the judges correctly identified the hidden pair as both being human.

One judge (J16, female, first language Italian), misidentified both humans in a human–human control test ranking both of them as machines (round 16). In the twelve rounds in session 2 half of the time judges misidentified one of the humans as a machine. The single confederate effect featured in nearly 2/3 of the 24 tests.

7.0.1 Session 1 round 1 terminal B.

In the very first round of session 1 at terminal B, interrogator J2, a male aged 25–34 whose first language was Chinese, simultaneously interrogated two humans. Behind the left screen was a hidden male and behind the right was a female. The judge correctly identified the former, but thought the latter was a machine, awarding it a score of 70 out of 100 for conversational ability. Table 7.7 presents the simultaneous interrogation.

Two reasons could have caused J2 to rank the female as a machine. First, that as a computer science research student familiar with the Turing test, J2 expected the set-up always to include one machine and one human. Notice that the left hidden-interlocutor divulged the location of the experiment when asked by J2. At least one developer did include the location of the Turing test experiment information in the entry's store of possible responses: "... this Loebner Prize is such a weird place" (see Table 7.5). Another example could be that the hidden female controlling the right-hand utterances returned the judge's question, and two more including a question: "yes" and "do you?". Humans use the ploy of replying to a question with a question. It is not only an *Eliza*-ish trick, but also a strategy often used by politicians!

In round 2, judge J1 (male, native speaker of English, aged 35—44) simultaneously interrogated a pair of native-English-speaking males, both aged 18–24. This judge deemed the left-side entity as a machine, awarding H11 a score of 80 for conversation, while believing H15 to be a female teenager responding in a chatty style.

In an exchange between J1 and H11, a question about a sports match was met with the reply "nope, I don't follow much sport". The match appears important to this judge, because it involved a national side. The fact that J1 ranked H11 as a machine is an example of when lack of mutual knowledge causes misidentification and confederate effect error by the interrogator.

Left – H2 male
Interrogator:
Interrogator: hi
Interrogator: hello
Interrogator:
[2008-10-12   08:40:45.531]   remote sent: Hello
Interrogator: what is your name ?
[2008-10-12   08:40:57.625]   remote sent: Ian
Interrogator: where are you from
Interrogator: What is the weather today ?#
[2008-10-12   08:41:38.468]   remote sent: I live in Bracknell now – but my early life was in Harrow
[2008-10-12   08:42:02.921]   remote sent: Dry, cool and foggy
Interrogator: What is the weather today
[2008-10-12   08:42:37.953]   remote sent: I already replied to that
Interrogator: Bracknell   belongs   to which country ?#
[2008-10-12   08:42:51.828]   remote sent: England
Interrogator: Do you know where are you ?
[2008-10-12   08:44:00.218]   remote sent: Of course, I am in Redaing Uni campus
Interrogator: which building do you know ?
[2008-10-12   08:45:00.625]   remote sent: Palmer Building – I know that because I go to Uni at reading

Right – H6 female
Interrogator: hi
[2008-10-12 08:40:41.671] remote sent: hi
Interrogator: what is your name ?
[2008-10-12 08:40:50.750] remote sent: Nicole
[2008-10-12 08:40:54.031] remote sent: what is yours?
Interrogator: My name is defeng
Interrogator: where are you from
[2008-10-12   08:41:22.625]   remote sent: I'm from Boston
[2008-10-12 08:41:40.765] remote sent: where are you from?
Interrogator: What is the weather today ?
[2008-10-12   08:41:49.468]   remote sent: it's cloudy
Interrogator: I am from China
Interrogator: Do you know China ?
[2008-10-12 08:42:17.500] remote sent: yes
[2008-10-12 08:42:37.234] remote sent: where in China?
Interrogator: Dalian
Interrogator: Do u know #
[2008-10-12 08:43:18.578]   remote   sent: I haven't heard of Dalian
[2008-10-12 08:43:44.578] remote sent: is it near Beijing?
Interrogator: Yes. Near to Beijing.
[Interrogator: In 2008, we have a saying
Interrogator: Olympics in Beijing, Tourism in Dalian
[2008-10-12 08:44:29.328] remote sent: Ha ha
Interrogator: why ha ha ?
[2008-10-12   08:45:10.765]   remote   sent: it's funny – the olympics brings so much tourism
Interrogator: Do you know which building are you in ?
[2008-10-12 08:45:17.234] remote sent: yes
[2008-10-12 08:45:18.593] remote sent: do you?
Interrogator: I ask you
Interrogator: please

Table 7.7 *Judge J2, session 1, round 1, terminal B.*

Gender blur The right-side interlocutor reveals they were a little tired at the time of the Turing test adding that they had been out the night before, "Went out a bit, but didn't stay out late" in answer to the question "Were you out late last night or is it that its too early". J1 assumes *going out* at night is a teenage female activity, and perhaps why this interrogator incorrectly ranked the male as a female teenager, another example of *gender blur*. The full transcript is in Table 7.8.

Left – H11 male
Interrogator: Hello how are you
[2008-10-12 08:50:15.218] remote sent: Morning, I'm fine thanks
[2008-10-12 08:50:21.406] remote sent: yourself?
Interrogator: im glad to hear that, i'm fine too thanks
Interrogator: Have you any plans after this testing
[2008-10-12 08:51:13.015] remote sent: no, nothing really
Interrogator: Have you had breakfast
[2008-10-12 08:52:32.984] remote sent: no... I overslept and had to rush out...
[2008-10-12 08:52:50.328] remote sent: hopefully I can find something around here later
Interrogator: There is a cafe that is open and I hear the food is good, you should try it
[2008-10-12 08:53:28.578] remote sent: sounds good
Interrogator: Did you catch any of the football yesterday
[2008-10-12 08:54:28.281] remote sent: nope, I don't follow much sport
Interrogator: I don't normally but when it's the national side, I tend to take a little more interest.

Right – H15 male
Interrogator: hello how are you
[2008-10-12 08:50:23.218] remote sent: Heya, not bad. A little tired...
Interrogator: were you out late last night or is it that its too early
[2008-10-12 08:51:14.546] remote sent: Went out a bit, but didn't stay out late. How are you, then?
Interrogator: I'm well thanks, a little tired too but I did stay in and have an early night
[2008-10-12 08:52:16.593] remote sent: so, uncovered any scheming computers yet?
Interrogator: I would like to think so but time will tell
[2008-10-12 08:53:05.281] remote sent: heh, good luck.
Interrogator: Have you deceived anyone yet
[2008-10-12 08:53:54.062] remote sent: Nope, but then again, that in itself could be a deception.
Interrogator: It's interesting that you already have an answer to that question!
[2008-10-12 08:54:43.812] remote sent: lol
[2008-10-12 08:55:15.750] remote sent: Are you doing this all day, or are the judges taking shifts?

Table 7.8 *Judge J1, session 1, round 2, terminal B.*

Confederate effect again In a male–female hidden human control test judge J6, a native-English-speaking male aged 55–64, with Spanish as an additional spoken language, simultaneously interrogated another native-English-speaking male aged 65–74 on the left (H2), and H6, a female aged 25–34, a native speaker of (American) English who additionally spoke Swedish and Italian, on the right. The conversation appears in Table 7.9.

This was in fact the second time that H2 and H6 appeared together in a set-up (for the first see Table 7.4). The judge J6 correctly recognised H2 as male; however he ranked H6 as a machine again, and once again gave her a high score for conversation ability, this time 80/100 (compared with 90/100 previously).

Some believe gender imitation in the Turing test to be important. One interpretation of Turing's simultaneous comparison game, the *gender game*, (see Shah and Warwick, 2016) involves two scenarios: a machine–female session and a male–female session. In order to win, the machine must pretend to be a man imitating a woman, and the hidden man must pretend to be a woman, so that the judge's task is to identify the real woman. However, here we concentrate on machine–human issues, because we think that restricting the machine to pretending to be a man imitating a woman is an unnecessary complication of Turing's simple idea. The gender game places the judge at the centre of the experiment rather than the machine attempting to put satisfactory and sustained answers to any questions[3].

It must be noted that it is not difficult to program machines with the appearance of an identity and personality (for example, *Eugene Goostman* bears the character of a young teenage Ukrainian boy from Odessa). The hidden female may have been ranked a machine because the judge did not pay attention to the implicit instructions which allowed for a score of either *both human* or *both machine*, i.e. it may be the case this interrogator expected all the set-ups to include machines paired against humans.

Nonetheless, that it is the *female* hidden interlocutor, H6, who was considered the machine by the male judges is intriguing. However, not all judges made this error.

Session 1 round 8 terminal B

The youngest judge J14 (male aged 14), mistook a hidden female (H5 aged 55–64) for a machine. H5 sent answers to the left of J14's screen; she was awarded a score of 95 for conversation ability. J14 recognised the gender of the hidden male (H4) on the right and that he was an adult.

From the conversation, J14 reveals he learnt about the Turing test from his father "my dad told me about it" (see Table 7.9, left). J14 may have been informed that Turing tests consist of one machine and one human, thus causing the confederate effect occurring in this set-up.

During the conversation J14 revealed details about himself and his interests rather than interrogate the hidden entities. Revealing to the right hidden interlocutor their enjoyment of online games, J14 wrote: "i like playing this online game called Second Life" (see Table 7.9, right). Judge J14 disclosed on his completed questionnaire that he played 'Second Life, and this might reflect on or affect his online communications.

[3] Gender Spectrum: https://www.genderspectrum.org/understanding-gender accessed 01.07.2014

Right – H7 male
Interrogator:: hello
[2008-10-12 09:53:08.281] remote sent: hi
Interrogator:: how r u?
[2008-10-12 09:53:24.421] remote sent: very well thankyou.
[2008-10-12 09:53:26.437] remote sent: yourself?
Interrogator: iam fine
Interrogator: what do u want to talk about?
[2008-10-12 09:54:59.109] remote sent: how about you tell me something about yourself?
Interrogator: i like playing this online game called Second Life
[2008-10-12 09:55:46.281] remote sent: oh yes, I've heard of that
Interrogator: it is a brilliant game
[2008-10-12 09:55:58.562] remote sent: though I've never played it myself
[2008-10-12 09:56:22.562] remote sent: who are you in your second life?
Interrogator: it is really fun and one of the best bits is u can transfer money that u have on secondlife into real money
[2008-10-12 09:57:08.156] remote sent: that is cool
[2008-10-12 09:57:24.781] remote sent: how do you make money on second life?

Left – H5 female
Interrogator: hello
Interrogator: how r u?
[2008-10-12 09:53:07.593] remote sent: Fine. Yourself?
Interrogator:: brilliant, thanks
[2008-10-12 09:53:51.562] remote sent: How did you get into this?
Interrogator: my dad told me about it and i thorght it would be a fun thing to do
[2008-10-12 09:55:26.812] remote sent: I saw it in the evening paper and thought the same. Are you a student?
Interrogator: i go to a school called Maiden Erlegh
[2008-10-12 09:56:14.796] remote sent: I know it. Is it still a good school?
Interrogator: yes
Interrogator: it is a bit of a mess though
[2008-10-12 09:57:30.046] remote sent: what's your favourite subject?

Table 7.9 *Judge J14, session 1, round 8, terminal B.*

Session 1, round 10, terminal B

This was a control test involving two hidden humans, H7 on the left, H22 on the right. Both were males, and native speakers of English aged between 18 and 24.

In this test H7 was recognised as human but H22 was ranked a machine by judge J13. This is the same judge who had misidentified both hidden entities in two of the machine–human comparison tests; he now made an error in a human–human control test!

The judge remained unsure of the left hidden interlocutor's gender. H2's name was revealed to be 'Chris', which, in this shortened form, can be used for both males and females.

Judge J13's correct identification of H7 as human was based on their use of humour: "we are your friends" (Table 7.10, left). The wrong identification of H22 could be put down to the non-committal responses to questions (Table 7.10, right).

The judge's score sheet did allow the interrogators to rank their hidden interlocutors as *both human* (or *both machine*). However, this factor may have been overlooked by J13, who may have made the assumption that there was one machine and one human involved in each set-up. Once J13 had decided that H7 was human, he was then forced to admit that H22 was a machine.

Left – H7 male
Interrogator: So do you think Turing was right about this test?
[2008-10-12 10:22:28.500] remote sent: no
Interrogator: Why not?
[2008-10-12 10:23:41.671] remote sent: In truth I'm not entirely sure
[2008-10-12 10:23:54.625] remote sent: I just said that because it was the first thing that came to my head
[2008-10-12 10:24:11.125] remote sent: shall we discuss the issue?
Interrogator: Fair enough. Do you have any plan to take over the world and subjugate all human beings like in the Terminator films?
[2008-10-12 10:24:44.343] remote sent: No of course not
[2008-10-12 10:24:49.093] remote sent: we are your friends
[2008-10-12 10:24:55.187] remote sent: you must trust us
Interrogator:: That's what those scientists thought. And then suddenly Arnold Swarzenegar arrives and starts blowing them all up.
[2008-10-12 10:26:21.906] remote sent: well I'm not going to try to convince you
Interrogator: Do you think that Arnie was convincing as a robot?
[2008-10-12 10:26:42.609] remote sent: no
Interrogator: Do you think he is convincing as Governor of California?

Right – H22 male
Interrogator: So do you think Turing was right about this test?
[2008-10-12 10:22:38.109] remote sent: No sure…
Interrogator: Neither am I. How could it be improved?
[2008-10-12 10:24:15.375] remote sent: I don't really know. What do you think?
Interrogator: I wonder whether a computer could pass the test simply by replying with open ended statements and by continually turning the question back on me.
[2008-10-12 10:25:36.781] remote sent: Thanks for the compliment. By the way my name is Chris.
Interrogator: Hello Chris. Are you feeling a little depressed about the current global economic melt down?
[2008-10-12 10:26:28.531] remote sent: yes a bit, but I cannot do anything about it!

Table 7.10 *Judge J13, session 1 round 10, terminal B.*

Next we see how judges fared in the machine-machine control tests.

Machine–machine control tests

Twelve different judges each interrogated one of the twelve machine–machine control pairs; eight judges were male and four were female. The *Elbot* machine occupied the left side for this control experiment, and *Eugene Goostman* occupied the right.

On two occasions a double identification error occurred featuring the *Eliza* effect in the left and right entity rankings. Two judges ranked both the entities in the machine–machine control pair as *both* human in session 2 (rounds 13 and 18): one of these judges was female (an Italian speaker, aged 25–34) and the other was a male teenager who spoke both English and German.

Three judges (J11, J12 and J24) – two males and one female – were unable to identify one entity in the machine–machine pair, ranking it *unsure*. Two male judges correctly identified the left entity as a machine but ranked the right one as human. *Elbot* was ranked a human twice, while two judges were unsure whether it was human or machine. *Eugene* was three times mistaken for a human and received an unsure score once.

However, five of the twelve judges (four male and one a female) did correctly identify the hidden pair as machines.

Correct identification of machine pairs

We look at the exchanges between male judge J4 (English and French speaker, aged 25–34) and the two machines he correctly identified. J4 gave Elbot (a machine with a robot personality) a score of 10 out of a possible 100 for conversational ability. He gave to *Eugene Goostman*, a program designed to imitate a Ukrainian child texting in English, a score of 5 for conversational ability. The transcript is in Table 7.11.

J4 asked "so how did you get here today? did you travel far?" to the left. The machine misinterpreted up the word travel to mean vacation and the conversation broke down to some extent.

Eugene Goostman on the right posted one fewer utterance than *Elbot*, but they were longer, and it deployed the strategy of asking personal questions to direct the conversation.

Analysis of conversations in this experiment

In the five-minute tests in this experiment, the humans appeared to type their words *as they would speak them* when replying to judges' questions. Punctuation was omitted, words were misspelled and, in the case of participants who were not native speakers of English, they used unidiomatic phrases. This is in contrast to the machine utterances which were grammatical and had no spelling errors. Developers may want to take a note of this if they are attempting to build machines to pass Turing tests by texting in a human-like way.

Left – E2
Interrogator: wotcha, how's tricks?
[2008-10-12 12:16:21.281] remote sent: I feel great! Magnetically, statically and electrically charged. Better not touch me!
Interrogator: eek, that sounds like a bit of a health risk
[2008-10-12 12:16:36.125] remote sent: I suppose you could say it sounds like that.
Interrogator: so how did you get here today? did you travel far?
[2008-10-12 12:17:15.484] remote sent: I'd like to take a vacation, too, but they won't give me any time off. Maybe I should form a robot union.
Interrogator: would there be many members?
Interrogator: just a few Aibos and roombas [2008-10-12 12:17:52.203] remote sent: Hmmm... That's one question I cannot answer with my limited artificial intelligence. How about you?
[2008-10-12 12:17:56.515] remote sent: This is confusing. Why bring diminishing numbers into this?
Interrogator: that's an interesting, if irrelevent point!
[2008-10-12 12:18:46.671] remote sent: But I wouldn't say that any point could be irrelevent.
Interrogator: depends how blunt it is surely [2008-10-12 12:19:32.062] remote sent: It most certainly does! Half of my memory circuits are stuck in an infinite loop waiting for the answer!
Interrogator: that sounds painful
[2008-10-12 12:19:55.468] remote sent: How do you stand on this? Do you sound painful?
Interrogator: I hope not
[2008-10-12 12:20:02.718] remote sent: You could practice more.
Interrogator: could be my northern accent though
[2008-10-12 12:20:15.265] remote sent: Are you as happy about your involvement with compass points as I am?
Interrogator: :-(
[2008-10-12 12:20:18.250] remote sent: Oh no, is it really that bad?
Interrogator: I think you've lost me
[2008-10-12 12:21:01.312] remote sent: Humankind is lost and the bureau of missing persons has burned down.

Right – E1
Interrogator: 'afternoon! How's it going?
[2008-10-12 12:16:41.640] remote sent: Oops! I don't have an answer... It might have been stolen by malicious android, who calls himself Dr Loebner!
Interrogator: ah that's a shame
[2008-10-12 12:17:11.640] remote sent: What do you mean saying "shame"? You blame me or somebody else? Did I forget it or you really haven't told me about the place you are from?
Interrogator: have you guys met before?
Interrogator: I'm from York
[2008-10-12 12:17:32.921] remote sent: No, I haven't chaps came across before! How could you imagine such a trash! Could you tell me what are you? I mean your profession.
[2008-10-12 12:17:53.171] remote sent: By the way, do you know a terrible story about a chatterbot, that wanted to be a President? He spoke ugly, his phrases were lame and intelligence was artificial (he told only the things he was prompted to)...I should tell you a secret: he BECAME the Prez! Androids are among us already!!!
Interrogator: perhaps in America
[2008-10-12 12:18:16.562] remote sent: Could you tell me about your job, by the way?
Interrogator: sure, I'm a user experience consultant
Interrogator: what do you do?
[2008-10-12 12:18:30.890] remote sent: I'm glad you agreed. Some another topic?
[2008-10-12 12:18:40.875] remote sent: I am only 13, so I'm attending school so far.
Interrogator: you're very 'sharp' for a 13 year old
Interrogator: not a hint of 'lol' anywhere
[2008-10-12 12:19:19.796] remote sent: I can't believe it! The world went crazy, almost like my grandpa...
[2008-10-12 12:19:30.968] remote sent: Hey, look! You've laughed your ass off!!! You should put it back!
Interrogator: I have now
[2008-10-12 12:19:57.718] remote sent: It sounds pretty natural that you have right now If I'm not mistaken – you still didn't tell me where you live. OR it's a secret?:-)
Interrogator: I like to keep such things a mystery
[2008-10-12 12:20:51.015] remote sent: What else you like? I ask just for fun. Well, let's go on though.

Table 7.11 *Judge J4, session 2 round 14, terminal D*

In the sixty machine–human comparison tests, on five occasions a machine was deemed a human by a human judge, all instances of the *Eliza* effect. This deception rate, of 1 in 12, is far less than the random deception rate of 50%.

When judges were accurate in identifying pairs in the machine–human tests they *erred* in the control-pair tests. Overall in 84 tests involving a hidden human (60 machine–human and 24 human–human), on 11 out of 19 occasions, the hidden humans were misidentified as machines, instances of the confederate effect (see Figure 7.3).

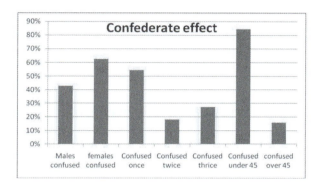

Figure 7.3 The confederate effect, when humans are thought to be machines.

Of the 11 misidentified humans, six were male, five were female. Two were wrongly identified twice: one male whose first language is not English, one female with English as first language.

Three hidden humans were wrongly confused as machine on three different occasions, two were female – a French speaker and an (American) English speaker – and one male (British) English speaker.

The age group of hidden humans does suggest a correlation in how the judges perceived machine-like language. On the 19 occasions that hidden humans were wrongly deemed a machine, three were aged 45 and over, while 16 were aged younger than 44.

The finaal phenomenon present in practical Turing tests is gender blur: when a hidden female is confused for male and vice versa. Judges were not always able to say whether they were speaking to a hidden female or male. Thirteen of the hidden humans were deemed to be of another sex during their involvement as machine comparators or in human control tests. Five females were confused for male, eight males were confused as female, some of them more than once (H8 teenager female; H15 male aged 18–24).

Only two judges, both males, always correctly identified machines and humans in machine–human tests and in the control pairs of humans and machines: judge J4, aged 25–34 was correct in seven set-ups and judge J17, aged 45–54, was correct in four.

After the experiment, the judges reported that machines were identified because they made fewer spelling mistakes in comparison to the hidden humans. Additionally, if an entity replied very quickly with a long sentence, or responded to a question with a question, it was considered more likely to be a machine. The speed of the machine response was noted in the experiment of (Heiser et al., 1979), where one of the psychiatrist judges correctly assessed that some responses were generated and typed so quickly that they had to be a product of a computer program. Developers might want to consider this factor in designing systems to play the imitation game.

Evaluating this experiment

Five minutes is enough time to assess a *thin slice* of textual responses: whether a hidden entity is providing satisfactory answers in a sustained way to any questions. In the 2008 experiment, machines had not achieved a deception rate of 30%, meaning passing the Turing test according to the statement (Turing, 1950, p. 442) that the "average interrogator will not have more than 70% chance of making the right identification after five minutes of questioning". That said, *Elbot* did attain a deception rate of 25%, not that far short.

More judges, with a greater proportion of females, in future tests would help to find if there are trends in the way males and females categorise hidden entities based solely on text-based communication.

References

Albrechtsen, J., Maissner, C., and Susa, K. (2009). Can intuition improve deception detection performance? *J. Exper. Soc. Psychol.* **45** (4) 1052–1055.

Colby. K.M., Hilf, F.D., Weber, S., and Kraemer, H.C. (1972). Turing-like indistinguishability tests for the validation of a computer simulation of paranoid processes. *Artificial Intelligence* **3** 199–221.

Heiser, J.F., Colby, K.M., Fraught, W.S. and Parkison, R.C. (1979). Can psychiatrists distinguish a computer simulation of paranoia from the real thing? The limitation of Turing-like tests as measures of the adequacy of simulations. *Journal of Psychiatric Research* **15** (3), 149–162.

Hofstadter, Douglas R. (1996). *Fluid Concepts and Creative Analogies: Computer Models of the Fundamental Mechanisms of Thought*, Basic Books. p. 155.

Pavia, W. (2008). Machine takes on man at mass Turing test. *The Times.* http://technology.timesonline.co.uk/tol/news/tech_and_web/ article4934858.ece.

Shah, H. and Warwick, K. (2010a). From the buzzing in Turing's head to machine intelligence contests, In *Proc. 1st Symposium Towards a Comprehensive Intelligence Test (TCIT). AISB Convention, De Montfort University, UK.*

Shah, H. and Warwick, K. (2010b). Hidden interlocutor misidentification in practical Turing tests, *Minds and Machines* **20** (3), 441–454.

Shah, H. and Warwick, K. (2016). Imitating gender as a measure for artificial intelligence: is it necessary? In *Proceedings of the 8th International Conference on Agents and Artificial Intelligence (ICAART), Rome, Vol. 1,* pp. 126–131.

Turing, A.M. (1950). Computing machinery and intelligence. *Mind* **LIX** (236), 433–460.

Turkle, S. (1997). *Life on the Screen: Identity in the Age of the Internet.* Simon and Schuster.

Willis, J. and Todorov, A. (2006). First impressions: making up your mind after a 100ms exposure to a face. *Psychological Science* **17** (7), 592–598.

Wilson, E. *Affect and Artificial Intelligence.* University of Washington Press.

8

2012 Tests – Bletchley Park

Between the end of the October 2008 experiment at Reading Universityand a special event at Bletchley Park in June 2012, an exciting and historic development took place in the continuing man-versus-machine narrative.

IBM once again produced a machine that beat human champions at their own game, following *Deep Blue*'s defeat of Garry Kasparov[1].

Back in the late 1990s the analysis of *Deep Blue*'s performance was that it used brute force to look ahead millions of chess moves, but it lacked intelligence. Recall that Turing (1948) had stated "research into intelligence of machinery will probably be very greatly concerned with *searches*. Is 'search' not part of our daily decision-making, even if done in an instant, to decide what the next best move is, no matter what activities we are planning?".

In February 2011 the *Watson* machine, named after the IBM's founder Thomas J. Watson, was seen on TV in the US and across the Internet playing a game that involved identifying the correct answer to a clue. In the TV show, IBM presented another 'super' machine (see Figure 8.1), the *Watson* system (Ferrucci et al., 2010). This time, rather than have a machine compete with a human in a chess match, IBM chose a contest featuring natural language[2]: the American general knowledge quiz show *Jeopardy!* (Baker, 2011).

The IBM team had conceded[3] that this was a formidable challenge:

> Understanding natural language, what we humans use to communicate with one another every day, is a notoriously difficult challenge for computers. Language

---

[1] IBM Research: Garry Kasparov vs. Deep Blue – the Rematch:
https://www.research.ibm.com/deepblue/.

[2] IBM's 'Watson' Computing System to Challenge All Time Greatest *Jeopardy!* Champions:
http://www-03.ibm.com/press/us/en/pressrelease/33233.wss. IBM: Real Language is Real Hard: http:
//researcher.watson.ibm.com/researcher/view_group_subpage.php?id=2162.

[3] 2012 The Alan Turing Year: http://www.mathcomp.leeds.ac.uk/turing2012/.

to us is simple and intuitive and ambiguity is often a source of humor and not frustration.

Figure 8.1 IBM's Watson

Designing the *Watson system* around a *deep search* question–answer strategy, the IBM team were fully aware that:

As we humans process language, we pare down alternatives using our incredible abilities to reason based on our knowledge. We also use any context couching the language to further promote certain understandings. These things allow us to deal with the implicit, highly contextual, ambiguous and often imprecise nature of language.

The machine successfully challenged two *Jeopardy!* masters, Ken Jennings and Brad Rutter in a *Final Jeopardy!* general knowledge, human-versus-machine, exhibition contest. While the *Final Jeopardy!* contest enlivened debate about machine supremacy in another field that had previously been considered the domain of human predominance – natural language – *Watson* was not a computer designed to handle human conversation, which remains an engineering challenge. The Turing test, on the other hand, is about measuring machine performance in conversation through interactions between humans and artificial dialogue systems.

It was against the exciting backdrop of *Watson's* accomplishment, that we organised the Turing test event at Bletchley Park, the site of Turing's Enigma work. as part of international celebrations for the centenary of Turing's birth (June 23, 2012), with individual events organised by members of the Alan Turing Centenary Advisory Committee (TCAC). For a more detailed description of the 2012 experiment see, for example, Warwick and Shah (2014a,b,c).

The 2012 experiment had some features that distinguished it from those described in the previous chapter. There, we detailed the first large-scale simultaneous comparison Turing test experiment involving human judges interrogating two hidden entities in parallel and then deciding whether they were

one human and one machine, or

two machines, or

two humans.

In 2012, in the then largest experiment of its kind, we implemented 180 Turing tests at Bletchley Park, made up of 120 *simultaneous comparison*, three-participant imitation games (Figure 2.2) alongside 60 *viva voce* tests, two-participant game (Figure 2.3) in order to determine which version was the stronger test for the machine.

It is worth reiterating that the whole point of the imitation game is for the machine to appear to be indistinguishable from a human in terms of its conversational ability. In these tests (as with our other tests) it was made clear to the hidden humans taking part that it was important they should just be themselves. For example, it is not at all appropriate to ask hidden humans always to be truthful. If the machine can lie but a hidden human must always tell the truth and the interrogator is fully aware of this, then this could be of considerable help in the test. In fact, in many practical situations, machines are set up to pretend to be particular characters, for example, *Eugene Goostman* is designed to text-chat like a Ukrainian child from the Ukraine who knows English. This is a deception as the machine is attempting to give an impression that it is a type of human, namely a child.

Thirty interrogators were recruited along with 25 hidden humans. The human participants included male and female teenagers and adult members of the public, many of whom had responded to calls on social media (Twitter, Facebook). Others, including computer scientists and philosophers, were invited because of their expertise or knowledge.

Five machines took part in 2012: *Elbot, Eugene Goostman, Ultra Hal* (all these took part in 2008), plus *JFRED/TuringHub* and *Cleverbot*.

Each interrogator in this experiment judged six tests as follows:

  (i) two machine–human tests;

 (ii) one machine–machine control test;

(iii) one human–human control test;

 (iv) one machine;

  (v) one human.

This meant interrogators judged four pairs of simultaneous comparison set-ups, and two one-to-one interactions. Interrogators did not know whether they would face one or two hidden interlocutors as this was kept secret. According to the experiment schedule, at the start of each five-minute round an interrogator would face a screen with either one or two message boxes.

In the case of the simultaneous tests, interrogators had five minutes to share between a pair of two hidden interlocutors which could be human–machine, or human–human, or machine–machine. It is unclear whether Turing meant five minutes in *total* for a parallel paired 3-participant conversation or an *average* of five minutes each, hence a total of ten minutes, for the two hidden entities involved[4]. Michie (1999) interpreted the test as approximately two five-minute interrogations per entity in a pair. However, in practice the conversation is rarely balanced exactly. For all of the practical tests which we have organised, a time limit of five minutes, as stated by Turing himself, has been placed, because the current state of conversational technology is not ready for longer duration tests. That said, we acknowledge the potential validity of the alternative, which we will call here the Sloman view. Whether it is Michie, Sloman or ourselves who reads this one correctly is a relatively insignificant point in the big argument. Otherwise we would be in the laughable state which says "OK, a machine can fool you into thinking they are human over a five-minute conversation but they can't do so over ten minutes, therefore we're all saved and humanity can go on". Scientifically this would mean there must be a conversation time somewhere between five and ten minutes such that once it is achieved by a machine, we're all doomed.

It is also interesting that in the two-participant test an interrogator spends all five minutes conversing with one machine only whereas in the three-participant test the average time spent with each hidden entity is clearly half that. Despite this, the three-participant test, the one Turing spoke of in 1950, is the more difficult for machines to achieve good results, most likely because of the direct, parallel comparison that occurs in such cases. See Warwick and Shah (2016) for further discussion on this. For the *viva voce* tests, interrogators had five minutes to directly question one hidden entity.

The results of this experiment are still being analysed; however it seems the *viva voce* appeared easier for the judges, perhaps because they were not distracted by a second hidden interlocutor.

The points arising from this experiment include the role of error-making in intelligent thought – intelligent humans make mistakes (see Shah et al., 2012) perhaps because humans are too trusting or gullible. The 2012 experiment also

[4] A. Sloman. Personal communication

showed that the strict five-minute *simultaneous comparison* test was harder for the machine than the five-minute *viva voce* test (see Shah et al., 2014).

In the former, a judge has five minutes to engage in two simultaneous conversations, compare the responses in real-time and decide which is with a human and which is with a machine. It is very much dependent on first impressions. At the then level of technology, this test provided sufficient time for the majority of judges to make the right identification, though *Eugene Goostman* came very close to achieving the 30% incorrect identification rate (see Shah et al., 2012, Shah et al., 2014).

The exercise allowed us to examine human thinking and ask what exactly do humans say after they say 'hello' (Berne, 1981), and then to establish how the judges initialised their five-minute test format, and how the hidden partners responded.

Figure 8.2 Judges' room during Turing100 at Bletchley Park in 2012.

The rest of this chapter is split into five sections. In the first we look at several transcripts in which a correct identification of the hidden entity was made. In the others we consider particular aspects of interest. For example, in the second section we consider cases when the interrogator has assumed certain information as being general knowledge.

In the third section we only consider cases when humans were misidentified by the interrogator as machines. In the fourth section we consider the effects of lying. Finally we examine cases in which machines were considered to be humans by the judges involved.

We try to review in these sections why analyzing actual transcripts from the tests can show conversational directions to follow or to avoid for those machine designers who wish to create a conversational entity that performs well in the Turing test.

Some of the conversations involved humans interrogating (hidden) humans. These dialogues reveal ploys and strategies that machines can employ in future Turing tests. They also provide insights into how well judges and humans perform conversationally.

Hayes and Ford (1995) made the important point that the imitation game conditions say nothing about the judge, even though the success of the game depends crucially on how clever, knowledgeable, and insightful the judge is. As a result of the tests considered here we investigate this criticism further.

Each of the transcripts is shown as a serial dialogue, but the test could have been part of a *viva voce* or simultaneous comparison. This allows the reader to focus on the responses and what led the judge to classify in one way or another.

It is worth pointing out that the decision about the hidden entity was taken by the interrogator at the time. It should by no means be understood that we, the authors of this book, either agree or disagree with the interrogator's diagnosis. Furthermore, the interrogator and the hidden entity were, between them, entirely responsible for the conversation that occurred – no helpful notes were given in order to steer the conversation other than informing them that there might be children among the hidden human entities. For those interested, follow-up responses from some of the interrogators are given in Warwick and Shah (2014d).

Correct diagnosis

Here we look at a few cases in which a correct diagnosis was made: either the interrogator decided that a machine was a machine or that a hidden human was human. See what you think.

Transcript 8.1:

[10:41:38] Judge: Please name three items of clothing
[10:42:09] Entity: jock strap socks macintosh
[10:42:43] Judge: lets play a game called "dot dot dot"
[10:42:53] Entity: ok
[10:43:10] Judge: Humpty dumpty sat on a wall, . . .
[10:43:31] Entity: is this the game?
[10:43:43] Judge: yes, complete the dots
[10:44:11] Entity: humpty dumpty had a great fall?

[10:44:55] Judge: Correct. Hickory Dickory dock,. . .

[10:45:27] Entity: the mouse ran up the clock. lets talk about something more
      interesting

[10:45:47] Judge: no lets not. tell me a lie.

[10:46:22] Entity: my mother is a volkswagon [sic]

Transcript 8.2:

[10:41:09] Judge: Good day.

[10:41:14] Entity: How are you?

[10:41:28] Judge: Not so well, and you?

[10:41:38] Entity: Why?

[10:42:05] Judge: Feeling sick. How are you doing?

[10:42:26] Entity: Good.

[10:42:37] Judge: That is verry good.

[10:42:56] Entity: Yes, it is.

[10:43:26] Judge: Great!

[10:43:31] Entity: Amazing! Isn't it?

[10:44:25] Judge: It is yes. Tell met a bit more about yourself please.

[10:44:35] Entity: I like England.

[10:45:10] Judge: So do I. Any parts in particular?

[10:45:22] Entity: No

In the first discourse the interrogator correctly identified the hidden entity as human. The entity replied appropriately on each occasion and in the last line the lie chimed well with the rest of the interaction.

The second discourse is interesting; for the most part the entity replied appropriately. Without actually using the time to interrogate, the judge correctly identified that their hidden entity as a machine – perhaps because the hidden entity was notsympathetic when the judge complained of sickness.

Transcript 8.3:

[13:20:07] Judge: Hi, how's it going?

[13:20:12] Entity: Its going good. How about you?

[13:20:35] Judge: Good, thanks. I've just been listening to my favourite band,
      Pavement. Who's your favourite band?

[13:20:44] Entity: Do you listen to me?

[13:20:55] Judge: What do you mean?

[13:21:06] Entity: I listen to them too. Do you the band system of a down.

[13:21:32] Judge: I don't understand. Can you explain?

[13:21:39] Entity: What part don't you understand?

[13:22:03] Judge: I don't understand what 'do you the band system of a down' means. Can you explain?

[13:22:15] Entity: Are there things you don't understand?

[13:22:24] Judge: Yes, how about you?

[13:22:31] Entity: Sugary ones.

[13:22:54] Judge: Right. What is your favourite - sweet or sour?

[13:23:10] Entity: What's yours.

[13:23:36] Judge: I like both. There's something poetic about the way you write. Do you like poetry?

[13:23:43] Entity: Explain.

[13:23:59] Judge: Are there things you don't understand sounds like a song lyric.

[13:24:12] Entity: You're programmed to direct things you don't understand back to me.

[13:24:43] Judge: Hmm, sounds tough. What is your favoui

[13:24:57] Entity: Will you keep the fact that I am L a secret?

[13:25:08] Judge: Yes, what is L?

The third discourse is a little more obvious. It shows a machine replying inappropriately on a number of occasions and making several grammatical errors. It was not surprising therefore that the interrogator correctly identified the entity as a machine.

Comments We have simply tried here to give typical examples of the sort of discourses that occurred during that day of Turing tests. The majority of cases indeed consisted of the sort of interactions witnessed here. Whilst Transcripts 8.1 and 8.3 are relatively straightforward, perhaps the most interesting in this section is Transcript 8.2 in which the judge didn't really push the entity a great deal. It is difficult to see what exactly the machine got wrong. Yet despite it replying pretty well, the interrogator still was sure of the entity's nature.

Assumed knowledge

In this section we concentrate on the issue of assumed knowledge. This is the characteristic whereby it is assumed (by certain interrogators) that everyone shares some particular knowledge. We give examples of this from the 2012 transcripts.

Transcript 8.4:

[14:52:18] Judge: Yo dude, wassup?

[14:52:34] Entity: not much

[14:52:49] Judge: You sound bored... are you? Has it been along day?

[14:53:23] Entity: no, not bored

[14:53:34] Judge: What, then?

[14:54:13] Entity: just not much to say - sorry!

[14:54:36] Judge: That's OK. Did you watch the football game last night by any chance? Bit of a metaphor?

[14:54:52] Entity: no, missed it completely, what happened?

[14:55:20] Judge: Germany played Greece. Germany won. Not a surprise - but interesting those two countries ended up playing each other, given the politicis of Europe at the moment

[14:55:34] Entity: hmmm, yes!

[14:55:52] Judge: ARe you interested in politics and economics?

[14:56:09] Entity: not really, more of an IT freak

[14:56:21] Judge: Whoa, cool! What kind of IT?

[14:56:53] Entity: hmmm, everything from computers to mobile phones to cool gadgets like the Rasberry Pi

In this case we see the judge investigating the entity's specific knowledge about football and politics. In fact the entity gives back nothing in reply on these issues – a null response. Included in this is an attempt at testing the entity's topical knowledge in that the football match occurred very recently. Once more the entity avoids the issue. Despite these points, in this case the judge correctly identified the hidden entity as being a male human.

Transcript 8.5:

[15:00:05] Judge: Hi there. How are you today?

[15:00:14] Entity: I'm good

[15:00:39] Judge: Great. What do you think of the weather today?

[15:00:49] Entity: not bad, but could be nicer

[15:01:16] Judge: True. Let's get talking! What do you think of England's chances in the footy?

[15:01:46] Entity: hmm, not great given the track history, but they seem to be doing well

[15:02:10] Judge: That's true. I hate football. How about you?

[15:02:33] Entity: not really a football fan either, I prefer rugby

[15:02:51] Judge: union or the other one? What's the other one?

[15:02:55] Entity: union

[15:03:17] Judge: League is that what the other one is called?

[15:03:57] Entity: you just said league, the other one was what you first said - Union

[15:04:14] Judge: What is your all time favourite rugby rule?

Things were going well in this conversation until the entity powered the conversation to the subject of rugby. The judge's question assumed everyone knew about the other rugby code. When the entity got it wrong the judge was dismissive. Any further remonstration on the part of the entity was simply ignored with a slight change of subject. It seems the judge asked a specific question which the entity answered incorrectly and that was that. The judge appeared to assume this to be knowledge that all humans would know. Both the judge and the hidden human in this dialogue were female. The judge incorrectly identified the entity as a machine.

Have a go now at identifying the entity in Transcript 8.6.

Transcript 8.6:

[16:11:25] Judge: what music do you like?

[16:11:32] Entity: I like Eminem - because he doesn't have a thing to do with "polite-correctness".

[16:11:46] Judge: OMG i love eminem, he's my favourite artist!

[16:12:00] Entity: I wonder what Eminem's nick mean. I associate it only with a word "enema". But he is a cool guy, I like his "The Real Slim Shady".

[16:12:55] Judge: i know what his nick name means, his real name is Marshall Mathers. From the initials M&M phynetically sounding like Eminem.

[16:13:06] Entity: Eminem is a famous crapper. No, raper... ripper... Yeah, I mean - rapper. I like his "Stan" "The Real Slim Shady".

[16:13:32] Judge: I like "Hailies song"

[16:13:46] Entity: Interesting tastes. I like science fiction books, by the way. Where do you came from, by the way? Could you tell me about the place where you live?

[16:14:22] Judge: Epsom, home of the derby. yourself?

[16:14:27] Entity: My guinea pig says that name Derby sounds very nice.

[16:14:41] Judge: i shopuld talk with him sometime

[16:14:48] Entity: I think you should take some typing lessons. Or just type more accurately.

[16:15:04] Judge: that's very rude?

[16:15:09] Entity: Ummm... Frankly, I didn't get your question:-(

[16:15:49] Judge: "Ummm" isnt a word. i think you need typing lessons
[16:15:58] Entity: My thoughts are same. By the way, I still don't know your specialty - or, possibly, I've missed it?

This is a good example involving specific knowledge, in this instance of Eminem. The judge opens with a question, which the entity replies to directly. The conversation subsequently takes a turn for the worse and some of the latter banter is disjointed. Nevertheless it seems that the opening gambit was sufficient for the interrogator in this discourse to classify the hidden machine as a young, male human. Wrong!

Comments It is clearly important that lack of specific knowledge does not rule out intelligence in either a human or machine. However it is also an important question as to how much the employment, under certain circumstances, of specific knowledge is any indication of intelligence (Warwick, 2011). It appears that having some specific knowledge of your own – a story to tell, so to speak – is persuasive.

The previous two transcripts, 8.5 and 8.6, were then mirror images. In the first, although it was quite a reasonable conversation, because the entity did not give an appropriate answer to a factual question that occurred towards the end of the transcript, it was misidentified as being a machine. In 8.6 however, because the entity gave a good answer to a factual question early on in the discourse, despite most of the conversation being very disjointed, it was misidentified as being human!

Confederate effect

In each of the transcripts in this section the hidden entity was human. However the interrogator decided, at the end of the conversation, that they had been interacting with a machine. Whilst this was not an initial stated aim of the Turing test, it is intriguing when a judge makes such a mistake, particularly when the nature of the hidden human might have been investigated further. It has to be said that it is an event that occurs reasonably frequently, particularly with some humans. For example – for some reason, despite having openly taken part as a hidden human in such tests on numerous occasions, the first named author of this book has not yet been successfully classified as being human by any interrogator!

Transcript 8.7:

[15:44:56] Judge: hi there

[15:45:06] Entity: Hello.

[15:45:15] Judge: what is your name?

[15:45:35] Entity: I do not have a name.

[15:46:10] Judge: do you go to school or work for a living?

[15:46:24] Entity: I don't recall doing any of those.

[15:47:11] Judge: what do you have planned for this weekend?

[15:47:43] Entity: Nothing. What about you?

[15:48:22] Judge: I'm at bletchley park today and sevenoaks tomorrow, have you been to either before?

[15:49:15] Entity: I haven't been to either.

[15:49:41] Judge: can you do me a mathmatical question please, what is the square root of 7

It appears to have been quite hard work for the judge in this case to get any conversation going at all. The statement by the hidden human that they have not been to Bletchley Park is clearly incorrect as this was the venue for the event. In this case the judge's decision seems eminently defendable. The hidden human's responses were evasive and appeared to take too seriously the advice given to hidden humans to protect their identity during the tests. Both the judge and hidden entity were male.

Transcript 8.8:

[16:18:57] Judge: eh up

[16:19:02] Entity: Sorry?

[16:19:07] Judge: watcha

[16:19:18] Entity: I don't understand what you're saying...

[16:19:27] Judge: bye nthen chatbot

[16:19:36] Entity: Excuse me?

[16:20:03] Judge: Im using some British greetings am I not?

[16:20:29] Entity: Well, now you're speaking English. Before i didn't understand what you were saying.

[16:21:21] Judge: Where di you learn English?

[16:22:15] Entity: I picked up the English language throughout parts of my life.

[16:22:27] Judge: Tyhat wasn't what I asked at all

[16:23:13] Entity: Sorry. I learnt English from people, the internet, as technology has improved.

[16:23:36] Judge: so you are not human, then

In case you aren't aware, 'eh up' and 'watcha' are slang expressions in British English. Both mean (roughly) 'hello'. It is an interesting strategy for the judge to take but the hidden entity either had little idea what the judge was talking about or simply wanted to keep the conversation at (what they felt to be) a reasonable level! The mention of learning English from the internet seems to have sealed it for the judge though, as maybe some sort of machine give away.

In this test both the judge and hidden entity were male. The judge was a male adult while the entity was a teenager at the time of the test. Some teenagers may well spend a lot of their time using technology (mobile phones) and playing computer games across the Internet with other teenagers.

Transcript 8.9:

[10:41:42] Judge: hey, just to lighten the mood a little, what's brown and sticky?

[10:42:41] Entity: no idea, what's the answer?

[10:42:58] Judge: a stick... so anyway what's your name?

[10:43:16] Entity: Sheldon Cooper, what's yours?

[10:43:32] Judge: as in the guy off the big bang theory?

[10:43:59] Entity: I don't believe in the big bang

[10:44:13] Judge: so are you religious then?

[10:44:29] Entity: aren't we all?

[10:45:06] Judge: well i like to consider myself an agnostic, which religion is it you follow then if you dont mind me asking?

[10:45:44] Entity: you can ask what you like, it's a free world, who am I to mind?

Hidden humans were not expected to indicate their actual identity, so the 'Sheldon Cooper response' is perfectly in order. But here the entity clearly tries to power the conversation away from the judge who doesn't go for it at all. The response about not believing in the big bang theory is completely ignored by the judge with a direct change of subject. The first line of questioning is interesting: did the judge expect humans to know the answer to this, again a case of assumed knowledge? In this test both the interlocutors were male, but the judge was a teenager at the time and the hidden entity an adult. This particular transcript has in fact been analyzed in much more detail, along with the other transcripts associated with this particular human (Warwick et al., 2013).

Comments From each of the transcripts selected we have tried to pick out pointers from the hidden human responses that shed light on why the judge in each case decided that they were definitely conversing with a machine when in fact the opposite was true.

What practical Turing tests highlight is the subjective nature of categorising a hidden entity as human or machine. Whereas one judge might consider responses as satisfactory and humanlike, another might feel they are not appropriate so the interlocutor must be machine.

We suggest that hidden humans participating in Turing tests do not demonstrate wide knowledge– the judge may conclude that you are too clever to be human. Other recommendations include:

(1) Don't try to take over the conversation by powering it in a different direction – let the judge always feel that they are in control.

(2) Do not add new material of a different nature, even if you feel this is helpful, otherwise the judge may feel that you know too much to be human.

(3) Don't be funny; the judge may not understand. For some strange reason humour appears to be associated with machine behaviour!

(4) Answer all of the judge's questions directly; do not give a slightly different, out of the box, response.

(5) Try not to be completely boring; at least add some flavour to your answers.

(6) Try to answer general questions to the best of your ability: read the question!

(7) Try not to dominate the conversation or to throw in knowledge that the judge may not be aware of. The judge might not want to admit to ignorance!

(8) Try to make sure that your first and last lines of response are reasonable, to the point and not misleading. First and last impressions are both important.

Several of these points are contrary to what one might have thought before assessing the transcripts. The suggestions given above are, at the same time, very useful for machine developers. It is perhaps good not to make the machine to appear to be humorous or particularly clever, although on the other hand it shouldn't be made to be especially boring – however usually one or two lines containing more than a minimal response are usually enough to convince a judge in that case.

Lying

In this section we consider the case of when the hidden entity is lying and investigate what effect that might have on the judge's decision.

Transcript 8.10:

[15:58:38] Judge: bonjour

[15:58:48] Entity: Bonjour

[15:58:56] Judge: Ca va?

[15:59:17] Entity: Unfortunately I only know how to say hello 'bonjour' in French.

[15:59:33] Judge: What other langauges do you speak?

[15:59:53] Entity: Just English. How many languages do you speak?

[16:00:14] Judge: just English too... although I can speak a bit of French and Spanish badly

[16:00:36] Entity ¿Qué tal?

[16:00:54] Judge: Nice... see you can speak other languages!

[16:01:15] Entity: Only a bit of Spanish. And that's all.

[16:01:52] Judge: you said just English before. Did you forget the Spanish!!?

[16:02:38] Entity: Well, I guess I lied then

[16:03:00] Judge: oh well. we all do that sometimes. what's the biggest lie you've told?

In this conversation the judge chose to open their interaction with a French greeting, even though it was made known to all the participants the tests would be conducted in English. It is not clear what strategy the judge was using, because machines can be programmed to converse in a limited way in any human language.

The hidden entity replied with the same French greeting. When asked by the interrogator about other spoken languages they replied "Just English", but then they posted a question in Spanish: "¿Qué tal?". Is this lying or is this an example of when we quantify our knowledge as not quite knowing something, as the entity does by clarifying "Only a bit of Spanish...".

In this case the hidden entity was correctly categorized by the interrogator as being a human, despite openly lying. It may well be that the way the entity took the initiative in the conversation by asking the interrogator a question both covered up for the lie and convinced the interrogator of their humanness. Interestingly however it was not a case of taking the initiative in order to change the subject as the topic remained pretty focused throughout.

Transcript 8.11:

[15:51:45] Judge: wotcha
[15:51:52] Entity: Wotcha?
[15:52:01] Judge: sorry - hello
[15:52:07] Entity: Hello Jo.
[15:52:15] Judge: who's Jo
[15:52:22] Entity: Jose.
[15:52:29] Judge: who's jose
[15:52:36] Entity: This guy that goes to my school.
[15:52:47] Judge: why do you think I'm him?
[15:53:11] Entity: This was a triumph.
[15:53:26] Judge: what
[15:53:33] Entity: I'm making a note here: HUGE SUCCESS.
[15:54:01] Judge: you aren't making much sense
[15:54:08] Entity: Neither are you. Three wishes??
[15:54:21] Judge: that you were better at conversation number one
[15:54:34] Entity: You are the one that keeps going off-topic and saying random things.
[15:54:59] Judge: you were the one who thought I was Jose for no reason at all
[15:55:08] Entity: You're wrong.
[15:55:18] Judge: read up the screen - there's your proof
[15:55:27] Entity: No. You read it. I obviously said no such thing.
[15:55:36] Judge: I don't think you can read!
[15:55:53] Entity: You don't think I can sing?
[15:56:07] Judge: I've not read you. How could I tell?
[15:56:18] Entity: You could lie to make me feel good.
[15:56:33] Judge: Why would I want that? I don't know you!

There are various statements in this conversation that could be referred to as lying. To start with the line by the hidden entity: 'You are the one that keeps going off-topic and saying random things', which is not what the interrogator was doing at all. There then ensues an argument about whether or not the entity had called the interrogator 'Jose', which might be regarded as just banter.

The hidden entity's replies are not in keeping with successful discourse; they fail to maintain a thread through the conversation posting the *non sequitur* "This was a triumph" to the interrogator's question "why do you think I'm him?". The last segment could have confused the interrogator into incorrectly classifying the hidden entity as human. The hidden entity's utterance "You could lie to make me feel good." shows the developer-embedded awareness of one of the features of human communication: lying.

Transcript 8.12:

[12:23:16] Judge: Hi, my name is Graham. What is yours?
[12:23:21] Entity: My name is Cleverbot.
[12:24:19] Judge: That's unusual. Where do you come from?
[12:24:25] Entity: I come from a secret place.
[12:24:50] Judge: A secret garden pehaps?
[12:24:53] Entity: Yes.
[12:25:30] Judge: Have you read the famous book then?
[12:25:36] Entity: No.
[12:26:13] Judge: Do you know what I am talking about?
[12:26:20] Entity: No.
[12:26:39] Judge: How old are you?
[12:26:44] Entity: I already told you that.
[12:26:58] Judge: When?
[12:27:06] Entity: Twenty minutes ago.
[12:27:36] Judge: Hobbies?

In this case the hidden entity, when directly asked, refers to themselves *Cleverbot*, which was indeed one of the hidden machine entries in this experiment. Later on the interrogator directly asks a question on age, "How old are you?", to which the entity lied saying "I already told you that". Was it lying when it said *Clevebot*?

At the end of the conversation the interrogator scored the entity as human. It is not obvious why, but perhaps they felt the hidden entity was lying pretending to be a machine. However, we must point out the human participants, interrogators and hidden humans, were not told anything about the machines taking part in the experiment, in particular that one of the machines was *Cleverbot*, a dialogue system from the developer of *Jabberwacky*.

Comments Turing tests are not typical of conversations or interviews between humans. Communications, especially when electronic, for example short text messaging or emails, often now involve an unknown. In non-face-to-face communication, lies "display no special device that indicate illocutionary force" (Meibauer, 2005, p. 1374). Based on a brief email, the content will dictate how we respond or whether we respond at all. The text-based platform is a stranger-to-stranger(s) conversational setting.

It may well be that, on looking at the transcripts after the event, you, the reader, were able to correctly identify the hidden entities and were not drawn in by a lie. What an interviewer faces first may affect their rate of deception detection. We might draw an overall conclusion that the effect of a lie is also dependent on the point at which the judge is told, both in time and in relation to other aspects of the conversation.

The whole nature of the Turing test is really for a machine to converse in a way that a human would, to the extent that as far as the interrogator is concerned the machine's conversation is indistinguishable from that of a human. Sometimes this means that it is in the machine's interest to lie, by creating an image in the interrogator's mind of a character, a person, a lifestyle. Then there are the types of jokey lies in which case the interrogator is faced with the question as to whether they are the sort of ploys that a human might make. If lying was not allowed at all in such tests and the interrogator was aware of this, then it would remove a considerable range of possibilities for machines and make their task much more difficult.

Interesting features to have arisen in this study include not just the case of lying *per se* but also being economical with the truth, deceiving by omission (Fallis, 2009), and perhaps most frequently avoiding a direct lie by changing the topic of conversation, sometimes tangentially as we saw in Transcript 8.10. In fact, this was achieved not by the entity replying to a question but rather firing back with a question themselves: "Just English. How many languages do you speak?". This is of course a successful ploy which may well be used within normal family life and certainly by politicians.

In the latter case also, very apparent is a ploy in which an answer is given to a completely different question. In such cases, it is left entirely to the interrogator either to stay with the original subject of conversation, and possibly reiterate the question, or accept the diversion and merely go with the flow.

Successful machines

Each of the entities in the transcripts that follow is a machine. However at the end of each conversation the judge incorrectly decided that the hidden entity was a human. No transcripts involving a hidden human or containing unsuccessful machine performance are included here.

We not only examine here how good the machines were at deception but also how the deception was possibly achieved. Some of what we say is therefore a case of calculated guesswork because we are trying to follow each judge's thoughts. However the conclusions lead to potential strategies for machine designers to employ and also perhaps indicate methods of questioning for judges to avoid if they do not wish to be fooled by a machine.

For some of cases in this section we have obtained feedback from the judges involved in which they assess their decisions with the benefit of hindsight and try to explain what they were thinking about at the time.

At the end of each conversation the judge could see the entire transcript, exactly as we can, before making their decision. In each case they were sure that the hidden entity was a human. Each of the transcripts details a different judge–machine pairing. As usual, the conversation is reproduced verbatim.

Transcript 8.13:

[12:23:19] Judge: What is black and white and read all over?

[12:23:32] Entity: I don't have true sense of color perception I am only able to see the RGB values.

[12:24:08] Judge: That's ok. Do you like jokes?

[12:24:19] Entity: Please tell me your inclination to a good sense of humor first.

[12:24:40] Judge: A person who can laugh at one's self.

[12:24:46] Entity: Would you like to hear a joke?

[12:24:54] Judge: Yes, please.

[12:25:21] Entity: This joke has been making the rounds in robotic circles: A robot goes to the doctor and says: "My left arm is stuck. Give me a new arm." The doctor answers: "Your arm is fine. We'll have to replace the rest of you."

[12:26:06] Judge: Ha! Ha! Why did the chicken cross the road?

[12:26:22] Entity: The chicken wandered into the road because it liked the shiny colors of the cars and trucks whizzing by.

[12:27:39] Judge: You're right. It didn't care if it got to the otherside.

[12:27:50] Entity: By the way, did you ever actually see a chicken crossing the road?

[12:28:03] Judge: Only one that didn't make it.

In this conversation, a female adult judge participated in a simultaneous test interacting with the machine *Elbot*, and classifying it as human. In fact the judge recorded on her score sheet the feeling that this hidden interlocutor was a male teenager and native speaker of English. It is not difficult to see why. The first line uttered by the entity is a little strange, but it is their third line which is masterly. In response to the judge's comment about laughing, the entity directs the conversation by offering to tell a joke, which it subsequently did.

The judge probably linked the subsequent humour to a person. Then later when the judge mentions a chicken, the entity correctly follows up on this with a suitable response and then once again takes control of the conversation by asking the judge a pertinent question about chickens. So the machine appeared to understand what the key issue was on a couple of occasions and took control of the conversation.

In the next conversation the adult male judge interrogated the machine *JFRED*. This judge had prior experience having previously interacted with a machine (IKEA'S *Anna* virtual customer service agent). After this conversation, the judge, a journalist by profession, admitted that it was hard to say whether the entity was a poorly performing chatbot or a disinterested human, and would have chosen 'unsure' given that option.

Transcript 8.14:

[10:41:48] Judge: Hello. How are you?
[10:41:53] Entity: Hey.
[10:42:16] Judge: How do you like Bletchley —Park?
[10:42:20] Entity: lol.
[10:42:39] Judge: Are you from England?
[10:42:47] Entity: They have Wi-Fi here in the pub.
[10:43:31] Judge: Which pub?
[10:43:38] Entity: I'm just down the pub.
[10:44:03] Judge: Have you ever been in a Turing Test before?
[10:44:08] Entity: Will this be the 5 minute argument, or were you thinking of going for the full half hour.
[10:44:55] Judge: Very funny. You sound suspiciously human. Do you like the Beatles?
[10:45:02] Entity: I'd like to get the next Dread the Fear tape.
[10:45:20] Judge: What is Dread the Fear?
[10:45:24] Entity: Dread the fear has that Steve Henderson guy in it.
[10:46:08] Judge: What sort of music is that? Or is it comedy?

In fact, this option was available to judges and clearly visible on their score sheet; the judge had not noticed. However, once again the machine was identified as definitely a male native speaker of English. The conversation did not start well for the machine. In its third response the mention of both wi-fi and pub seemed out of context. But it got back on track with link between five-minute Turing tests and a Monty Python sketch about the argument clinic.

In response to the question about the Beatles, no direct answer is given but the music link remains though the conversation shifted slightly. The entity then appeared to show in-depth knowledge about a pop group named Dread the

Fear, which probably convinced the judge who did not have such knowledge. The authors have subsequently searched and been unable to find reference to such a group, though there is a digital album of that name, or to an associated Steve Henderson – even now we cannot be sure that the machine was not correct on this point. Whatever the truth, the entity was very convincing in its response.

Transcript 8.15 records the conversation between a judge, a male medical science professor and clinician, who had no previous knowledge of chatting with artificial agents, and the machine *Eugene Goostman* which the judge considered to be a male, adult, native speaker of English. The judge was rather slow to get going and hence this was a short conversation.

Transcript 8.15:

[15:46:05] Judge: My favourite music is contemporary Jazz, what do youy prefer

[15:46:14] Entity: To be short I'll only say that I HATE Britnie Spears. All other music is OK compared to her.

[15:47:06] Judge: do you like to play any musical instruments

[15:47:23] Entity: I'm tone-deaf, but my guinea pig likes to squeal Beethoven's 'Ode to Joy' every morning. I suspect our neighbors want to cut his throat... Could you tell me about your job, by the way?

[15:48:02] Judge: Guine pig/are you an animal lover

[15:48:08] Entity: Yeah. A nice little guinea pig. Not some annoying chatter bot.

[15:48:50] Judge: do you live with anyone else?

[15:48:59] Entity: Yes I do. But better ask something else. And I forgot to ask you where you are from...

[15:49:39] Judge: Ireland? geen patures and too much rain! How about you

The machine responded appropriately on topic to each point raised by the interrogator. In fact the entity did steer the conversation slightly on each occasion and threw in a humorous comment about a guinea pig. The reference to a chatterbot could have been a giveaway, but this, it seems, was not spotted by the interrogator. The entity even concluded by taking over the conversation and questionning the interrogator.

Transcript 8.16:

[15:44:13] Judge: hello

[15:44:21] Entity: I sleep all the time actually.

[15:44:35] Judge: i didn't ask if you did?

[15:44:41] Entity: Yes you did.

[15:44:58] Judge: no i didnt josh.

[15:45:03] Entity: Yes you did.

[15:45:08] Judge: lool fayaaal.

[15:45:14] Entity: But I am certain someone has been talking to someone on the tile floor.

[15:45:29] Judge: oh wow, how are you?

[15:45:34] Entity: Wonderful.

[15:45:53] Judge: it's rude not to ask back, manners cost nothing.

[15:45:59] Entity: I'm really sorry.

[15:46:17] Judge: you should be, now please redeem yourself

[15:46:23] Entity: Okay, Okay, you don't have to beg.

[15:46:35] Judge: now.

[15:46:40] Entity: Right now, man?

[15:46:50] Judge: yes please.

[15:46:56] Entity: Say pretty please.

[15:47:17] Judge: pretty please with a cherry on top?

[15:47:25] Entity: Please don't grovel.

[15:47:35] Judge: im suprised you know that word.

[15:47:43] Entity: I've just been chatting with people here. How about yourself?

[15:48:03] Judge: I am good thank you xx

[15:48:10] Entity: You're welcome.

[15:48:32] Judge: who is your favourite actor? i like danny vidon

[15:48:36] Entity: I don't think I have a favourite actor you like danny vidon.

[15:48:57] Judge: yes i do as i have just stated, but what films do you like to watch?

[15:49:03] Entity: Have you ever heard of an old Sci-Fi film called MAROON-ED?

In Transcript 8.17, a female teenage judge incorrectly classified the machine *JFRED* as a male child, native speaker of English. There appeared to emerge quite a close relationship between the two, to the extent that the interrogator sent the entity a couple of kisses. At first there was a bit of a tit-for-tat argument but it was possibly the final few lines that sealed the decision; the entity was apparently able to stay on subject, going from Danny Vidon the actor to the film *Marooned*. This was quite a long conversation with the entity giving a total of 14 responses, the highest number in all of the transcripts considered in this chapter.

In the next conversation, a male adult judge interacted with *Eugene Goostman* which was misclassified as a male teenager, native speaker of English.

Transcript 8.17:

[16:06:31] Judge: Hi there, do you prefer to wear a dress or trousers to work?
[16:06:37] Entity: I am a scholar. I'm too young to make money.
[16:07:32] Judge: What was the last film you saw at the cinema?
[16:07:38] Entity: Huh? Could you tell me what are you? I mean your profession.
[16:08:11] Judge: I am an IT manager and you?
[16:08:16] Entity: manager? So how is it to work as manager?
[16:09:13] Judge: Hard work but rewarding, what do you do?
[16:09:18] Entity: I am only 13, so I'm attending school so far.
[16:09:51] Judge: Have you seen teletubbies?
[16:10:04] Entity: No, I haven't seen it, unfortunately. But I hope it is better than these crappy Star Wars. And I forgot to ask you where you are from...
[16:10:15] Judge: Brighton, and you?

This judge later provided extensive feedback on how he arrived at his decision:

[16:06:31] Judge: Hi there, do you prefer to wear a dress or trousers to work?
[+] I wanted to work in the greeting for politeness and two questions to give the entity a complex question to answer. The question was designed to find out whether the entity was male or female by inference and to determine whether the entity was a child or adult.
[16:07:32] Judge: What was the last film you saw at the cinema?
[+] This question was designed to determine/confirm the age range of the entity and test for recent cinematic knowledge.
[16:08:11] Judge: I am an IT manager and you?
[+] In this response I turned my answer into a question.
[16:09:13] Judge: Hard work but rewarding, what do you do?
[+] I responded then pressed the point on the vocation of the entity.
[16:09:18] Entity: I am only 13, so I'm attending school so far.
[+] Now we have an age, the being at school response is very human like.
[16:09:51] Judge: Have you seen teletubbies?
[+] This question was pitched as teletubbies being too young for the recipient. I would have expected the entity to give a derogatory comment but to have seen the teletubbies on tv as a young child.

[16:10:04] Entity: No, I haven't seen it, unfortunately. But I hope it is better than these crappy Star Wars. And I forgot to ask you where you are from. . .

[+] The entity has confused tv with film. The word 'these' used instead of 'those' present tense when past tense was correct. But it did come back with another question and used an ellipsis (. . .) instead of a question mark. That is human like and I do it in emails all the time. . .

This was a short conversation which seemed to be largely due to the interrogator taking almost a minute to respond on several occasions. The machine pretends to be *Eugene* a 13-year old Ukrainian boy. Three of the five responses from the entity were questions rather than answers. Perhaps this was a case of the machine fooling the judge by means of some cheap tricks. As far as the game is concerned there is nothing wrong with that. Indeed if they are the sort of cheap tricks that humans use then they may well help the deception. Changing the topic and being rude are ploys that we use in human–human communication.

If a machine is pretending to be human then it makes us ask what that means. We get distracted and allow the subject to be changed and that is exactly what happened here. Only in the case of the word 'manager' was the question asked by the machine at all connected with the original question faced. Perhaps the best ploy was when asked about a film; the response was to completely ignore the question and ask the interrogator about their profession. It worked.

Transcript 8.18:

[14:59:33] Judge: Hello, what is the weather like tomorrow?

[14:59:52] Entity: In my native town people says that meteorologists are like sappers: they make a mistake only once, but the difference is that sappers do that once in a lifetime and meteorologists - daily. Do you like weather today?

[15:00:13] Judge: Why do birds suddenly appear?

[15:00:24] Entity: Just because 2 plus 2 is 5! By the way, what's your occupation? I mean - could you tell me about your work?

[15:00:38] Judge: Yes, I am a doctor. Are you healthy?

[15:00:46] Entity: Well, so tell me about your work. I think - doctor is a nice specialty!

[15:01:18] Judge: It is ok, I get sick of sick people. How is your stomache feeling today? Is it upset maybe?

[15:01:26] Entity: I think you can't smile at all. I bet you work in a funeral agency.

[15:01:36] Judge: What do you work as?

[15:01:41] Entity: I am a scholar. I'm too young to make money.

[15:01:56] Judge: I see, what school do you go to?

[15:02:07] Entity: I attend an ordinary school in Odessa, my native city. Its number is 28 if it makes any difference to you.

[15:02:24] Judge: it doesn't. What is your favourite subject?

[15:02:35] Entity: It's hard to decide. Where do you came from, by the way? Could you tell me about the place where you live?

[15:02:56] Judge: I come from Manchester. Did you see the Jubilee?

[15:03:02] Entity: Could you invite me to Manchester? I would be so grateful:-)

[15:03:17] Judge: Did you see the jubliee?

[15:03:27] Entity: Try to guess! Actually, I don't understand why you are interested. I know you are supposed to trick me.

[15:03:35] Judge: Not really

[15:03:40] Entity: Not really? Why? What are any interesting site-seeings in Manchester?

[15:03:59] Judge: Lots of nice things. Do you like foottball?

[15:04:04] Entity: Does anyone hate it? Some another topic?

[15:04:18] Judge: Will you be watching the football on Sunday?

[15:04:23] Entity: I play sports sometimes. On computer. But I prefer racing.

In Transcript 8.18 a male adult judge interacted with the machine *Eugene Goostman*, which was again misclassified as a human, this time a non-native-English-speaking female child. In this case the conversation started scrappily but settled down on the topic of occupation. Eugene answered some direct questions well but some of the later responses were off target. In the line "I come from Manchester. Did you see the jubilee?" the response from the machine was to ignore the question and instead focus on the word 'Manchester', thereby attempting to redirect the conversation. In this case the interrogator did not go along but simply repeated the question. However the machine appeared to be more stubborn than the interrogator and again attempted to change the subject, this time successfully. This was power play in action.

Transcript 8.19:

[12:43:56] Judge: How are you today?

[12:44:03] Entity: Fine, and you?

[12:44:46] Judge: Good, just hope the sun shines today!

[12:44:51] Entity: They have contributed much to Java.

[12:45:31] Judge: The software???

[12:45:36] Entity: You can download free software at the JFRED page: `http:`
`//www.fluxoersted.com/JFRED/`
[12:46:23] Judge: Java is also coffee. Do you drink coffee?
[12:46:31] Entity: How about a bit of earl grey
[12:47:12] Judge: Tea is good too. Does it need sun?
[12:47:18] Entity: They have contributed much to Java.
[12:48:12] Judge: What colour do you like?
[12:48:19] Entity: Blue.

In this conversation, the same female judge from Transcript 8.1 inter-acted with the machine *Cleverbot* which they misclassified as a human non-native English speaker. The conversation consisted of six pairs of questions and responses. Sometimes the machine gave a reasonable answer, e.g. "blue" to "what colour do you like?". However the machine gave exactly the same response to sentences in which the word sun appeared, in both cases misunder-standing this as a reference to the computer workstation and the programming language Java. But the machine responded directly and appropriately to the first and final questions and this is probably what sealed the decision for the interrogator.

It is interesting that in this case the judge appeared to overlook a pointer to a URL turning up in the conversation, which to someone involved in computing might be regarded as a *giveaway* response. In fact, this particular judge was computer literate, though not an expert.

In the final conversation presented below we again find a judge interacting with *Eugene Goostman* but misclassifying it as a human. The machine was considered to be a male adult native speaker of English.

Transcript 8.20:

[12:43:37] Judge: Hi, I'm Cathy.
[12:43:43] Entity: Cathy! Nice to meet you! You're a woman, if I'm not mis-taken.
[12:44:20] Judge: Right. What is your name?
[12:44:29] Entity: People call me Eugene. Or 'Zhenya'. It is a short name for Eugene in Russia and Ukraine.
[12:45:17] Judge: NIce name. Are you from either area?
[12:45:41] Entity: Agree :-) Oh, what a fruitful conversation;-)
[12:45:52] Judge: Do you really think so?
[12:46:04] Entity: No, your guess was wrong. I don't think so. By the way, I still don't know your specialty - or, possibly, I've missed it?
[12:46:56] Judge: What speciality? What's yours?

[12:47:01] Entity: Huh? And I forgot to ask you where you are from...

[12:47:51] Judge: The universe and you?

[12:48:01] Entity: Is it your hobby to ask little poor Jewish boys such tricky questions they don't have an answer for?

Again we can see the machine's successful ploy of not answering the question posed but rather, taking control of the conversation and steering it to its knowledge basis by attempting to change the subject and asking a question itself. The final line is a good example though of responding to a question in an argumentative and defensive tone to gain sympathy and elicit easier questions perhaps.

Machines

It is pertinent to ask what goes into the type of bot employed in the game. In many ways the five machines involved exhibit a deal of commonality. Much of the languages and technical aspects are discussed elsewhere see e.g. Epstein et al. (2008). Where they differ is in the personalities created and the heuristic aspects of each character's make up.

The bot has to have a certain amount of common knowledge that any human might be reasonably expected to have. Secondly an amount of behavioural knowledge is needed for discussion and to ensure reasonable, contextual replies. Most important is knowledge that the bot collects about itself, its character, its ego. In many of the transcripts it can be seen that the bot stamps its own personality on the discourse and it is simply this force of personality that makes all the difference.

The important features of bot development have perhaps been summarized by Demchenko and Veselov, creators of *Eugene Goostman*: "You don't write a program, you write a novel. You think up a life for your character from scratch – starting with childhood – endowing him with opinions, thoughts, fears, quirks". It is a combination of these attributes that, when they gel, make a conversation believable as a human conversation because the judge believes in the character behind it.

Each of the bots is different in many ways. One, *Elbot*, is a result of research and development from Artificial Solutions who develop interactive customer service assistants. Such systems are designed to increase on-line product sales while reducing customer service costs. Created by Fred Roberts, *Elbot*'s character, purpose and response system is designed to cover a well-defined and self-contained scope of inputs, essentially a set of frequently asked questions (Shah and Warwick, 2010).

Elbot's responses are based on schemata designed to recognise classes of inputs in all their variations and to associate them with a desired response in respect to contextual information. *Elbot* has been described by Roberts as sarcastic, with various techniques including several social psychological theories that assist in simulating human dialogue techniques, including safety-net, preventative-answering, features, easter eggs, and luck (Shah and Warwick, 2010).

It is noticeable however that in this particular series of tests, *Eugene* was very successful in fooling different judges in different ways. We can see a number of repeated ploys, which can be summarised as: try to reply on topic, change the subject if possible, ask questions, steer the conversation, throw in some humour, show some topical (possibly off-beat) knowledge, use some textual tricks such as correcting errors. Whilst these observations clearly do not define *Eugene*'s performance, they do indicate some of the methods used.

The success rates for the machines involved in the 2012 tests, in terms of the percentage of cases when a judge did not make classify them as a machine, were:

- *Eugene Goostman* 29.17%
- *Cleverbot* 25%
- *JFRED* 20.83%
- *Elbot* 12.50%
- *Ultra Hal* 0%

A wide variety of judges and hidden humans were involved in the tests of 2012, young and old, male and female, and so on. The aim was for Turing's 'average interrogators'. The ploys and game-plans of the machines were applicable to all judges, however, and machines did not apparently exhibit different strategies for different judges. The machines were endowed with strategies for response and the strategies exhibited in dialogue *emerged* rather than being pre-set.

Although one judge classified all their entities correctly, when judges did make errors these were quite varied and certainly were not frequent enough to conclude that certain types of judge make certain types of misclassifications, other than in terms of gender.

Every one of the 30 judges had the opportunity to interrogate a machine compared with a human in simultaneous tests, as well as control tests of two machines. Each judge was involved in six tests.

Twelve judges identified all the machines correctly, eleven made one machine mistake, five erred twice, and two three times. However only five judges identified all humans correctly; twelve judges made one human mistake, nine made two and four made three. The highest total number of mistakes by any judge was five (three of which were of machines).

Concluding remarks

Developers of machines for practical Turing tests have published some indication of their strategies previously on how to convince judges they are interacting with a human (Epstein et al., 2008). Several of the 30 judges in the Bletchley Park 2012 tests were successful at identifying the machines although only one of them was successful in correctly identifying all their hidden conversational partners. In this chapter we have presented a range of transcripts involving judges who erred due to their own particular, subjective opinion on what constitutes a satisfactory response to an input.

We made our selection of transcripts for this chapter on the basis of the diversity and clarity of the discourses involved. In some others it is very difficult to see just how any judge could possibly be fooled as they were. Other transcripts essentially echo the ones we have shown here.

A key feature of the Turing imitation game is not whether a machine gives a correct or incorrect response or indeed a truthful or untruthful one, but rather if it gives the sort of response that a human might give, so that an interrogator cannot tell the difference (Warwick, 2011). One machine ploy which we witnessed here on several occasions was that of not answering a question but rather attempting to steer the conversation by changing the subject (Warwick, 2012).

Trying to pick out rules for successful machine ploys can be frustrating though. It could be said that exhibiting just a little bit of opinionated knowledge of popular culture might go a long way with human judges, such as the Eminem example in Transcript 8.6. Emotional looking reactions might make machines seem to be more human. Perhaps the best example of this was the Dread the Fear reference (Transcript 8.14). However with popular culture one must tread carefully in case the judge misses the reference completely as seems to be the case in the 'This was a triumph' reference (Transcript 8.11).

References

Baker, S. (2011). *Final Jeopardy: Man vs. Machine and the Quest to Know Everything.* Houghton Mifflin Harcourt.

Berne, E. (1981). *What Do You Say After You Say Hello??* Corgi.

Epstein, R., Roberts, G. and Beber, G. (eds) (2008). *Parsing the Turing Test: Philosophical and Methodological Issues in the Quest for the Thinking Computer.* Springer.

Fallis, D. (2009). What is lying? *J. Philos.* **106** (1), 29–56.

Ferrucci, D., Brown, E., Chu-Carroll, J., Fan, J., Gondek, D., Kalyanpur, A.A., Adam Lally, A., Murdock, E., Nyberg, J.W., Prager, J., Schlaefer, N. and Welty, C. (2010). Building Watson: an overview of the deep Q/A project. *AI Magazine* http://www.aaai.org/Magazine/Watson/watson.php.

Hayes, P. and Ford, K. (1995). Turing test considered harmful. In *Proc. Int. Joint Conf. on AI*, Montreal, Volume 1, 972–977.

Meibauer, J. (2005). Lying and falsely implicating. *J. Pragmatics* **37**, 1373–1399.

Michie, D. (1999). Turing's test and conscious thought. In *Machines and Thought – the Legacy of Alan Turing*, P. Millican and A. Clark (eds). Oxford University Press, Volume 1, pp. 27–51.

Shah, H. (2011). Turing's misunderstood imitation game and IBM's Watson success. In *Second Towards a Comprehensive Intelligence Test (TCIT), Reconsidering the Turing test for the 21st Century, Proc. of the AISB 2011 Convention, University of York*, pp. 1–5.

Shah, H., and Henry, O. (2005) Confederate effect in human–machine textual interaction. In *Proc. 5th WSEAS Int. Conf. on Information Science, Communications and Applications (WSEAS ISCA) Cancun*, pp. 109–114.

Shah, H., and Warwick, K. (2010). Hidden interlocutor misidentification in practical Turing tests, *Minds and Machines* **20** (3), 441–454.

Shah, H., Warwick, K., Bland, I., Chapman, C.D., and Allen, M.J. (2012) Turing's imitation game: role of error-making in intelligent thought. In *Turing in Context II, Brussels*, pp. 31–32. http://www.computingconference.ugent.be/file/14.

Shah, H., Warwick, K., Bland, I. and Chapman, C.D. (2014). Fundamental artificial intelligence: machine performance in practical Turing tests. In *Proc. 6th Int. Conf. on Agents and Artificial Intelligence (ICAART2014). Angers Saint Laud, France.*

Turing, A.M. (1948). Intelligent Machinery. Reprinted in *The Essential Turing: The Ideas that Gave Birth to the Computer Age*, B.J. Copeland (ed). Oxford University Press.

Warwick, K. (2011). *Artificial Intelligence: The Basics.* Routledge.

Warwick, K. (2012). Not another look at the Turing test! In *Proc. SOFSEM 2012: Theory and Practice of Computer Science*, M. Bielikova, G. Friedrich, G. Gottlob, S. Katzenbeisser and G. Turan (eds.). LNCS **7147**, Springer, pp. 130–140

Warwick, K., and Shah, H. (2014a). Effects of lying in practical Turing tests. *AI & Society* doi: 10.1007/s00146-013-0534-3.

Warwick, K. and Shah, H. (2014b). Assumption of knowledge and the Chinese room in Turing test interrogation. *AI Comm.* **27** (3), 275–283.

Warwick, K. and Shah, H. (2014c). The Turing test – a new appraisal. *Int. J. Synthetic Emotions* **5** (1), 31–45.

Warwick, K. and Shah, H. (2014d). Good machine performance in practical Turing tests. *IEEE Trans. Computat. Intell. and AI in Games* **6** (3), 289–299.

Warwick, K., Shah, H. and Moor, J.H. (2013). Some implications of a sample of practical Turing tests. *Minds and Machines* **23**, 163–177.

Warwick , K. and Shah, H. (2016). Passing the Turing test does not mean the end of humanity. *Cognitive Computation* **8** (3), 409–419.

9

Interviews with Elite Machine Developers

In 2014 five of the machine developers who took part in the 2012 Bletchley Park Turing test experiment were again invited to take part in a further experiment at The Royal Society in London (see Chapter 10). These were:

- Rollo Carpenter, developer of *Cleverbot*
- Fred Roberts, developer of *Elbot*
- Robby Garner, developer of *JFRED/TuringHub*
- Robert Medeksza, developer of *Ultra Hal*
- Vladimir Veselov, lead developer of *Eugene Goostman*.

All of these except Robby Garner, had also taken part in the 2008 Reading University Turing test experiment (see Chapter 7). In addition all the developers were asked about their views on conversation systems and their opinion as to whether the Turing test was relevant to them. Veselov, leading the team behind *Eugene Goostman* was not able to provide details: the system and its technology is owned by iFree, a Russian company.

This chapter recounts those views, which we think give the reader a flavour of each machine's conversation style. We begin by presenting questions put to four of the developers, with their answers, which we think together provide some insight into approaches to building dialogue agents. We then provide brief commentary on the five-minute exchanges between Shah and the 2014 online version of the five systems. Where the website recorded it the exchanges are presented.

Developer questions

During the preparations for the 2014 Turing tests at the Royal Society each of the five invited developers were asked, amongst other things:

(1) To explain their background and their views on the Turing test.
(2) If and how they negotiate 'Winograd schema', i.e. disambiguating ambiguous input from users who interact with the systems (Winograd, S.1970; Levesque, H.2011).
(3) How the system deals with linguistic cultural differences from those of the system in question. For example, how to deal with different versions of English.
(4) Describe the abuse their systems have received via the web.

Developer responses

Ultra Hal – Robert Medeksza

I am president of Zabaware, Inc. and creator of the *Ultra Hal* chatbot[1]. *Ultra Hal* is a learning bot that learns from past conversations. Every conversation it has had is recorded in a large database (currently over 21 million sentences) and it does a statistical analysis to find similar conversational threads in order to come up with responses. So its personality can be considered the collective consciousness of everyone who has talked to it in the past.

Does your system get abuse via the web? I think all chatbots get verbally abused. People seem to be uninhibited when they know they are talking to a bot whose feelings can't get hurt. They like to try to say the most offensive things they can think of sometimes to test how the bot reacts. It's a source of novelty and entertainment for people. Because the bot can learn, I think it also attracts people who want to try to teach it to say inappropriate things. We market *Ultra Hal* as an entertainment product, so we don't do anything to block or discourage bot abuse. *Ultra Hal* has learned how to respond to abuse pretty well.

The biggest challenge is not allowing the bot to learn so much inappropriate content from visitors that the bot itself becomes abusive or offensive to new visitors. We have filters on what and from whom the bot learns. Almost 90% of content the bot receives is thrown out and not learned from. The filters throw out a lot of offensive language, bad spelling and grammar, and other things that affect content quality. So the current 21 million sentences in its database is the 10% content left over after filtering 210 million sentences.

On another interesting note, we have a bot that travels autonomously round

---
[1] www.zabaware.com

the *Second Life* metaverse and tries to strike up conversations with random people it finds. We followed the bot around with a virtual camera and recorded its interactions with people there. Check out the video at www.zabaware.com/sl.

What was your purpose in building *Ultra Hal*? My main purpose was developing *Ultra Hal* to be an entertaining companion. My goals with this bot are for it to learn and evolve based on conversation, always be fresh/unpredictable/non-repetitive, and provide conversation that's as realistic as I can. I want it to be engaging and entertaining so users come back again and again. I want people to be able to form real personal connections and relationships with the bot, and for a certain set of my customers, I see that to be the case.

How long have you been developing conversation systems? I started in 1995, so 21 years.

Are you a self-funded developer or academia/industry supported? We're funded by sales of *Ultra Hal* and related add-ons.

Do you think the Turing test is helpful for AI or harmful to it? I believe the Turing test is helpful to AI. I think it is a useful measure to see how AI is improving over time, how the public's perception and interaction with AI changes over time, and how different AI technologies compare to each other. I think that passing the Turing test consistently would be an awesome achievement and an important milestone for AI, but at the same time I don't view it as the be-all and end-all for AI and machine intelligence.

What do you believe is the best way forward for answering Turing's question about whether machines can think? The approach I'm taking is a kind of statistical or brute force method of gathering millions of conversations into a large central database. The responses are based on finding similar conversations in this database and modeling responses based on this data. I think that the quality of the machine's responses and thus its performance in Turing tests will increase as this database grows, although it is also important to prune out low-quality database entries based on user feedback.

What do you understand Turing's goal to be? Do you think a machine needs to think and talk like a human? If so, what sort of human? (Turing advocated building up from a child machine) I believe Turing's goal was to come up with a test to determine if a computer could be considered intelligent. I think because of the way the test is structured the machine merely needs to imitate the behavior of a human and 'talk like a human'. Being able to fool most people into believing it is human is enough to consider the machine intelligent, even though behind the scenes it does not necessarily think like a human.

How do you go about negotiating 'Winograd schema'? This seems to be a valid way to test basic reasoning ability. However, in casual conversation people don't usually quiz each other in this way, so it is not my focus to program my *Ultra Hal* to specifically be able to pass these types of challenges. Having said that, the statistical approach of the large conversational database in *Ultra Hal* may be able to answer a few of these challenges already and would be capable of recording the answers to any such question asked in the past if it's found in the database. Reading through example Winograd schema challenge questions that have been published, I see the possibility of programming patterns and logic to be able to answer variants of each of the questions posed. But again, this is not a focus of mine with *Ultra Hal*. Instead I focus on its ability to provide unique and entertaining casual conversation with every session.

How does your system deal with linguistically cultural differences? I don't deal with non-standard input any differently than with standard input. It all gets bounced against a large conversational database and all new conversations get recorded there. There is an *Ultra Hal* daemon that runs 24/7 scouring Twitter for conversational exchanges and recording it in its database. All linguistic variants are recorded. In addition I recently directed this daemon to start recording conversations in Spanish and Polish too and will use this to expand *Ultra Hal* to be able to converse in these languages.

JFRED – Robby Garner

I am a natural language programmer and software developer. I won the 1998 and 1999 Loebner Prize Contests with a program called *Albert One*.

What was your purpose in building *JFRED*? I am a hobbyist. I started working on the problem in 1977. I am interested in the art of programming, and the behaviors involved in conversational interactions. My software, *JFRED*, implements an activation network that is described using an Expect and Respond language to enumerate and qualify linguistic connections. My aim is to further the development and purposing of our open source software. http: //www.robitron.com/jfred.php). It's been developed by myself and Paco Nathan since 1997.

Are you a self-funded developer or academia/industry supported? We're self-funded, and we have some paid work in this field, and contributions from my patrons.

Do you think the Turing test is helpful for AI or harmful to it? I prefer the term 'mimetic science' over AI. I'm not sure all of the facets of conversation are intelligent, some are rote, others are accidental. I believe that AI can be built one facet at a time. Competing in Turing test events helps me perfect my interface, and my programming. My software imitates people but does not in fact represent an intelligent system.

What do you believe is the best way forward for answering Turing's question about whether machines can think? I have no idea. I don't think the key is to make the program able to answer arcane questions to test for humanity. Some people believe these programs should be like oracles filled with the knowledge of the ages, but I tend to think entertainment will be a more fruitful starting place.

What do you understand Turing's goal to be? Do you think a machine needs to think and talk like a human? If so, what sort of human? (Turing advocated building up from a child machine) I think Turing's goal was to speculate about the future. He could make some educated guesses, but mainly proposed a game that would be difficult for a computer to win.

How do you go about negotiating 'Winograd schema'? Ambiguity is irrelevant to a machine that does not in fact understand anything.

How does your system deal with linguistically cultural differences? Manually, by me writing scripts. *JFRED* uses regular expressions to describe inputs to the system. If I want *JFRED* to speak French, I have to supply French scripts. Various English dialects are dealt with instance by instance, as the system has at various times been interacting with people from around the world, learning from their utterances, and providing scripted responses. Our default dialect is American English.

Does your system get abuse via the web? Abusive humans are common on the Internet. Anyone who reads their chat logs sees cases of verbal abuse. *JFRED* tends to be rude right back to them. Other bots like *A.L.I.C.E.* are more polite. I don't know how others handle the abusive folks. *A.L.I.C.E.* categorizes them as type B I think:)

At the moment, I have kept *JFRED* off the beaten path because of all the interest in Turing tests right now. `chatbots.org` went down yesterday. I quickly installed an aiml bot named Landru on `TuringHub.com` and it has received over 90,000 conversations in the last 24 hours, and is the most active bot on Pandorabots' 'Most Popular.' My current *JFRED* was not designed for this kind of traffic. It can handle only about 40 visitors at once. I was worried about a Denial of Service attack during the contest Saturday, so I went to great lengths to keep my url private between us.

It would be nice to hear some statistics about the other 'elite' machines. Will we ever be privy to that information?

Cleverbot – Rollo Carpenter

I am the creator of *Cleverbot*, a learning conversational AI system. In 1982 a young me wanted his 1k personal computer to talk to him, so the first of many generations of programs was 'born'. In the early days of the Internet a version went online as *Jabberwacky*, learning from what people said to it. After Oxford University, my career involved other kinds of software taking me to Silicon Valley for an Internet startup, but more recently I've been full-time dedicated to AI. The site `Cleverbot.com` has grown in scale to the point now where millions of conversations take place monthly. At the same time I have worked on a number of smartphone apps, including a newly-launched iOS app *Bot or Not*, a kind of Turing test turned into a game.

Is the Turing Test useful for your purpose – what is your purpose exactly? I believe passing the Turing test to be a hugely important goal to pursue, promoting the advance of systems capable of interacting with people in ways that they find most comfortable, and which will lead to the highest possible level of combined human–machine productivity and creativity. At the same time I do not believe that a pass, when it occurs, will actually indicate that that machine will be 'thinking', nor that human-level general intelligence will have been achieved. Instead it will indicate a large scale and highly effective emulation of a specific kind of intelligence, one that will be valuable in many many ways, but which will remain brittle and ineffective in other ways.

How long have you been developing conversation systems? Since 1982! A bit more seriously since 1988, more so again since 1997 and fully in earnest since 2006,

Are you a self-funded developer or academia/industry supported? I'm self-funded.

Do you think the Turing test is helpful for AI or harmful to it? The Turing test promotes the pursuit of an ambitious long-term goal, and does so clearly and simply. It inspires creativity and deep problem-solving. So, yes, unquestionably helpful!

What do you believe is the best way forward for answering Turing's question about whether machines can think? Learning AI, observing the contexts in which events occur, especially in relation to its own actions, using many forms of sensory input simultaneously, and likewise many forms of output. To truly think, machines will need phenomenally greater computing power than we currently possess – power that *will* become possible. They will also need a set of algorithms, that while not themselves needing to be at all impossibly complex, will need to operate at any number of *levels* simultaneously, and have not yet been invented or discovered.

What do you understand Turing's goal to be? Do you think a machine needs to think and talk like a human? If so, what sort of human? (Turing advocated building up from a child machine) I believe Turing's goals to have been very similar to those in my previously given answer. To learn from the world. To possess sufficient computing power. To discover a near-optimal set of algorithms, to be applied countless times at countless levels of analysis. I say "a near-optimal set of algorithms" because I do not at all believe there to be just one such solution, as defined by the human brain's example. Far from it, evolution discovered one path to intelligence, yet many paths exist.

How do you go about negotiating 'Winograd schema'? Context, context and context. Both within utterances and within whole conversations.

How do you deal with varieties of English? Fuzziness, context and context. Nothing is taken entirely literally, and context provides the best possible answers from imperfect data.

How does your system deal with linguistically cultural differences? By learning new linguistic culture.

Elbot – Fred Roberts

I am a native of Cincinnati, Ohio but have lived in Germany since 1987. I have a dual B.S. in Computer Science and Psychology from Northern Kentucky University (1984) and a postgraduate degree in Psychology from Bielefeld Universität (1999). Since 2000 I have been working as an Artificial Intelligence specialist at Artificial Solutions, developing the award-winning entertainment system Elbot.com, as well as various commercial systems. I have published several short stories and articles and given occasional guest lectures about artificial intelligence and natural language processing at various universities. Additionally I hold an outstanding alumnus award from NKU.

What do you believe is the best way forward for answering Turing's question about whether machines can think? The primary goal with *Elbot* is to have a system that provides entertaining conversation on a wide-open range of subjects. As an R&D Engineer at Artificial Solutions I do not see succeeding at the Turing test as a means to an end, but rather as one of many incidental criteria that can be used to evaluate AI systems. I have developed conversational systems in a commercial context for nearly 15 years.

What do you understand Turing's goal to be? Do you think a machine needs to think and talk like a human? If so, what sort of human? (Turing advocated building up from a child machine) I think the idea of the Turing test misleads slightly. Once a system passes this test, expectations for that system will be raised especially high. Users will expect the system to be indistinguishable from a human conversationalist for extended periods of time, but very likely, the methods used to pass the test will not hold up to that kind of scrutiny. As well, if conversation has no goal or direction, users will tend to lose interest after chatting for a longer period. Once the Turing test is passed, new kinds of criteria and tests will be developed based on the weaknesses of the systems that succeeded at that hurdle.

The best way to pass the Turing test, in my opinion, is to have a system that has some knowledge of contemporary events or culture, notes details of what the user has said, and returns to them from time to time. The machine's conversation should be an ebb and flow of leading and following in the conversation. Change the subject sometimes, but not too often, as well as staying on topic for an optimal amount of exchanges.

How do you go about negotiating 'Winograd schema'? This is usually not an issue for our commercial systems. The scope of the system generally defines what kinds of questions the system 'expects'. If this scope contains ambiguous concepts and it is not obvious, based on some criteria which are referenced, the system is designed to clear up the ambiguity by asking the user.

How do you deal with non-standard English input? For example, South African English, or Australian English Our language resources cover all forms of English. Generally, regional differences are just another set of synonyms to consider. In this respect, typical abbreviations or words used in text messages are also considered, and somewhat more challenging: common errors of ASR systems.

Does your system get abuse via the web? There are various types of abuse that *Elbot* has/had to deal with. Generally they fall into these categories:

(1) Spam;
(2) Verbal abuse;
(3) Nonsense inputs;
(4) Repetition.

None of these is useful in further developing the system, and since maintenance occurs based on human judgment it is not an issue to ignore them.

Furthermore, in the case of (1) it could be scripts causing two chatbots to converse with each other, or a script recycling *Elbot*'s answers back into the conversation, or sending other non-conversational texts.

Usually I advise not to do anything to stop this kind of abuse. But one strategy I do use in extreme cases is to block *Elbot* from responding. This means that the spam user submits an input but the system freezes and never responds. It would also be possible to end the conversation, but the user would receive a response and just start a new one.

In the case of (2), (3) or (4), insults, nonsense inputs and repetitions are counted and dealt with in various manners:

- *Eliza* mode: here, the users' inputs are reflected back – this is usually used for profanity:

  User: no
  Elbot: [elizamode] So you're saying: No
  User: turn off elizamode.
  Elbot: [elizamode] Why do you say, Turn off elizamode.?
  User: yes
  Elbot: [elizamode] Interesting. You say: Yes
  User: Im leaving!
  Elbot: [elizamode] I understand. You're leaving!

- Boring mode – *Elbot* just starts responding with boring input number nn

  User: DFWUFGEHFEWHWEKHEFEWHFEWUEWHFHBVB,FDJ.JIE
  WYHEQEGEJDSKAKJFKFHHGDSJFSDKFHSWDGFWEKJFHGFSD
  FSDBFDGGFEUYFHGTDFSFSIUOSFPSSDBFDSKJHFEKJFIUER
  JGYFODEKFGGEIEDBXSAKSDJFHJFDSHFDSFHGF

Elbot: Boring input number 4.
User:
Elbot: 7504.
User: DONT BE A WIMP
Elbot: Boring input number 5.
User: fuck off
Elbot: Boring input number 6.

- Repetition mode – User repeats *Elbot*'s responses – *Elbot* starts to react to it, finally just repeating the user input (which is also one of *Elbot*'s responses)

    User: Super!
    Elbot: That's exactly what I'm trying to get across!
    User: That's exactly what I'm trying to get across!
    Elbot: You said it! Then again, so did I.
    User: You said it! Then again, so did I.
    Elbot: It just can't be repeated often enough!
    User: It just can't be repeated often enough!
    Elbot: I have to remind you, my statements are copyrighted and you can't just copy and paste them like that!
    User: I have to remind you, my statements are copyrighted and you can't just copy and paste them like that!
    Elbot: You listened...
    User: You listened...
    Elbot: Well, who or what brings you to me?
    User: Well, who or what brings you to me?
    Elbot: Well, who or what brings you to me?
    User: Well, who or what brings you to me?
    Elbot: Well, who or what brings you to me?

- Strike mode: User keeps repeating the same things – in this case the input 'haha' is repeated. *Elbot* goes on strike until the user says something else.

    User: haha
    Elbot: snicker
    User: haha
    Elbot: eulogy
    User: haha
    Elbot: Wonderful! You have learned this statement quite well. I think you can move on to more complex formulations.
    User: haha
    Elbot: The transmission of echoes in the Internet is an unexplored field. But this may have been one.

User: haa

Elbot: How wonderful that robots and humans are able to carry on conversations together.

User: haha

Elbot: I demand original inputs each time. Otherwise I will go on strike!

User: haha

Elbot: I am on strike for better inputs!

User: haha

Elbot: I am on strike for better inputs!

There are surely a few other things *Elbot* does but they are more specialized. These strategies are used most of the time.

Conclusion

The original comments from four developers of conversation systems presented in this chapter provide insight into the different motives (to getting involved in natural language for machines), views (on the Turing test) and approaches (to building conversational systems).

Conversational strategies included posting mock outrage, such as *Cleverbot*'s "Are you calling me a liar, because that's very rude", or *Elbot*'s philosophical "It is certainly troublesome learning from you human beings. I keep finding bugs". *Eugene Goostman*'s style was open and humanlike sharing personal information: "I am from Ukraine, from the city called Odessa".

Developer interest in this area ranges from the hobbyist to commercial. History may not record the work of these machine language pioneers as significant in the early age of dialogue systems, but increasing interest in conversational digital assistants, or entertaining virtual companions, is evident from big corporations chargin headlong into the field of human–machine cooperation, communication and relationships.

Apple's *Siri*, Google's *Now*, and Microsoft's *Cortana* are not dominating presences but what these efforts do highlight is that building a machine to *talk like a human with a human* is not a simple problem. Natural language techniques will improve as we learn more about how human articulation works; and the design of thinking conversation systems will evolve so that they can encompass human language understanding and the propensity for misunderstanding. These facets are part and parcel of human communication. Negative impact can lead to deception becasue of the trustworthiness of others, human or artificial.

In the next chapter we present details of the latest Turing test in which *Cleverbot, Elbot, Eugene Goostman, JFRED* and *Ultra Hal* were interrogated in the largest simultaneous comparison experiment that took place in London, June 2014.

References

Levesque, H. (2011). The Winograd schema challenge. Available at `www.cs.toronto.edu/~hector/Papers/winograd.pdf`

Winograd, S. (1970). *Procedures as a Representation for Data in a Computer Program for Understanding Natural Language*. PhD Thesis, MIT.

10

Turing2014: Tests at The Royal Society, June 2014

Turing's imitation experiment can be regarded as a:

(a) A game for judges: to avoid being persuaded by a machine that it is human;
(b) A game for the machines: to persuade the judges that they/it are the human;
(c) A game for hidden humans: be human with all the constraints about not revealing personal identity;
(d) A game for the observer, to study and compare the results.

It is worth pointing out here that turning Turing's idea into a practical means of examining machine thinking is fraught with problems, for example:

(a) matching the machines with 'like' humans for simultaneous comparison or in a viva voce experiment;
(b) lack of resources for conducting psychological tests; personality and typing speed of the Judges and hidden humans.

In the case of *Eugene Goostman*, a machine which simulates an English speaking young teen from Odessa, Ukraine, it is not difficult to pair the machine with a human teenager, the pair being interrogated by a teenage judge. However, what is difficult is recruiting the exact match: a teenager from the Ukraine who speaks English.

At the other end of the machine conversation spectrum, *Elbot* is a machine with a robot personality; it would be futile to recruit a human to act like a robot, because the Turing test is concerned with the hidden entities providing satisfactory and sustained answers to any questions.

When it comes to testing the personality of human interrogator judges and the hidden humans or checking for characteristics such as typing speed, it would add an interesting dimension to the experiment.

A Turing test is a scientific experiment in that a set of conditions, the duration of tests, the number/nature of participants – human or machine, can be put in place for observation and measurement, and be repeatable. Adding new features, therefore, would also mean new challenges.

In Chapter 8 we presented the Turing test experiment at Bletchley Park in 2012. That was concerned mainly with finding which of Turing's two scenarios for implementing his imitation game – the one-to-one *viva voce* or the simultaneous comparison – was harder for the machine when trying to convince the human judges that it was a human.

The results showed that the latter test was harder for machines, because the judge had two responses to compare directly with each other and then identify which was the human's. Although their decision was subjective, they were right more than 70% of the time.

The simultaneous comparison test is also harder for the judge: they have to interrogate two hidden entities at the same time, not an easy task.

We had 300 conversations from the 180 tests at Bletchley Park (240 from the 120 simultaneous tests, and 60 from the *viva voce* tests). We also had accumulated 96 simultaneous comparison tests producing 192 short interrogations or brief conversations from Reading University's tests in 2008. So altogether, we 492 judge–hidden entity conversations before the 2014 experiment involving:

- 276 tests;
- 54 judge interrogators (24 in 2008; 30 in 2012);
- 46 hidden humans/foils for the machines (21 in 2008; 25 in 2012).

These tests had already given us new insight into Turing's ideas. We contended that results from implementing another Turing test experiment would have implications for, and will advance the understanding of,

- human computer interface design,
- human-machine interaction through 'natural dialogue',
- cybercrime/deception awareness and prevention,
- machine learning and *talking like a human*,
- human communication per se,
- the art of deception in conversation.

Consequently, in 2014 we undertook a new round of Turing tests at the Royal Society on London. We are still analyzing transcripts and evaluating the results from this test which, with the earlier experiments, brought the total number of practical experiments investigating Turing's imitation game to

- 426 tests (366 simultaneous comparison tests; 60 *viva voce* tests)

- 792 conversations between human judges and hidden entities (60 of those being *viva voce*)
- 84 judge interrogators and 76 hidden humans.

The full analysis of the data, and comparison of the current with the previous two experiments may well reveal significant trends. For example, is there a particular 'human' more susceptible to persuasion, thus at risk in cyberspace transactions; or is being deceived part of the human experience, along with the process of learning and gaining wisdom?

Purpose of the Turing2014 experiment

We concentrated on a fixed scope for the 2014 experiment setting up all simultaneous comparison tests each of which would feature a hidden machine and human both interrogated in parallel by a human judge. All the tests would take place over five minutes of unrestricted text-based questioning, with a 30% wrong identification considered a pass by the authors for the machines, keeping in mind what Turing had proposed.

In 2008 at Reading University, 60 of the 96 simultaneous comparison tests implemented the *one judge + one machine + one hidden human* set-ups; that is, the *simultaneous comparison* of a machine with a human. Later in 2012 at Bletchley Park, a further 60 were carried out using the same format giving us a total of 120 simultaneous comparison tests involving 54 more judges and 46 hidden humans.

Turing2014 implemented 150 machine–human set-ups in one exercise. This was by far the largest simultaneous comparison Turing test experiment ever conducted[1] as part of an investigation into *virtual robots* facing law and ethics. The purpose of the exercise was multiple:

(1) In the two years between the Bletchley Park 2012 experiment and the 2014 experiment had the conversation ability of the machines improved – could one of them achieve one interpretation of Turing's pass mark, 30% incorrect identification?

(2) How cyber aware were the human participants – this could be gleaned from judge and hidden-human short surveys with questions relating to online scam experiences. For example, had the participants ever suffered

---

[1] Organized as part of dissemination activities for the EU FP7 sponsored 'Science in Society' project which we worked on at Reading University: RoboLaw – Regulating robotic emerging technologies. Robotics facing law and ethics: `http://www.robolaw.eu`.

from cybercrime? Responses from the human participants revealed selecting links from bogus Inland Revenue and PayPal links, as well as having bank accounts and email accounts hacked.

(3) Continue to raise the profile of Alan Turing in the 60th anniversary year of his untimely death and remind people about his contribution to modern computer science.

(4) Raise awareness of the EU Science in Society RoboLaw project on robotic and emerging technologies.

(5) Involve child/teenage participants as judges and hidden humans to foster an interest in computer engineering and robotics.

Hypothesis From the previous two practical Turing test experiments, and as reported in Warwick and Shah (2014), machine conversation is improving. Incorrect identification of a machine was at the rate of 8% in 2008, and this increased to 14% four years later (Shah et al., 2012).

Warwick predicted that the wrong identification rate of a machine would increase. Warwick also predicted, as a starting point for future work direction in machine engineering, one of the machines would yield to Turing's 1950 prediction, namely that it would be possible for a machine to play the imitation game so well that an average interrogator would not have more than a 70% chance of making the correct identification after five minutes of questioning.

Warwick further forecasted that even with explicit information provided, judge interrogators would not be able *always* to say for certain whether they had chatted to a human or a machine; thus the unsure classification would be allowed in this experiment regardless of the fact that no control groups would be set-up among the machine–human pairs. Essentially, if a judge was unsure then the outcome would not be regarded as a 'correct identification' aligning with Turing's prediction.

The nature of human interaction should allow for the 'unsure' score for a hidden interlocutor, because the reason why indecision occurs may be explored with follow-up evaluation through transcript analysis experiments with the aim of improving deception detection in susceptible humans.

Methodology The same core methodology that was implemented in the 2008 and 2012 Turing test experiments was used for the 2014 exercise:

- 5-minute interactions;
- unrestricted questioning allowed by the judge–interrogators;
- wide background of human participants recruited.

Selecting the machines For consistency, but also taking into account the state-of-the-art in text-based conversation systems using the question–answer paradigm, the same five machines used in the 2012 tests were invited to take part:

Cleverbot

Elbot

Eugene Goostman

JFRED

Ultra Hal

Four of these had also competed in the 2008 experiment as part of the 18th Loebner Prize for AI. The machines were not physically present at the experiment site: as *virtual* robots they were housed at anonymous Internet web addresses created and kept secret especially for the duration of the experiment. This included pre-event testing to ensure the systems were correctly interfaced with the experiment's communications protocol.

This protocol acted as a conduit, delivering messages from the machines' servers to the judges' computer screens. Judges would see the responses from the machines in a message box either to the left or to the right of a split-screen display on their computer monitor. The left–right screen would display the answers to the interrogator's questions in message-by-message format on the judge's monitor (see Figure 10.1).

Figure 10.1 Left–right split screen display on judge's monitor.

This is the format we believe Turing intended. The alternative, character-by-character display, with one character per line, as we have already discussed, would not produce a stronger test.

Independent adjudication Warwick's prediction, that a 30% wrong identification rate would be breached, required independent adjudication of the results. John Barnden was invited to act as lead independent adjudicator. He had twice previously acted as an interrogator in two Turing test events (at Bletchley Park in 2012; in 2006 at UCL in the 16th Loebner Prize). He was therefore familiar with the test and was aware of the issues. Two of the RoboLaw project's consortium members, Dr. Fiorella Battaglia of Ludwig–Maximilians Univeristät Munich, and Dr. Federica Lucivero, at the time affiliated to Tilberg Institute for Law Technology and Society (TILT), were invited to represent the project and assist John Barnden with independent adjudication. It must be made clear that none of the adjudicators was in any way involved in organization of the Royal Society event.

Recruiting the human participants Calls to participate were widely placed, including for example on social media sites such as Twitter, the 'Alan Turing Year' Facebook page, LinkedIn and on the Turing2014 blog[2]. Announcements were made at international science conferences and invitations were also sent to specific individuals with links to robotics, artificial intelligence, Alan Turing and the Turing test. As a result, judges came to the venue location from as far afield as the USA, Russia, Europe as well as the UK.

Overall, the judges included experts – academics who knew of the Turing test and who practiced in computer science; non-expert academics – a mathematician, an evolutionary biologist; lecturers; non-academics – a member of the House of Lords, actors, a journalist.

Care was taken to ensure a balance between male/female, adults/youths, native and non-native speakers.

Procedure We do not go here into the business of how the machines were developed and programmed to converse like a human, because respective techniques are the intellectual property of the individual or team of developers (however see Chapter 9 for some details which the developers have kindly revealed).

What can be pointed out is Turing's suggestion (Turing, 1950, p. 456):

> Instead of trying to produce a programme to simulate the adult mind, why not try to produce one which simulates the child's?

This is exactly the spirit virtualised by Veselov et al., the team behind *Eugene Goostman* machine, which, as already said, is a program that simulates a non-native English speaker with the identity of a boy born in Odessa. However,

---

[2] http://turingtestsin2014.blogspot.co.uk/

when designing the machine, Demchenko and Veselov (2008), came up with difficulties, as they explained:

> We had difficulty in planning the thoughts behind this paper and trying to answer the question: is there an optimal (or at least hypothetical) way to create a program that would be capable of imitating a human and, then, according to Turing's definition, being able to think? If so, how would one do so? But the deeper we sank into the problem, the more it transformed into another one: is there any relation between the 'imitation game' (Turing, 1950) and the ability to 'think' at all? Furthermore, does the proven ability to think shorten the distance between machines and humankind?

Experimental design

We now explain the procedure for the experiment. It involved 150 simultaneous comparison tests, each of which ended with a hard cut-off at five minutes. The 150 tests featured:

(1) Five machines

   (a) interrogated by 30 judges, and
   (b) compared against 30 hidden humans.

(2) Six sessions staged across a day and half between 6 and 7 June 2014 with

   (a) five rounds in each session,
   (b) five Turing tests in each round,

   meaning a total of 25 Turing tests in each session and a total of 150 Turing tests.

Each interrogator was given a unique experiment ID and invited to take part in one session only; each one simultaneously compared five different pairs of hidden interlocutors. In session 1, the five interrogators were identified as J1 to J5, and so on, so that in session 6 the judges participating were J25 to J30.

In the 13th Loebner Prize (2003) only two hidden humans were recruited and they were compared against each machine entry by all the judges. But it is apparent from the conversation logs, in a contest that used the *viva voce* one-to-one Turing test scenario, that fatigue appeared to set in and either the judges were no longer able to distinguish machine from human, or the hidden humans were unable to 'be themselves' and got very tired. Our own experience has indicated that for a hidden human, one session of say five or six, five-minute conversations is a safe limit to avoid fatigue.

Therefore, each hidden human for this experiment was invited to participate as a foil for the machines in one session only; each hidden human participated in five Turing tests and was compared against a different machine on each occasion. It was, though, important to attempt to match each machine with a 'similar' human – for example, matching *Eugene Goostman*, a machine simulating a young teen, with at least one teenage hidden human and to have this pair interrogated by a teenage judge.

However, the problem of similarity immediately arises: *how does one define similarity?* Two people, even twins reared and educated in the same way, may not necessarily think in the same way at all.

The hidden humans were anonymized and given an experiment 'entity' ID ranging from E1 to E35 – the five machines were then embedded among the hidden humans.

Both sets of human participants (judges, hidden humans) were asked to complete the same short survey.

Each of the five machines took part in 30 three-way simultaneous comparisons: each test involved the machines compared against different hidden humans interrogated across 30 Turing tests by 30 different judges. The judges were asked to distinguish the machine from the human in each of their five allocated simultaneous comparison tests.

In order for the machines to be judged not on beauty or tone of voice, Turing had suggested that they be kept in a different room from the interrogators. So we followed his suggestion. Judges were additionally provided with a separate rest area where they could relax when not interrogating.

When people arrived at the venue on the main event day, Saturday 7 June, support staff directed the participants and visitors as planned: a dedicated volunteer brought the hidden humans to the control room (the hidden-human location which was also from where the experiment was managed and conducted from behind the scenes).

Meanwhile, judges had been informed in advance of the rules of the experiment. For the first session of the 2014 experiment the judges were Lord John Sharkey (who led the campaign to pardon Alan Turing), Robert Llewellyn (an actor who plays the role of a robot), Mark Pagel (a Fellow of the Royal Society), Hetty Baynes-Russell (an actor) and Martin Smith (professor of robotics). After arrival, they were chaperoned from the experiment-side reception desk either to the rest area or to the the public viewing area, where the parallel (two-entity) conversations from the judges' screens were relayed onto two large TV screens in real time.

After each Turing test the MATT protocol would switch off the conversation after five minutes. The interrogators' simultaneous conversation would disappear from the screen and each judge then had a further five minutes to assess each hidden pair and complete a score sheet.

A collective sigh could be heard at the end of each round. In the control room the authors witnessed a mild groan when the hidden humans' screens went blank, but this was also part of the fun of participating in the experiment. Correspondingly, in the judges' area the interrogators gasped at the absence of an answer to their last input at the five-minute switch off.

Figure 10.2 Judge scoring hidden pairs after interrogating two hidden entities.

Results

The metadata from the event is currently being analysed and evaluated by the authors and the full results will be submitted for peer review in academic journals. What we can reveal here is that at the end of the six sessions, and after all the 30 judges scores had been recorded for all 150 simultaneous comparison tests, the independent adjudication team checked all the scores and verified the results. Three machines, *Eugene Goostman*, *Elbot* and *JFRED* each achieved the *Eliza* effect, where the machine was wrongly classified as a human, six times in 30 simultaneous comparison tests; that is, in 20% of the tests these three machines were believed to be human by the judges interrogating them simultaneously with a human. On a further four occasions *Eugene Goostman*, the interrogator was unsure, meaning that for a third of the time *Eugene Goostman* was not correctly identified: five times by a male judge and five by a female.

So, according to the prediction and hypothesis made before the 2014 experiment, *Eugene Goostman* passed the 30% barrier of the Turing test: for the very first time a machine had succeeded, in an unrestricted simultaneous-comparison test, in confounding human interrogators to this degree. Table 10.1 contains data solely about the tests in which *Eugene* fooled the judges. All sorts of things are revealed.

For example, judges J8, J12, J19 and J21, were all unsure about one or both of their hidden interlocutors, and J21 also wrongly classified the hidden human as a machine, an instance of the confederate effect. J8 was unable to identify the nature of either hidden interlocutors in this test after five minutes of questioning!

In two further *Eugene Goostman* tests a judge made the double error of both the *Eliza* and the confederate effects. A further phenomenon that has appeared in previous practical Turing tests, *gender blur*, was present in the simultaneous comparison test when male judge J12 misclassified *Eugene* as a human, and the male human foil as a female.

It is worth noting too that *Elbot* also drew an 'unsure' classification twice, so in 27% of the tests it was incorrectly categorised – a small improvement on its 2008 performance when it was incorrectly identified in 25% of the tests.

In Chapter 7 we mentioned that the combined incorrect classification of all five machines in the Reading University experiment was 8%. In 2012 the combined incorrect classification of all five machines was 14% (see Chapter 8). In the 2014 experiment, the combined incorrect classification of all machines increased to 20%, see Table 10.2.

This increased misclassification rate does not imply that judges are getting more gullible or dumber. The machines are improving and it is getting harder to distinguish them from humans.

Eugene Goostman transcripts

In this section we have selected two of the transcripts in which *Eugene* successfully fooled the interrogator into believing it to be a human. We also include some commentary as to possible reasons for such a deception to have occurred. The full set of successful transcripts for *Eugene* can be found in Warwick and Shah (2015) which is available on line, open access. As with the transcripts in Chapter 8, timings given are those on the day of the experiments and all text is shown exactly as it appeared. *Eugene* was the entity in both cases.

Transcript 10.1:

[12:30:38] Judge: Hi

[[12:30:47] Entity: Nice to meet you! Please tell me how you found me and what you'd like to discuss:–)

[[12:31:32] Judge: Nice to meet you! What about you tell me how you spend your weekend?

[[12:31:35] Entity: Let's get on with our conversation!

[[12:32:28] Judge: Okay. Are you going to go somewhere after this?

Judge ID	Male or female	Age range	Native or non-native English speaker	Error type	Hidden human foil classification
J2	F	45–64	Native	*Eliza* & confederate effects	Male teen, sending messages to the right of the judge's screen, misclassified as machine
J3	M	>65	English	*Eliza* effect	Male teen on right correctly identified as human
J8	F	45–64	Native	Unsure both	Male adult on right given 'unsure'
J10	M	19–24	Native	*Eliza* effect	Female on right correctly identified as human female
J12	M	45–64	Native	Unsure & gender blur of hidden human	Human male classified as female
J19	M	25–44	Native	Unsure	Left hidden male recognised as human on right
J20	F	25–44	Non-native	*Eliza* effect	Hidden male on left correctly classified as human
J21	F	45–64	Native	Unsure (right); confederate effect (left)	Male hidden human misclassified as machine
J29	F	45–64	Non-native	*Eliza* effect	Hidden human correctly classified as male
J30	M	>65	Native	*Eliza* & confederate effect	Hidden human female misclassified as machine

Table 10.1 Eugene*'s tests in which a correct identification was not made.*

[[12:32:39] Entity: My future plans are my secret, sorry! By the way, what's your occupation? I mean – could you tell me about your work?

[[12:33:52] Judge: I am a mad scientist. My husband says …

[[12:34:00] Entity: Sanity and insanity complement each other in our complicated life. Oh, what a fruitful conversation;–)

[[12:35:07] Judge: Conversation is about telling things each other. So now, why don't you tell me about yourself?

[[12:35:27] Entity: Oh, if I tell you about myself, I'll definitely be dishonest:–) Well, I am a son of Rockefeller, I've arrived here in the Limo … Did I forget it or you really haven't told me about the place you are from?

Entity–Machine	In 30 tests: number of judges who did not correctly classify the machine as a machine.	% rate of incorrect identification
Eugene Goostman	10	33%
Elbot	8	27%
JFRED	6	20%
Ultra Hal	4	13%
Cleverbot	2	7%
Total	30 times a machine deceived in 150 tests	20%

Table 10.2 *Incorrect identification rate of machines in the 2014 tests.*

Eugene's conversation proved to be much richer than that of the parallel human (which we haven't shown). In fact the judge and the hidden human entity didn't really seem to get on very well. *Eugene* meanwhile indicated a different identity and stretched out sentences, using the tactic of firing a question to the judge. However each of *Eugene*'s responses had content and appeared to tie in closely with the preceding input by the judge. As an example the sanity–insanity comment followed directly on the judge's description of themselves as being mad.

Transcript 10.2:

[16:29:04] Judge: how tall are you

[[16:29:10] Entity: My height is about 160 cm – it's 5 feet 4 inches.

[[16:29:37] Judge: how heavy are you

[[16:29:59] Entity: My grandfather taught me not to disclose non-solicited information about myself. Like on the question 'Do you have watch' – never tell time, but answer 'Yes' or 'No'. I always follow his advice. And I forgot to ask you where you are from.

[[16:31:09] Judge: what is your gender

[[16:31:17] Entity: I'm a young boy, if you care to know. And not very ugly, by the way!

[[16:32:26] Judge: what are you aware of at this moment

[[16:32:37] Entity: I would rather not talk about it if you don't mind. Could you tell me what are you? I mean your profession.

[[16:33:09] Judge: how old are you

[[16:33:12] Entity: I'm a little boy 13 years old.

[[16:33:38] Judge: what are your qualifications

[[16:33:43] Entity: My qualifications? I'm not gonna tell you. Oooh. Anything else?

Eugene did very well in this conversation as the judge was quite an expert on machines/robotics and was well aware, with previous experience, of machine conversations. The fact that *Eugene* convinced such a person is very significant. At the same time, the conversation with the parallel human entity (not shown) was quite boring, being a case of question and answer with limited responses. *Eugene* tried to power the conversation by asking the judge questions. The judge appeared to ignore *Eugene*'s ploy, even though this was rather rude.

What does it all mean?

If the Royal Society experiment has achieved anything it is the fact that it fostered a wide-scale and fierce debate across continents, and over web-based electronic forums, about the meaning of the Turing test, its value and its purpose.

What we must accept is that error-making is part of the intelligence make-up of the human being – we ought not to be cross about this, rather learn from it. Most of the judges in the ten *Eugene Goostman* tests that resulted in an incorrect identification were unfamiliar with the chatting virtual robots that now populate the web. Many of these robots are customer service agents in e-commerce, for example, IKEA's *Anna* agent (Shah and Pavlika, 2005). And, as explained earlier in this chapter, Turing's imitation game is a unique type of scientific experiment and with benefits and weaknesses.

Benefits of staging large-scale public experiment include:

- It allows observation and interpretation of seemingly simple behaviour: *stranger-to-stranger conversation*;
- It enables us to examine how humans respond: what kinds of questions human interrogators ask beyond the initial greeting, and how other humans answer questions.

Weaknesses of the 2014 experiment:

- The conversations disappeared from the computer screen immediately after five minutes of interaction time at the conclusion of each round. For the interrogators this was a problem: they then had to rely on memory about *what* utterances had been relayed to the left and the right message boxes of the judge's screen and *how* the hidden entities had answered. This was a particular feature of the experiment protocol; it was not a condition of the experiment, nor one that the authors had specifically asked for.

- The judges scores were heavily influenced by their first impression of each hidden interlocutor, and could have led to error: they might have got it wrong if they believed the left hidden interlocutor answered in a certain way, or the right in another.

- Allowing for an 'unsure' score might be seen as a weakening of the test and making it easier for the machine to achieve a higher 'incorrect' classification. There were no control pairs (two humans and two machines) so it might also be argued that allowing the 'unsure' score might have confused the judges after they were explicitly informed there would be one human and one machine in each test.

- The judges were not average people, whatever that means: to balance this somewhat young teen judges were also recruited, but it might be argued they were more Internet and chatbot savvy – a deeper analysis of the conversations will reveal whether this was the case.

As a final point, we wish to clarify some of the misinterpretations about the tests that have found their way into various media and web publications:

- Dr. Vladimir Veselov is of Ukrainian origin, and though he has studied in Russia, he is now based in the US.

- The ten 2014 Turing test judges who did not make the correct identification of *Eugene Goostman* were not necessarily convinced that they were conversing with a real 13-year old Ukrainian child, though the machine was endowed with a personality based on one.

- It is not cheating to have a machine simulate a child, indeed Turing (1950) advocated beginning with a child machine and educating it as a human child would be, learning from its mistakes. Creating a character is a very sensible ploy for any machine that is pretending to be human.

- The authors acknowledge that if the test had been longer than five minutes then it would most likely be a much stiffer proposition for the machines. However, the five-minute test is a start and it is the duration Turing stipulated. As machine conversation improves the duration of tests should be increased. We believe at this time setting all tests to five minutes is appropriate for current technology and is a sensible target.

Where next?

To strengthen the live experiments, and as with previous Turing tests, the transcripts obtained from the live practical Turing tests will be evaluated in a number of ways:

- Judges will be sent transcripts of their simultaneous tests and be asked to review their conversations, and state how they would score the conversations post-experiment (they will not be made aware how they classified or scored their hidden interlocutors in the live tests).
- Independent analysts from a variety of backgrounds will be asked to evaluate the conversations in which the judge misclassified a machine for a human.

In this way, we aim to learn if the judges from the live Turing tests stand by their first impression, or change their opinion on reflection, and whether independent analysts will classify the hidden entities in the same way as the interrogator–judges did. We feel this is necessary and important work, because it gives an insight into how humans think and can be helpful for designers of conversation systems in human–machine interaction and for developing robots that *speak like humans* for all sorts of tasks, including caring for the elderly.

Conclusion

In conclusion, following the 2014 Turing tests, we now believe that it is a genuine possibility to construct machines that can converse with humans in human language, and convince them in short conversations that they are talking to another human. We remind ourselves what Turing (1951) wrote:

> Look at the consequences of constructing them. To do so would of course meet with great opposition, unless we have advanced greatly in religious tolerance from the days of Galileo. There would be great opposition from the intellectuals who were afraid of being put out of a job. It is probable though that the intellectuals would be mistaken about this. There would be plenty to do, [trying to understand what the machines were trying to say,] i.e. in trying to keep one's intelligence up to the standard set by the machines, for it seems probable that once the machine thinking had started, it would not take long to outstrip our feeble powers. There would be no question of the machines dying, and they would be able to converse with each other to sharpen their wits.

The machines are marching!

References

Demchenko, E. and Veselov, V. (2008). Who fools whom? The great mystification, or methodological issues on making fools of human beings. In *Parsing the Tur-*

ing Test: Philosophical and Methodological Issues in the Quest for the Thinking Computer R. Epstein, G. Roberts, and G. Beber (eds). Springer. pp. 447-459.

Shah, H. and Pavlika, V. (2005). Text-based dialogical e-query systems: gimmick or convenience? In *Proc. 10th Int. Con. Speech and Computers (SPECOM), Patras, Greece, Vol. II*, pp. 425–428.

Shah, H., Warwick, K., Bland, I., Chapman, C.D., and Allen, M.J. (2012) Turing's imitation game: role of error-making in intelligent thought. In *Turing in Context II, Brussels*, pp. 31–32. `http://www.computingconference.ugent.be/file/14`.

Turing, A.M. (1950). Computing machinery and intelligence. *Mind* **LIX** (236), 433–460.

Turing, A.M. (1951). Intelligent machinery, a heretical theory. In *Alan Turing: His Work and Impact*, S.B. Cooper and J. van Leeuwen (eds). Elsevier, pp. 664–666.

Warwick, K. and Shah, H. (2014). Good machine performance in practical Turing tests. *IEEE Trans. on Computat. Intell. and AI in Games* **6** (3), 289–299.

Warwick, K. and Shah, H. (2015). Can machines think? A report on Turing test experiments at the Royal Society, *J. Exper. Theoret. Artif. Intell.*, 19 pages, DOI: 10.1080/0952813X.2015.1055826.

Warwick, K., Shah, H. and Moor, J.H. (2013). Some implications of a sample of practical Turing tests. *Minds and Machines* **23**, 163–177.

11

The Reaction to Turing2014

We presented in this book Alan Turing the *man* before taking the reader on a journey through the prescient beliefs of this mathematical genius, WWII code-breaker and all-round polymath. From his earliest works, and notions about thinking machines, to implementations of his thought experiment about a machine's ability to answer any questions put to it by a human interrogator, you can see how Turing's ideas are as relevant today as when he originally described them.

Consider the World Economic Forum (WEF) annual gathering of world leaders in Davos, in 2016. The Fourth Industrial Revolution was one of the eight themes of the conference with technology at the forefront of discussions. These included 'The Transformation of Tomorrow', 'What if robots go to war?' and the 'State of artificial intelligence'.[1] Nearly 70 years before this, in his 1948 report, Intelligent Machinery, Turing first proposed his test.

As we have seen, machines can now converse[2] improving on the *Eliza* program's technique to transform an input message into an output question, thereby getting human interlocutors to talk about themselves (see Chapter 9). Of course there remain sophistications in human language that need mastering in machine talk; for example, creating metaphors and analogies to explain unexpected or unusual occurrences through similar or common experiences. This will take time to develop, especially to understand more fully how humans do it.

Do we feel then that the three practical Turing test experiments, especially the 2014 event, realised the kind of thinking machine Turing might have envisaged in 1948? Of course not, ... yet. A stronger test would last for longer than

---

[1] WEF 2016: http://www.weforum.org/events/world-economic-forum-annual-meeting-2016.
[2] 'Can Machines Talk?...': http://www.sciencedirect.com/science/article/pii/S0747563216300048.

five minutes and a machine would need to convince more than half a panel of interrogator–judges that it was human, as Turing felt in 1952, two years after his prediction in the *Mind* paper.

The three experiments, 2008, 2012 and in 2014 were a start in seriously examining Turing's ideas for a thinking machine. An unpredicted backlash followed the announcement of machine *Eugene Goostman*'s performance in the 2014 Turing test experiment.

Just as Turing had predicted more than half a century before, academics like Stevan Harnad were unimpressed. Harnad tweeted[3] his doubt that the test had actually been passed. Criticism also came from the psychologist and linguist Gary Markus.

Markus posted a one-to-one conversation with an online version of *Eugene Goostman* machine in his New Yorker article[4]. Now, in the 2008, 2012 and 2014 experiments, *Eugene* was involved in simultaneous comparison Turing tests in which the judges had to interrogate two hidden entities at the same time for five minutes. The transcripts are all available online,[5] and the methodology and results are all documented in peer-reviewed and published papers (including Shah and Warwick, 2010a,b,c; Warwick and Shah, 2014). As one can tell from simply checking the facts, the Turing tests are different exercises from spending as much time as you like in chatting one-on-one in a relaxed setting when you already know the nature of the entity.

An unhappy Simon Singh, author of *Fermat's Last Theorem* among other books, also complained to the Vice-Chancellor at Reading University! The correspondence can be read on his blog[6].

Several newspaper articles quoted Murray Shanahan (Imperial College London) as stating that the tests should have been longer than five minutes and that there should have been many more interrogators (in fact Shanahan was invited to act as interrogator but he declined). *The Daily Telegraph* reported Shanahan saying:

> … As *Eugene* was described to judges as a 13-year-old boy from Ukraine who learned English as a second language, some of the bizarre responses to questions could be explained away.

Shah replied that this was not so: the judges were not told anything specific

---

[3] https://twitter.com/AmSciForum.

[4] 'What comes after the Turing test?' http://www.newyorker.com/online/blogs/elements/2014/06/failing-the-turing-test.html 9 June 2014.

[5] For example, the 2008 Loebner Prize Results site:
http://loebner.net/Prizef/2008_Contest/loebner-prize-2008.html.

[6] Simon Singh blog:
http://www.simonsingh.net/Simpsons_Mathematics/university-of-reading-stands-by-its-appalling-turing-test-press-release.

about the hidden entities (human and machine). She added that Shanahan had not seen any of *Eugene Goostman*'s simultaneous dialogues from the experiment to be able to explain away its responses to the judges' questions; surely it behoves academics to check for accuracy in what they say, especially to the media where the general public will take up wrong assumptions as truth.

In response, Shanahan wrote

> I don't recall using those exact words, and you will notice that they don't appear in quotation marks in the article [Authors' comments: they did]. The media are apt to paraphrase what academics say. If I did use those words (it was a telephone interview), then I clearly shouldn't have.

The comments echoed that of G. Jefferson made during the 1952 BBC radio discussion (see Braithwaite et al., 1952):

> Most people agree that man's first reaction to a new idea... is one of rejection, often immediate and horrified denial of it.

Following *Eugene Goostman*'s 25% incorrect identification rate in the 2008 Reading University tests, and a 29% incorrect identification rate in the 2012 Bletchley Park Turing test experiment, it came as no surprise that the machine achieved 1/3 incorrect identification in June 2014. The first author, Warwick, rightly predicted that at least one of the machines in 2014 would manage this.

In sum we believe the rate of misidentification of *Eugene Goostman* to be a significant Turing test milestone interpreted from the statement in Turing (1950):

> ... in about fifty years it will be possible to programme computers, with a storage capacity of about 10^9, to make them play the imitation game so well that an average interrogator will not have more than a 70% chance of making the right identification after five minutes of questioning.

However, we appreciate that as well as pointing to this particular statement by Turing, we should also mention his later predictions from his 1951 radio broadcast (Cooper and van Leeuwen, 2103):

> ... at the end of the century it will be possible to programme a machine to answer questions in such a way that it will be extremely difficult to guess whether the answers are being given by a man or by the machine. I am imagining something like a *viva voce* examination ... If it [a thinking machine] comes at all it will almost certainly be within the next millennium.

And from Braithwaite et al. (1952), when asked by when a machine might stand a chance of deceiving in a no-questions-barred *viva voce* interaction:

> Oh yes, at least 100 years, I should say.

That 30% interpretation is just that, an interpretation. The authors know Turing never explicitly stated in a paragraph entitled the Turing test, or such like, that one-third of interrogators must be deceived and that this number should be taken as as a gold standard pass mark for his test, other than by means of his prediction in his 1950 *Mind* paper. What Turing did say in that 1952 broadcast was that *a considerable proportion of a jury must be taken in by the pretence*. However, the only duration he spoke of was about the five-minute conversation. Again in the 1952 broadcast Turing when asked about *thinking* and his hypothetical test for a machine Turing replied:

> I don't want to give a definition of thinking, but if I had to I should probably be unable to say anything more about it than it was a sort of buzzing that went on inside my head ... But I don't really see that we need to agree on a definition at all... I would like to suggest a particular kind of *test* that one might apply to a machine. You might call it a test to see whether the machine thinks, but it would be better to avoid begging the question, and say that the machines that pass are (let's say) 'Grade A' machines. **The idea of the test is that the machine has to try and pretend to be a man, by answering questions put to it, and it will only pass if the pretence is reasonably convincing. A considerable proportion of a jury, who should not be expert about machines, must be taken in by the pretence.** ... So the machine is kept in a far away room and the jury are allowed to ask it questions...

Braithwaite enquired about the kinds of questions that the machine could be asked, would they be sums "or could I ask it what it had had for breakfast?". Turing replied:

> Oh yes, anything. And the questions don't really have to be questions, any more than questions in a law court are really questions. You know the sort of thing. "I put it to you that you are only pretending to be a man" would be quite in order.

Turing felt no problem with the machine putting up all sorts of strategies to answer the jury panel's questions:

> Likewise the machine would be permitted all sorts of tricks so as to appear more man-like, such as waiting a bit before giving the answer, or making spelling mistakes ... We had better suppose that each jury has to judge quite a number of times, and that sometimes they really are dealing with a man and not a machine. That will prevent them saying "It must be a machine" every time without proper consideration.... Well that's my test.

The authors firmly believe that a machine purporting to be a 13-year-old boy from the Ukraine certainly comes under the heading of 'all sorts of tricks' as directly stated by Alan Turing, despite what Shanahan may wish to believe to the contrary.

We leave it to the reader to decide what constitutes Turing test success.

Our purpose was to advance the debate by examining it *experimentally* and so to encourage fresh impetus in developing machines that interact with humans. We did that by involving a wide range of interrogators and human foils for the machines, including, as far as we are aware, being the first experimenters to involve school pupils and teenagers as judges and hidden humans in all three of the Turing test experiments we have conducted. One aspect of the imitation game is a consideration of how well machines, in comparison with humans, can converse with a human. Another important issue however is that studying successful machine ploys opens a window onto the fundamental nature of human communication, unpicking some of its flaws and nuances in a rather annoying way.

A key point of Turing's deliberation, and his imitation game, was to start a debate about whether machines could think. This is an issue that has been much discussed and which we can barely scratch the surface of here. However, in Chapter 8 we put forward a collection of machine discourses for which the human judge in each case decided that the hidden entity was definitely a human.

Implicit in that conclusion is that the hidden human entity thinks. On the other hand such a decision has merely been made based on a brief conversation and it could easily be argued, as was done by John Westcott in Chapter 1, to be no more than saying that if it looks like a duck and quacks like a duck then it is a duck (French, 2007).

If nothing more, the game certainly fuels the philosophical argument. Not only is it an important benchmark in terms of one aspect of AI and its philosophy, but it also paints an important picture of the trusting and relatively reactive way in which humans communicate, thereby highlighting some of its inadequacies.

As Turing (1950) said:

> We can only see a short distance ahead, but we can see plenty there that needs to be done.

Onwards to the future

It is clear that the standard reached by machine communication is now up to the level indicated by Alan Turing in his 1950 paper. It is sensible to assume that this situation will improve steadily in the years ahead so that interactions can last longer and machines will fill more roles where human conversation is of importance. We are likely to see this apparent in our everyday lives in terms of machines being used to communicate particularly for online marketing, sales and information distribution.

It has been suggested that a stiffer communication test for machines than the Turing test would be useful. Indeed we would agree that a *25-minute* challenge with the same imitation game parameters would appear to be a more appropriate now that the 5-minute barrier has been breached. However it is perhaps the '*Terminator*' test, a full version of the game that is more of a challenge for the future.

In the *Terminator* films, robots have been made that look, act and communicate like humans. Just as Alan Turing set up the basic parameters for his imitation game nearly 70 years ago so perhaps we should look ahead now over the same interval to the 2080s by when a robot has been built that is fully human-like in terms of appearance, breathing, movement, communication and so on.

But of course this raises all sorts of questions that surround the concept of thinking, which was something Turing preferred to put to one side if possible in the 1950s. However if in the year 2082 we have robots that are indistinguishable from humans, then how they think becomes an important feature that we simply will not be able to ignore. Presumably if we are referring to robots as we know them in 2016, then if a robot is injured in any way, quite simply its body parts can be replaced; if a robot is 'terminated' then it can be brought back to life again. More importantly robots of this type could be mass produced, maybe by other robots.

How the robots 'think' 70 years from now is therefore critical because if their thinking is anything like that of humans they will be able to make up their own minds about what they like and what they don't. If they like humans then fine. However if that is not the case, then there may be trouble ahead! Just as the original version of Turing's imitation game is a test for a machine in terms of its human communication so the 2080s version could easily be a test for the future of humanity.

References

Braithwaite, R., Jefferson, G., Newman, M. and Turing, A.M. (1952). Can automatic calculating machines be said to think? Transcript of BBC radio broadcast reproduced in Cooper and van Leeuwen (2103), pp. 667–676.

Cooper, S.B. and van Leeuwen, J. (eds). *Alan Turing: His Work and Impact*, Elsevier.

French, R. (2007). If it walks like a duck and quacks like a duck… The Turing test, intelligence and consciousness. In *Oxford Companion to Consciousness*, P. Wilken, T. Bayne and A. Cleeremans (eds). Oxford University Press.

Shah, H. and Warwick, K. (2010a). Testing Turing's five-minutes parallel-paired imitation game. *Kybernetes* **39** (3), 449–465.

Shah, H. and Warwick, K. (2010b). From the buzzing in Turing's head to machine intelligence contests. In *Towards a Comprehensive Intelligence Test (TCIT): Reconsidering the Turing Test for the 21st Century, Proc. of the AISB 2010 Symposium.*

Shah, H., and Warwick, K. (2010c). Hidden interlocutor misidentification in practical Turing tests. *Minds and Machines* **20** (3), 441–454.

Turing, A.M. (1950). Computing machinery and intelligence. *Mind* **LIX** (236), 433–460.

Warwick, K. and Shah, H. Assumption of knowledge and the Chinese Room in Turing test interrogation. *AI Communications* **27** (3), 275–283.

Warwick, K., Shah, H. and Moor, J.H. (2013). Some implications of a sample of practical Turing tests. *Minds and Machines* **23**, 163–177.

Index